To

LEON

With all my Best Wishes

We Three Were All Alone

by
Barney Wagner

DORRANCE PUBLISHING CO., INC.
PITTSBURGH, PENNSYLVANIA 15222

ISBN #0-8059-3973-3
Printed in the United States of America

First Printing

For information or to order additional books, please write:
Dorrance Publishing Co., Inc.
643 Smithfield Street
Pittsburgh, Pennsylvania 15222
U.S.A.

ACKNOWLEDGEMENTS

This being my very first major writing venture, I obviously needed the encouragement and support of others. With that foremost in mind I wish to thank the following people.

Michael Bybee for encouraging me to go forward with this project and for helping me tell my story.

Jodi Mathis, the legal secretary in my son's law office, for typing my autobiography with her computer and for being so very patient and courteous.

My many friends who upon learning of my project kept urging me to go ahead.

Last, but of course far from being least, to my lovely wife, Rose, and my dear son, David, without whose support, love, and encouragement this autobiography would never have been possible.

To all you readers and good people for wishing to read this autobiography, a great big
THANK YOU!

Barney Wagner

We Three Were All Alone

I was working out at my gym on the treadmill a few months back when one of the guys came by to chat while I was walking. He asked where I was born and how I came to be in the U.S. He kept this up the next few workouts, and one day he said, "You know, Barney, you should seriously think of writing a biography on your life since I find it interesting, and I think many others would too." I resisted at first, but he kept on telling me to do it. Finally I've decided to give it a try, and so this is for you, Michael, since you were so sure it would be interesting for others to read.

It all began for me on March 20, 1918, in the large industrial city of Manchester in northwest England. Both my parents were Polish immigrants who had come to England with just one child, my oldest sister, who was just four years old at the time. The year they arrived, I believe, was 1910. The house in which I was born was an old, but large, four bedroom, and at that time I had three older brothers and one older sister. Eventually another boy and two more girls came after me, so we were a family of eight children with two parents and my ailing maternal grandmother. My grandmother passed away when I was eight years old, and I missed her very much since she was so very good to all of us children. I have never forgotten her.

The neighborhood in which we lived was a tough one, and you had to be tough to get along with the other kids. We all loved sports, but our main reason for living, in those times, was being able to play football (soccer). How well I remember rolling up wads of paper, packing it, and tying it with string to use as a football since we couldn't afford to buy one as little kids. We didn't have the money like kids have today. I'm happy that it is better for kids these days. Anyway, we would use our jackets spread apart for goalposts and let the game begin, and sometimes we would even play by the light from an old lamppost in the evening shadows. Those really were the days. I can clearly remember a time when I was about eight years old and already an avowed soccer addict. On Saturday afternoons from August until April I would find a good local amateur soccer game to attend.

On this particular Saturday the team I had chosen to watch was St. Lukes, a really good team. I remember taking up a standing position behind the goalkeeper's net of the opposing team. There was this young red-headed youth playing center forward (Striker) for St. Lukes who possessed a shot like a bullet.

On this one play the referee awarded a penalty kick to St. Lukes, for which a player takes twelve yards from the goalkeeper. The name of the player who took the kick was Hughie Green, the red-head with the devastating shot. His shot went past the goalkeeper, right through the net, and hit me square in my solar plexus! I went down in a heap, and the next thing I remembered was a couple of Red Cross ambulance men hovering over me whilst I was flat on my back.

Being a fairly tough young kid, I was able to get back up eventually and watch the finish of the game. When I got home I told my mom what happened, and as Mom always did in most cases those days, she rubbed some warm olive oil on my stomach. Needless to say I awoke the next morning after a somewhat restless sleep with a giant-sized tummy ache which eased off after a couple of days. I must confess I never watched another game standing behind the net of any goalkeeper. The nice ending to this incident in my young life was that Hughie Green sought me out after the game and presented me with the game ball. By the time I was twelve years old, I was playing soccer for my school, and I was also on the cricket team. I was getting to be very good at both sports.

My next oldest brother, Joey, who was three years older than me, was the schoolboy Fly Weight Boxing Champion of England at thirteen years old. Our family being Jewish, he also fought for the Jewish Lads Brigade Boxing Team, which is equivalent to the USA Premier Scouts. He then turned pro and began to rack up lots of wins. One day someone came to our house to ask that we pick up Joey's jock straps, which he forgot, and take them to the gym where he trained. I was elected to do that, and when I got to the gym my brother told them who I was. His trainer suggested I put the gloves on and go one round with my brother. Reluctantly I agreed, and after about thirty seconds I was flat on my back and literally did see stars out of a blue sky. My brother was indeed a good fighter, and had he stayed in focus with conditioning and living right, he would no doubt have won the Fly Weight Championship of Great Britain. He was beaten in a semi-final elimination bout.

I can also recall a time in my boyhood days when I was twelve years old and had been studying for my Bar Mitzvah for almost a full year. Most of you readers I'm sure know the meaning of these two words, but just for the many who don't, the Bar Mitzvah is the Sabbath Day which corresponds to a Jewish boy's thirteenth birthday, at which time he is required to chant the weeks reading (Haftorah) from the pulpit for all the congregation of the Synagogue to which his parents belong. It is on this special day, when the boy has fulfilled all of the teachings, that he then, in the eyes of God, becomes an adult and is accepted as such by all Jewish people.

Anyway, it was once again a Saturday afternoon, and I was watching a soccer game locally between two teams, the names of which I can't recall. It was a very cold, blustery day in Manchester, but as cold as it was I never liked wearing an overcoat. I was just wearing a wooly sweater. I watched the game from the sideline at about mid-field and stayed there the full ninety minutes until completion of the game.

I began to walk away but could hardly move, and I just sort of stumbled to the ground. I was literally unable to walk. Not being far from our house, someone went for my dad, and he came along shortly after. He lifted me on his back in a type of fireman's carry and took me to the Northern Children's Hospital, which was only about a five-minute walk from the grounds.

Upon reaching the hospital, I was immediately given an examination by a fairly young resident, and he informed my parents that I was being detained overnight for a further and more complete examination the following morning.

I was a little surprised when just before noon the next morning a lovely-looking young lady in a pure white three-quarter coat with a stethoscope around her neck approached the bed in which I was laying. She told me her name was Dr. Evelyn Chisholm and that she was about to give me a thorough exam.

The examination took what seemed like a full hour, and when the doctor was finally done she called in both my parents. They had been waiting in an outer corridor. I can clearly remember the doctor telling my parents that I had contracted a rather severe form of rheumatism mainly in both my legs. She prescribed two types of liquid medication and released me from the hospital, but she advised my parents to have me stay home, preferably in bed, for about three weeks and then return to the hospital for further examination. The doctor also told them that it was quite possible that my growth could be affected by all of this. I've always wondered if this was something she said in jest or whether she was being serious. Anyway, the truth of the matter is that I never really did grow that much after that, and at my tip-toes I am five feet four inches tall. Other than that I made a complete recovery.

I remember also my teacher Rabbi Cohen, who is now deceased, coming to the house, sitting by my bedside, and going over my Haftorah. Since I was only less than two weeks away from my Bar Mitzvah, he came by every day. I felt myself getting a little better and stronger each day, and when the Sabbath Day of my impending manhood arrived, I was able to go to the Synagogue helped by my parents. Though feeling very weak and extremely nervous, I was able to get through the ceremony. I was told by my Rabbi that I had performed my Bar Mitzvah with flying colors, so to speak. This of course turned out to be a day in my life that I will always remember.

All of my life, as far back as I can recall, I've always had a tremendous love for music. Although I don't think of myself as being a good singer, I have no trouble carrying a tune, and I enjoy singing. I'm reminded of the many evenings during my service in WWII that I spent in the Sergeant's Mess when the other sergeants and myself were called upon to perform in any way we were capable—either playing an instrument, singing, or even stand-up comedy. Since my N.C.O. friends knew I was Jewish, they would ask me to sing some Jewish songs, and I would oblige with a rendering of "My Yiddisher Mamma" and sometimes the Jewish (Israeli) national anthem in Hebrew. Surprisingly it always seemed to go down very well, and they all seemed to enjoy it.

All of this, of course, is leading up to how I first became interested in singing. I believe I must have been about ten years old when I first began singing. It all came about because of my thirteen-year-old brother Joey having joined the choir at the New Synagogue, the one to which my parents belonged. He had told me that all the choir boys received a monthly payment of two shillings and six pence, equal in those days to about forty cents. But the money would buy you some candy, soda pop, and chocolates, with enough left to get you into a decent cinema. All in all it was not too bad of a deal.

All I had to do to enroll in the choir was to have the choir leader listen to my tiny soprano voice. Surprisingly, to me at least, I was told after my test that I was now a fully pledged member of the choir and eligible for rehearsals and proper Sabbath and Holy Day services. After a period of about two months, I felt very confident. I enjoyed singing and always looked forward to the services.

It was about this time that a major problem arose in my young life. My soccer skills had earned me a regular place playing the right wing position on my school Shield Team, which is the equivalent of a freshman team but in Elementary School. We played one game a week throughout the autumn and winter. Games were mostly played in mid-week directly after school at about four o'clock.

When the important cup games came along, they sometimes had to be played on a Saturday morning at eleven o'clock. It was than that my situation became a little dangerous since I couldn't be in two places at the same time.

One particular Saturday morning, I had been selected for the school team to play an important cup game at a ground about a mile from the synagogue. Match time was for 11:00 in the morning. Synagogue services started at 9:00 and generally finished around 12:00 noon. Being eager to play and not wanting to be absent from choir, I hit on the idea of dressing ready for the game. I put on my noisy soccer shoes and quietly slipped out of the house, headed for the synagogue. Of course I had taken the precaution of putting loose every-day clothing over my soccer togs so it wouldn't be detected.

About half way through the morning synagogue service, I complained to the choir master that I had a bad stomachache and needed to go home. Naturally I was excused and retired to the choir dressing room, shedding the cap and gown that choir boys wore. I then ran the whole mile or so to the ground where we were due to play. It certainly worked out great that first time, but there were to be no more after that since my mother quickly found out about it and gave me a thorough tongue lashing in her native language (Polish), which most of us understood one way or another. After that first episode, I requested our sports master at school to not select me for any more Saturday games.

Nevertheless, just to close this part of my school days, it was only a couple of years later that I was chosen to play in a cup final on a professional ground on a Saturday. My dear mom allowed me to take off choir and play in the game.

Incidentally, speaking of my mother, perhaps it may be of some interest to you to know that she was born in a small suburb just a couple of miles west of Warsaw. Both her parents were dairy farmers. She had one brother, who I knew as my Uncle Jack. My mom's name was Rachael Greenberg. She also loved to sing, especially to us kids when we were all very young. She was an amazing woman. She was so very quick in all that she did. I think I favor my mother in that respect. She was such a good person and extremely honest. What a wonderful job she did bringing up eight children. As time goes by, I seem to think so much more of my dear mother.

As for my wonderful dad, his full name was Morris Wagner. He was not a huge man. He was just about average height and always very clean and well groomed. I truthfully can never remember him uttering a swear word, even when any of us misbehaved, which we sometimes did. To be quite truthful, neither of our parents ever laid a hand on us kids when we were out of line. Just a few well-chosen words were spoken. And even though the words were hardly ever spoken in English, they were still enough to keep us on the right path.

My dad was a rainproof machinist by trade, and he would always bring home work he could do on his machine that would greatly help supplement his weekly wage. As for us kids, we were always there helping him turn the sou-wester hats with ear flaps from the wrong side to the right side, fold them correctly, count them, and pack them in cardboard cartons ready to be shipped out. Those really were the good old days. My parents were such good people, and I've missed them. I think of them very often. Incidentally my dad was born in the town of Lublin, a town with a much smaller population than Warsaw.

Meanwhile my life was moving on. I was a very educated and wise fourteen-year-old and beginning my first full-time job since leaving school—it was as a printer. I began by sweeping up floors, cleaning ink off the machines, brewing tea for the other workers, and so on, but all the time I was learning and asking questions and doing little odds and ends. After about ten or twelve months, I felt I could tackle anything in the printing shop. I really felt I'd made great strides in my young life and was ready for whatever job the printing shop asked me to do. However a few months later my boss, who owned the shop with seven employees, came by one day and asked me to stop into his office. He sat me down and began to talk to me, as a father does to his son. He said he thought I had great potential to go far in my trade and was recommending me to a position as a Compositor with the M/C Evening News, the city's leading newspaper. I went for the interview and was told I had come well recommended. I was to report for work the following Monday morning. I remember running all the way home, about two miles, to tell my parents of my big break, which indeed it was. Just imagine, I was not yet fifteen years old and working for the newspaper read by all of Manchester.

I went to work on that Monday morning all eager to get going, with my new printer's navy blue apron and the lunch my dear mom had packed for me. I was met by a nice middle-aged man around forty years old or so, and he said how terribly sorry he was to have to tell me that I couldn't start work. The reason he gave me was that they were a union shop, and in those days it seems you had to be sixteen years old to work in their union. I was just flabbergasted. It was one of the few times I really broke down and cried, but still it didn't help, and I felt as if I'd let myself and my parents down. I got so angry that I vowed I'd not be a printer anymore, and so I began a trade in which three of my older brothers were working, upholstering furniture. I didn't know the first thing about it, but I soon became very good at it and very fast. After about two years, I was making more wages than my three brothers. I must say they all were proud of me doing so well. We all gave our wages to our parents, and they gave us our weekly allowances.

Meanwhile I was getting to be very good at sports, especially soccer and cricket. At age sixteen, I was playing for a junior farm team of one of the good pro teams. It was when I was at this stage of my life that I got involved in show business. My youngest brother, Sonny, along with three other boys, all between the ages of seven and thirteen, and a training coach got together a Mills Brothers type of act. One newspaper called them the youngest Mills Brothers act in the world. They were pretty good until their coach had to quit for heath reasons. Since I loved music and knew all of their routines, having been to their rehearsals and shows, I was asked by them if I would take over as manager and coach in addition to my full-time job of upholstering. I agreed to accept the job and changed their act completely, naming them the Melody Four and purchasing uniforms of blue sweaters with "M/F" embroidered in white along with white flannel pants and white shoes.

The act began to take off, and we were all over the place, finally getting a good spot on a radio show. By then it was 1937. Hitler had been taking over countries one by one, and war clouds were all over Europe. My dad asked me to accompany him to Poland to bring one of my many cousins to England. Dad had all of his family in Warsaw, and Mom had some family there too. In all there were seventeen members of the family living in Warsaw. We got our passports and reported to the British Consul for our visas. The consul said to my dad, "We can get you to Poland, but because of the Hitler regime there would be no guarantee of getting back here." He strongly advised us not to go. My dad talked it over with my Mom, and we did not go. It was somewhere around the early part of 1939, and things in Europe were not looking good at all. Hitler had already taken Poland, and a declaration of war by the British government seemed almost inevitable. This is the time frame of which I wanted you readers to be aware.

During one of the evenings of the crisis we were undergoing, my dear mother got all the family together. Those who were present were my mom, dad, five of us boys, and our three sisters. She then told us she was going to read us a letter she had just received from the Red Cross Agency. It must have been written in Polish since my mom could neither speak or read English. We understood very little of my mom's native tongue, so she read the letter to us in Yiddish, which is a Jewish dialect form of conversing. We all were fluent in speaking and understanding Yiddish since our parents used this to communicate with us in our daily lives.

The contents of the letter were shocking, to say the least, and my poor mom just kept crying throughout the letter. To put it all in as few words as possible, the letter said that all of our family of relatives, seventeen in all, must be assumed to have perished under the Nazi Regime. Not too much else was added other than to say further confirmation would be forthcoming at a later date.

I can clearly recall the events of that evening, and after the letter was read we all broke into tears, with only one exception. That exception was my brother Joey, the boxer. He was a tough kid, and I can honestly say I never ever saw him cry, even when my mom passed away. Not to say Joey was a bad kid. He really was always very nice to all of us. Anyway, it turned out to be one of the saddest evenings of my life. My poor parents never got over the loss of their brothers, sisters, nieces, nephews, and aunts.

It wasn't too long after receiving the letter that a large cardboard carton arrived at our house via parcel post from a division of the Red Cross containing various pieces of clothing said to belong to our lost ones. We never did find out find where they came, but we assumed they had to discard their clothing before entering what they thought to be communal baths. The baths were really chambers of death. It is just something we will live with for the rest of our lives. We never received any further information other than what we had been told. Shortly after came the Holocaust in Poland. We were devastated when the Red Cross gave us proof of what happened there. My parents never really recovered from the shock.

It was now 1938, and the small upholstering shop in which I worked had grown tremendously and had moved to a larger building with a crew of thirty employees. At age nineteen, I was the lead upholsterer.

It was now January 1939, and my lifetime friend Jack Gore and I jointly purchased our very first car, a 1930 Morris Minor. Boy, was that ever a relic. We nursed it and polished it since it was our very own treasure. Owning a car in England those days was considered a real luxury. Meanwhile things were going great for me. I was getting rave reviews on my soccer and cricket, but especially my soccer. I had visions of maybe one day making it with the big boys. My upholstering was keeping our family in good shape along with the income brought in by my brothers, who also did their share. The Melody Four were getting better and becoming well known.

Then a day came I remember so very vividly. I was working on the car changing a tire outside the house and had the old Philco Radio on loud so I could hear the news. It was the morning of September 3, 1939, somewhere around eleven or twelve o'clock. Neville Chamberlain was speaking, and it was a declaration of war! I had no idea at that time what it would mean to our family, but just four months later came my calling up papers for conscription. I was the first one in the family to be called up, and I remember being told to report to Fullwood Barracks in Preston, Lancs, which was only thirty miles from Manchester. I vividly remember having a farewell evening with the family, and it wasn't easy for me or any of us since we didn't know what would happen.

It was on a cold, dreary, very foggy February morning in 1940 that I took off on a train from Victoria Station in Manchester telling my tearful mom not to worry since I wouldn't be far away—I would probably be home for a weekend leave. Boy, was I ever wrong! The barracks was just a reporting depot. Arriving there in the dark winter evening, shivering and hungry, we were all served a small bowl of soup that looked awful and by all accounts tasted the same, though I did not have any. About an hour afterwards, we were all on a train with plenty of coaches to accommodate over two hundred fifty conscripts. We traveled to a desolate coastal spot in Scotland called Stranraer, where we were then loaded on to a troop ship bound for Belfast, Ireland, at a huge army depot called Palace Barracks in the town of Holywood, County Down. This was where we were all equipped, though not completely, since there was a shortage of almost all army clothing and equipment. But that never stopped us from our intense six weeks of army training, and it was intense since there was an urgency of which nobody needed to be reminded.

I would like to get back to the time when I departed Manchester by train to report to Fullwood Barracks in a town called Preston. As I may have previously stated, it was in the wee hours of the morning somewhere around three o'clock, and they served us this horrible looking soup. I knew then that I was in deep trouble as far as food was concerned.

Both my parents being Orthodox Jewish people, they had brought us all up on the Jewish Dietary Laws with regard to all edible food. Without going too deeply into this subject, I can certainly tell you a few of the things we were not allowed to eat.

Anything that came from the body of a pig, such as ham or pork, was strictly taboo. The only fish we could eat had to have scales and fins. That meant we did not eat any catfish, for example. There are, of course, many other types of food we did not eat, and so my dilemma during my years in the army was knowing how to cope with this problem. If I tell you that during my first two years in the army my main food was bread (dry) and tea, I would not be stretching a point. However, shortly after that, when I became a full-fledged sergeant and ate in the Sergeant's mess, I was able to indulge in this luxury of having my bread toasted and served with jam. I felt like I'd suddenly become a very wealthy person. Anyway, I did manage to get by.

Incidentally I was always having army buddies rushing to sit next to me in the dining hall because they could always count on me giving them my meal with the exception of the two slices of bread. I certainly had plenty of friends at meal time.

Since I am discussing army issues, now would be as good a time as ever to talk about army pay. As a private soldier, my weekly pay was fourteen shillings a week, which at that time was the equivalent of approximately one dollar and twenty-five cents. I had made permanent arrangements for my parents to receive exactly half of my weekly pay. I somehow managed to survive on the seven shillings a week with which I was left.

Pay Parade in the British army is a very ceremonial event, and I can imagine that it is even more so today than when I served. As I recall, Pay Parade in our battalion took place every Friday morning at 11 a.m. It generally took place in a large room with a fairly lengthy table at one end at which sat a high ranking officer, more often than not a captain, and on one side was a quarter master sergeant flanked on the other side by a clerk who was either a lance corporal or full corporal.

When your name was called from the ranks, you would respond with a

"Sir" and swing smartly to attention. Then you proceeded to march smartly to the pay table, come to a halt facing the captain, and deliver a very smart salute. Your pay would be handed to you by the officer. You would receive it with your right hand, transfer it to your left hand, salute the officer once again, and then come back to attention, do a smart about turn, and march briskly back to rejoin the ranks.

I have to tell you that I spent many hours practicing marching up and saluting for my pay, and I really got to be very good at it and received many a compliment from various pay officers. I often wonder what the present day Pay Parade is like in the British army.

Upon completion of recruit training, I was made a platoon leader although I was still an ordinary private. Then came the really tough eight weeks of Advance Training, and it was upon completion of this that I was made a lance corporal, which means I was an NCO (non-commissioned officer) with one stripe. Most of the boys with whom I'd completed my training were shipped to different areas of active combat and sad to say I never saw some of them again. Incidentally I was an infantryman in the elite Durham Light Infantry (DLI), and I was chosen to remain in the training depot and be an assistant platoon instructor of small arms, field tactics, aircraft recognition, and gas warfare protection. I never dreamed I would become somewhat of an expert in any of this, but somehow it did happen.

One day, I believe it was in 1940 in the late summer, we were told most of us would be going to Solihull near Birmingham in the midlands, not too far from Coventry. We were given a great send off by all the local Irish people, especially the girls, as we marched the two miles from the barracks to the train depot led by a large Irish bagpipe band. It was a real thrill for me and very moving too. There was no barrack in Solihull. We were billeted in scattered homes. We were there for further heavy intense combat training, and we were put on alert. It didn't take long before we were in an action of sort.

I was with another lance corporal at a cinema called the Odeon watching "Gone with the Wind". Suddenly the movie was interrupted by a screen slide flashing "All personnel of the DLI report immediately to company headquarters in full field equipment to draw one blanket and await orders." Yes, it was the beginning of the Battle of Britain in the air. We were being bombed all over the country, but especially in Coventry, which is where we were sent. Our job was to keep up the supply of ammunition for the ACK/ACK guns. It was hard work, and we kept it up until we were almost out of ammunition. By then it was almost dawn. The German fighters and bombers had ceased and had either been shot down or returned to their base. Losses were very heavy, but since the Royal Air Force had outfitted themselves so extremely well, even with the heavy loss of planes, personnel, and especially property, it was by our British government's acknowledgment a true victory. I can really say that it was from this point on in WWII that England began to slowly assert itself as a military power that would in the end be victorious. True, we may be just a tiny country, but our army, air force, and navy are really great.

In the morning, after the air raids on Coventry, I was in charge of a twenty-man squad helping clean up the rubble and searching for possible buried bodies. One incident stands out in my mind, and it is one I will never forget, although I rarely talk about WWII. We were all working and doing whatever we could when a young lady in her early thirties approached us. She was wearing just a light coat and absolutely no other clothing since it was all burned by an incendiary bomb in her home. She even told me her pajamas had burned since she was sleeping at the time of the raid. She asked me if I would try to locate her mother, and she directed me to an area where she thought their home had been. I, along with my squad, began our search. I came upon the woman's mother under a load of bricks which were still red hot, and I pulled her out. I covered her with blankets since she was dead, mostly by suffocation I thought. Shortly after the daughter came by. You have to remember that she had lost her home, her belongings, and her mother. All she could think about was getting two huge containers of tea for my boys. How's that for courage? I swear I don't even know how she managed to acquire the containers of tea, but it was so deeply appreciated. I felt sorry to convey the news of her mother, but she was a gritty one. That was a true example of the courage of the British people in WWII, in which we were almost alone for what seemed such a long time. We were all so happy when we were joined by the troops of the good old USA. One almost knew the war wouldn't last much longer once that happened. Looking at that fine young lady, it was so difficult for me to believe that in spite of her cheerful smiling face and how she had gone out of her way to get my men some refreshments, she had literally lost everything. Her home, her mother, and almost all of her property were lost.

I say she lost almost everything because she had asked me to keep an eye open for a fairly large cardboard carton containing a forty-eight piece tea service. It was a brand new set she had just purchased, not even unpacked, and she told me each piece had this picture of Lady Godiva sitting on a horse imprinted into it. It was shortly after I found her dead mother that one of my men found the unharmed carton under a pile of burnt clothing. She was so happy to get it back. I'll never forget her.

It was during the next few days of continuing the massive clean up that my left knee came in full contact with the corner of a red hot brick. My knee was severely burned, bruised, and swollen. I was checked into a hospital just outside of

Walsall near Birmingham, where I stayed for four days. The scar on my knee, however, is a permanent, constant reminder to me of the bombing of Coventry in WWII.

Remember when I told my mom when I was leaving for service that I'd probably be home by weekend? Gosh was I ever wrong. It was about two years before I got my first seven-day leave. Crossing the Irish Sea from Ireland to England was dangerous too because of U-Boat activity, but I guess I got lucky. I just wanted to get that little bit of knowledge in.

After recovering from the bombing raids and eventual clean-up but no rebuilding, we were told we were being shipped en-bloc by train to a place on the southeast coast of Wales called Fishguard, right on the coast itself. What a desolate spot. But compared to where we would be sent later it was heaven. It was here in Fishguard in 1941 that I was promoted to full corporal (two stripes) meaning I was second in line to my sergeant in charge of a platoon of thirty-six men. We spent our time mainly field training and shooting on the range with all types of small arms weapons, and I was really getting to be an expert shot on both rifle and machine gun. In those days it was the 303 Rifle and the Bren machine gun we used.

After almost eight months in Fishguard, we were once again moved. This time we moved to an even more desolate spot in Wales, which was also on the coast, in a small town called Treardurr Bay, where I was to remain for about one and a half years. I was selected by my commanding officer to attend a six-week instructors advanced course at the British Army School of Small Arms in Bisley-Hythe, which is in Surrey, a county in England, in the south outside of London.

I did extremely well on this course and was given a grade of "distinguished," which is the highest grade given, and not many were given at that. My commanding officer was elated when I got back, and I was promoted to full sergeant (three stripes). In a way I was sorry all this happened since my progress had come under the scrutiny of the war office, and they gave orders to my CO to have me report to the Western Command School of Weapon Training. I was given a further promotion to that of SIM (Sergeant Instructor of Musketry), and my position in the school was as a full blown instructor to teach NCOs and high ranking officers the correct method of instruction for recruits and advanced personnel. I was indeed sorry to have to leave my original unit, the DLI, and all the men with whom I had been stationed for such a long time.

Going to the Western Command School was also my first experience serving with women in the service. It was a brand of the service called WATS (Women's Auxiliary Territorial Service); we called them ATS for short. Actually they were made up of mostly young girls between the ages of eighteen and twenty-three, and what a great job they did. Mostly they were responsible for administration and cooking, but they were non-combat. They were such a great part of the victory of WWII, and I want to emphasize this point.

Meanwhile things back at home had changed radically since the day I said farewell to my mom, dad, brothers, and sisters. My older brother, being unfit for the service because of a physical defect, was working in an aircraft factory. My two other brothers were both in the army. In Great Britain during peace time, married women were mostly housewives. Now the war and Hitler were upon us, and the married women were nearly all working on jobs for the war effort and what a great job the women did. Also there was "total blackout" in the evenings, and people had difficulty finding their way since it was a 100 percent blackout. Petrol was severely rationed, as were all types of toffee and chocolates. Food such as peanuts, bananas, eggs, and meat were almost invisible. In spite of all these shortcomings, the mood of the people of Great Britain was very much upbeat, with an unwavering confidence in our Royal Family and the cabinet led by Prime Minister Winston Churchill, or as he was more commonly known to his people, "Winnie." What a great leader he turned out to be.

Please forgive me if I seem to digress sometimes, but I am trying to recall events that happened some fifty years ago all from memory, so I hope you'll bear with me.

Reverting back to my family, the only ones left at home were my parents and my youngest brother, Sonny. Two of my sisters were married, and my youngest sister Sonia, the baby of the family, were evacuated by government order and living in the seaside town of Blackpool with a nice family. She was only eight years old when evacuated, and I remember spending a full day with her on one of my rare leaves (furlough) from the army. She was such a great kid, and she held up very well being away from her parents and siblings.

Of all the main towns that had been under siege by the German Luftwaffe, the worst hit were in the midlands, where all the ammunition and gun factories were located. These were towns like Coventry and Birmingham, northwest towns such as Manchester and Liverpool, and of course London and many of its suburbs. During one of the raids on my hometown, Manchester, the largest hospital in the town was completely shattered by HE bombs. Some patients, doctors, and nurses were killed. My parents' home was right next to the hospital, and my mom was thrown to the floor by the shock of one of the explosions. It is sad to say, but she was never the same after that, and she passed away just a few years later. I do believe the shock contributed to her passing on at a seemingly early age of sixty-five. My mom was quite a lady, and as I go along in life I realize more and more just how great she was.

So it was just our youngest brother, Sonny, helping out at home and doing all he could to keep up the spirits of my mom and dad.

It was now 1944, and the events of the war were now beginning to swing in our (the Allies) favor. As for myself, I was just becoming one of the leading instructors at the army school, I vividly remember one occasion on a humid summer day. I was instructing the class in bayonet fighting and had taken off my battle dress jacket. My braces (suspenders) were off my shoulders, and I had my sleeves rolled up. I was demonstrating the thrust-parry and withdrawal of the bayonet. The training went well on this session, and during the lesson I had noticed a crowd of about a dozen civilians crowded around my commanding officer, about thirty or forty feet away, looking on. I completed my instructional period and went on with the rest of the work for the day.

The following morning, I was ordered to appear before my CO. I was a little scared, but I couldn't think of anything I'd done wrong to warrant this. When I marched in to see the CO, he at once told me to stand at ease, and he then began to tell me why he had sent for me. It seems that a VIP, visiting the school to observe what was happening in the army school, had asked the CO about me and my background. The VIP made the comment, if I remember it correctly, "As long as we have boys in our service of this caliber we will do just fine." So my CO was commending me. If felt great. I really had debated about relating this incident since I'm not a boastful person by any means, but I wanted to be as good a soldier as I could be. It turned out I got to be very good. Incidentally, that VIP was Winston Churchill!

I was singled out to test new weapons, two of them being the PIAT (Projector Infantry Anti-Tank), which is a shoulder held, barrel-type gun loaded by a number two soldier from the rear of your shoulder. The PIAT was capable of putting an enemy tank out of action and maybe even destroying it from a distance up to one hundred feet. Another weapon I had to test fire was the Sten Gun. The Sten Gun was a crude looking sub-machine gun weighing one and a half pounds invented by two officers—Lt. Sawyer and Lt. Taylor, the weapon was developed at the Ammo Depot of Enfield, thus the name STEN. It became the commandos' main weapon on their many raids. It was capable of approximately six hundred rounds a minute with a thirty round magazine, and it was a 9mm weapon.

It was almost 1945, and the beginning of the end was in sight for Hitler, even though the Japanese forces were still going strong. I had been married since July 2, 1944, and my wife, Rose, was living with my mom and young brother in Manchester.

How I met my wife you may find interesting, at least I hope so. I went home on a three-day leave from the army school to be with my parents and my brother, Sonny. It was the second day of my leave. It was early afternoon, and I decided to take a brisk walk to the Ritz dance hall in the center of town, which was about two miles from our house. I was hoping that maybe I'd run into some of my friends who would be home on leave. I was well on my way walking down the main road leading to town when I was hailed by the driver of a sleek new black Jaguar. Next to the driver was a person in civilian clothes who I recognized as the private in charge of the NCO's canteen shop at the army school. A canteen shop is equivalent in some respects to the American PDX stores. Anyway, the private and the driver were brothers-in-law and there was this young girl in the back of the car whom they introduced as their cousin. She appeared to be very young, very dark skinned, like her skin was tanned, very slim, very pretty, and somewhat on the shy side, not saying even a word. The two boys asked me for directions to a wholesale house where they could purchase cloth for suiting. Having concluded my directions, we each went our separate ways.

To be truthful about how all this happened, I must tell you that a couple of days after getting back to the army school off my leave the private, who I knew only as Nat Morris, sought me out when I was off during the evening. Nat asked me point blank if I'd taken any notice to the young girl in the back of the car, and if so, did I wish to meet with her. Since there was a war going on, and me not being a ladies man, sports and music were more interesting for me. Nevertheless, I agreed to meet her, and as luck would have it I had to cancel without giving any notice since I was selected to instruct night firing on that particular evening. I felt bad letting her down, as I would anyone. We arranged to meet another time, and we did eventually get to see each other. The very first time we went out together she looked even better than the first glimpse I had of her in the Jaguar when they were driving around Manchester.

Anyway, we went to see a movie on our first date, and I enjoyed just being with her. She was a rather quiet girl, but when she did speak it was very meaningful. After a very pleasant evening we agreed to meet again, and of course she turned out to be the girl with whom I would spend the rest of my life. As for my married life, that is another story in itself, but as of this time of my writing, we have our fiftieth wedding anniversary coming up. We are hoping to celebrate in England since the show business side of the family wishes to put on a great show and celebration for us. Come next July, all being well, we will do just that, and July is just about six or seven months away.

I'd like to go back a little if I may to the time when I had just been promoted to full corporal. It was in Palace Barracks Holywood, Northern Ireland. It seems that a prisoner in the MP detention cells had escaped and had been picked up at his home in Manchester by the local police. His name was Pvt. Albert Green, and I had known him well in peace time since he was always driving posh cars. My friend and I went driving around with him sometimes. He wasn't a bad sort of chap, he just liked the good times. He was mischievous sometimes, but he was definitely not the criminal type. My name was posted on Battalion Orders to report to Ardwick Green Barracks in Manchester to pick up Pvt. Albert Green from the MP's and bring him back to Northern Ireland. I was joined by a lance corporal for escort duty. During the war it took almost two days to get to Manchester, and when Pvt. Albert Green first saw me, his eyes lit up. I thought I might be in for a rough time, but I was dead wrong. He said to me that had it been anyone other than me, he would have attempted to escape. He also told me he was very hungry and skint (broke). So I took him along with the escort to my mom's house, which wasn't more than a fifteen minute bus ride, and decided not to handcuff the prisoner, which I was supposed to do. My mom was surprised and rather shocked but still happy to see us with our full equipment and carrying rifles. I also holstered a pistol. It must have been a little frightening for her. However, she made up a nice meal in no time, plus she prepared lots of sandwiches for us to take on the journey back by train to Scotland and then by boat to Ireland. I also gave Pvt. Green a little cash to get him by. We got back to the barracks in Ireland with no trouble, and I learned much later that Pvt. Green had been discharged from the army as being "Unfit for Service."

Getting back to my duty in the Western Command School, I should mention that it was located thirteen miles northwest of Liverpool and close to the seaside resort of Southport. The school was located in a small town called Hightown, and it was sometimes referred to as Altcar Rifle Ranges. There is an issue I would like to talk about which, truthfully, I had not even thought about until now, and that has to do with racial feelings. I was thinking back on some of the things that happened during my years of Army service, and I remember this particular incident very clearly because it is something I can never forget.

During my boyhood years growing up along with all my brothers and sisters, I can never remember our parents mentioning anything about different races or religions. However, they did teach us kids to be good Jewish children and to following our faith. They did not try to turn us away from children of different faiths, and so my growing up with other children was never a problem.

Well I must return to what happened one particular time in the Army. I had been at the Western Command School for nearly three years. Being one of the leading instructions, I was assigned a group of twenty-five ranking men and officers of the U.S. Air Force stationed in Warrington, a small town where the U.S. Air Force was based. It was all a part of prepping for invasion by the allied forces, and my orders were to teach these men as much as I possibly could during a ten-day crash course. Then they in turn would be able to instruct all of the men on their base on all the weapon training they had learned in the course.

On the day the U.S. Air Force men arrived at the school, I went down to the railroad station to meet them. I introduced myself as their instructor for the course and informed them of what would be taking place over the next ten days.

However, I was totally unprepared to see twenty-five black men. I must say at this point that I had never before been exposed to black people since they were very few and far between in England.

After escorting the men to the school and placing them in the Nissan Hut allocated for their sleeping quarters, I began to think about the best way to let the group know I was not only their instructor but also their friend.

I should explain that a Nissan Hut is the same as a Quonset Hut in American terminology. I should also point out that all school instructors were billeted in special quarters, and each instructor had a room all to himself.

After some thought I approached the senior officer in charge of the U.S. Air Force group and asked him if he would allow me to sleep in the Nissan Hut along with the others for the duration of the course. He was very surprised, and a big smile broke out on his face as he readily agreed. Indeed he thought it was a great idea.

That was my way of getting closer to the men, and it was after this that I was not only able to get 100 percent of their attention but so much extra effort from them. By the end of the course, they were well trained and ready to pass on all they had learned. They were a great bunch of young men, and our parting was a little on the sad side. Of course I never was able to follow their trail after leaving the school, but I have to believe that they performed whatever was asked of them.

I often think of this episode in my life whenever I read of anything racial in newspaper columns. It all seems so senseless to me. After all we are all God's children.

V.E. Day happened, I believe, sometime in late 1945, and I happened to be visiting my wife and her parents in Liverpool. They lived just around the corner from the Cellar Pub where the Beatles, all local lads, would perform on a regular basis in later years. There was singing and dancing going on in the streets, and as I walked along with my wife people would come up and thank me and hug me. You'd think I was personally responsible for our victory. Still, I did understand how they felt and it made me feel good.

Only the Japanese Imperial Army was now fighting us, but it wasn't too long after that they too surrendered to our government. Peace was now complete, and it was 1945. Still, being the type of instructor I was, I was kept in the army by the war office until 1947. The army school was dispersed in 1946, and I was sent to Chester in Wales to finish my army service with the Manchester regiment. I was finally demobilized at an army depot in Oldham, ten miles from my hometown. I was given a set of civilian clothing plus a character reference and discharge papers, and that was all. I was given no fringe benefits or cash as is the custom I think in the American military forces. So now I was a civilian on reserve if another emergency were to break out.

I would like to mention that during the last three months at Chester I came across an army bulletin informing us that personnel who had been away from their civilian trades for more than three years could apply to brush up on his skills by obtaining a part-time job working 9:00 a.m. until 4:00 p.m., but they must find their own job. The employer would be notified that no payment need be made to service personnel. I found a nice small upholstering shop in Chester with just four employees doing mainly reupholstering. I was given a start by the owner, who was a very nice elderly gentleman. I took to the work very quickly, and my skills had not diminished by much. At the end of the week, on a Friday, when the workers were given their wages, he came to me and said, "I know I don't have to pay you anything for your work here, but you are a good worker and if it's all right with you I'll give you union rate wages until you finish in the service and I'll be happy to have you here." Naturally I was delighted, and so for the last three months in the army I was drawing two paychecks and my wife was able to save money for us. Meanwhile my wife, who had been living with my mom and my brother for some time, had been working at a large department store in Manchester called C & A selling toys. She only weighed eighty-five pounds, and she was considered not physically suitable for the war effort.

Now I was a full-fledged civilian. It was 1947, and I had to think about what I wanted to do with my life. My musical group, The Melody Four, had outgrown themselves and disbanded. However, my brother, Sonny, had teamed up with his girlfriend, Pam, as a piano, ukulele, and vocal duo. They later married and coached, produced, and promoted a cast of twenty calling it "The Sonny Warner Show." (My brother changed his name from Wagner to Warner during the war because he thought people might think he was German.) The Sonny Warner Show is still going as strong as ever today, though with ever-changing talent, and they have appeared on radio, tv, and even put in a couple of shows before members of the Royal Family. Pam and Sonny now have three grown sons who are all married with children. One of their boys, Brian, has his own band called "The Lemon Tree" which is one of the top stage bands in Great Britain. Some of the children performed on The Sonny Warner Show. You can see that show business is in the family genes.

Coming back to civilian life after almost seven years in the army was certainly a little more difficult than I imagined. I'd been through so much in all the time away from home that I'd led myself to believe I was capable of doing anything. The stark truth, however, was that I was now an ordinary civilian looking for work, but I was also seeking to find myself and what I wanted to do. It is true that I was offered my old pre-war job again. I also pondered whether or not to pursue a show business career. I decided against both of these options. I was twenty-seven, and I thought it was too late to pick up my soccer career.

My oldest brother, Louis, who had been working during the war at Faireys Aviation plant, had been released after the cessation of war and was doing upholstering repairs and renovations in a small room above a drapery (clothing) shop owned by his wife. He had much more work than he could handle alone, so about two weeks after my release from the forces, I decided to become his full-time partner. Lucky for both of us, it turned out to be a wise decision. The work was plentiful, and we were fast becoming known for our high standard of work. My brother was a good worker. He was very clean and very steady on the job. I was a very fast worker and well acquainted with all the modern up-to-date methods of upholstering due to my having brushed up on everything while working at that small upholstering factory during my last three months in the service. Now it was beginning to pay off for my brother and me. I was also good at seeking repair work and estimating time and costs. In addition to all of this, my old pre-war employer asked me if I would do some sub-contracting work for him producing new upholstered furniture. They had a license issued by a branch of H.M. Government called The Board of Trade which allowed them to make new furniture. It began during the war when materials were scarce. The materials were still scarce, and so the licenses were not easy to be had.

I began to reflect on what my brother and I had achieved during the first six months of our partnership. We were certainly making money. So far we were able to get enough work, but I knew eventually the work would stop coming since not everyone wants old furniture reupholstered when they can purchase new furniture for very little difference. So after discussing it with my brother, I came to the conclusion that to go forward in this business we needed three things. First of all we needed a much larger shop in which to work. We also needed a telephone, which in those days was about impossible because of the lack of equipment and a long waiting list. Finally we needed a Board of Trade License to produce new furniture, which I knew was not going to be an easy task since they were not issuing any new licenses.

So with all of this in mind I took it upon myself to try to achieve all three tasks while my brother kept on working upstairs above the little shop. I presented myself at the telephone company's offices on a Monday morning and spoke to a male representative. Although he was sympathetic to my cause, he told me all he could do was put me on the list of people waiting. We were looking at a two-year wait. I asked him if I could talk to a supervisor and he agreed. I was shown in to an office where a pleasant-looking lady was sitting at her desk. I pleaded my case, telling her about my years in the army, how we were finding it extremely difficult to operate our business with no telephone, and how I believed I deserved some extra consideration. She turned out to be so very nice and supportive, and she promised to make our request for a telephone on top priority. Within two weeks we had our telephone.

It then occurred to me to try for our new furniture license using the same course of reasoning. The Board of Trade was so very obliging, and I was really surprised when they agreed to give us a license. We then proceeded to look for a larger shop and got lucky in a very short time. The new shop turned out to be a small factory where they had been working on war products, and it was spacious, all on one floor with a rear loading dock.

We then started by traveling on the road in a small car we had just purchased for the business. Our orders were beginning to come in so we had to employ, to begin with, three male upholsterers and one female upholsteress.

It was now the beginning of 1949, and our business was growing fairly large. We had been on a monthly rental basis in our factory since the owner had plans for the plant in the future. It happened that one day he came in to tell us we would have to vacate the premises since he was going into the business of producing a material called Dura-Glit contained in metal containers. Dura-Glit was an excellent product for cleaning brass, chrome, etc. We were rather shocked since we were right in the middle of our busy season. I even remember this owner's name, Mr. Hardman. We pleaded with him to let us stay on at least until we could find a suitable place. He was such a very nice man, and he turned out to be very good to us. He had some property just about one quarter mile away on which he said he had decided to build, and he asked us if we would care to purchase the building and property. He also offered to allow us to continue where we were until the new building was completed. We agreed on a price, and he proceeded to go on with the building, which he completed in just about four months. It turned out to be one of the best deals we ever made. It was very spacious with separate restrooms and some spare land which our employees used on their mid-day break to play pick-up soccer.

It was 1950, and our employees now were up to two upholsteresses and six upholsters, including my brother, Joey; my brother, Louis; and myself. Our work force was now up to ten people.

I'd like to go back in time, if I may, to 1944, when my wife and I got married. She had told me often before our marriage that she had a grandmother and many uncles, aunts, and cousins living in Portland, Oregon, U.S.A. There was also an older sister who was married to an ex-GI. It seems they had always wanted my wife, when she was single, to join them. As soon as we were married, we got an open invitation to live our life in Portland. However, I wasn't too enthused since we had everything going for us in Manchester. I had a good wife; a good partnership business; all my brothers, sisters, and both parents; plus all my sporting interests, especially soccer and cricket, so we turned it down.

However, my wife's mother, who had been in ill health for many years, passed away not too long after the German surrender. After that my father-in-law, who was deeply affected by her passing, was asked by his family in the U.S.A. to join them and bring his family along too. I believe it was 1948 when my wife's father, along with his two sons and three daughters, left Liverpool by boat for permanent residence in the U.S.A. This left my wife and one other sister whose husband also didn't fancy taking the big step to the U.S.A.

To bring you back up to date, the year was 1952. Business was good, and we had just purchased our very first home in a suburb of Manchester called Prestwich. It was a really nice home. Our one and only child, David, who was born in 1947, was almost five years old and had some new friends with whom he could play soccer and cricket. Nearly all kids in England, both boys and girls, grow up playing and watching these two sports. He was also doing extremely well in school and was just a great kid. I guess we all feel that way about our children, and that is certainly understandable.

We were constantly being asked to seriously think about joining my wife's family in Portland, Oregon. However, I still didn't want to do that, mostly because it would be difficult for my brother to run the business alone. So we just kept plugging along. I also didn't relish leaving my dad, brothers, and sisters.

It was somewhere around Christmas 1952 when we got a letter from my wife's oldest brother offering us, as he put it, probably the last chance for us to go to the U.S.A. since he would have to arrange for a sponsor to sign to bring us over and an affidavit stating he would ensure our livelihood and not be a burden to the state. In those days there was a huge waiting list to immigrate to the U.S.A. In addition to a sound sponsor, other conditions for immigration included a consulate interview, strict physical examinations with X-rays, and a currency limit entering the U.S.A. of 300 pounds sterling which was then equal to approximately $450. You had to pay for food and other supplies on the trip to the states out of that money. It was illegal to exceed that amount.

I gave the offer a lot of thought. I pondered over it for weeks and discussed it with many of my peers in the business. We finally agreed to accept the offer to live our lives in Portland, Oregon, U.S.A. I envisioned myself getting a job with my wife's uncles, who had this huge store selling not only furniture, electrical appliances, and hardware, but also sporting goods. It was the latter where I expected to fit in nicely. At that time I never knew that sporting goods in the U.S.A. included all types of firearms, which of course would be second nature for me since it hadn't been that long since I had been away from firearms.

Now came the extremely difficult task of having to tell my brother, Louis, of my plans. To say he was shocked is putting it mildly. I've often wondered if maybe I didn't handle it very well, but in hindsight I just can't think of any other way I could have done it.

We received our papers for entering the U.S.A. in early March 1953. We booked passage at the earliest possible date which was May 29th, sailing on HMS Queen Elizabeth leaving Southhampton (England) for New York.

Meanwhile I did all I could to make things in the business easier for my brother to handle. Since I did bench work, buying, selling, and the book work, it was not going to be easy for him. I loved my brother very much. I began to feel so bad about the whole thing, but my brothers and sisters were all in favor of what I was about to do.

Now we had to sell our home, but fortunately it was a nice home. In those days homes were hard to come by, especially a house like ours. We were able to find a very nice family to purchase our home who also understood our position and agreed to allow us to stay on in our home until the week we were due to leave Manchester.

Sad to say, just a few weeks before we were to leave, my mom took sick, and I called in the family doctor. He indicated to me that things didn't look good and referred me to an internal specialist. The doctor's name was Mr. Ordman. In England doctors are called Mr. if they are specialists. Anyway, Mr. Ordman came to our house to see my mom, and turned out to be an ex-classmate of mine. He told me how terribly sorry he was but there was nothing he could do for her. It was just a matter of days. She died just two days afterwards. It was just a few weeks later that my family and I would be leaving England, and it was a sad time all around.

Eventually, the time came to say good-bye to my dad, brothers, and sisters, and it was a tearful farewell. We boarded the boat train at Victoria Station in Manchester and were on our way to Southhampton, a three and a half hour overnight journey, arriving at the pier at four o'clock in the morning. We were then put in line to go through customs and an examination of our papers. Finally we were allowed on board the Queen Elizabeth at about six o'clock in the morning and we were to sail at 8:30 a.m.

We had great accommodations and the boat itself was exactly all it was hyped up to be—literally a floating city. It had been used in WWII for transporting troops, and upon cessation of hostilities the boat had been completely refurbished and renovated. We were on its maiden voyage since being in dry dock since 1948. Coincidentally, our voyage had us on the Atlantic the day our Queen Elizabeth had her coronation. They made a special dinner celebration on board that day, and I still have the menu which I've kept all these years. A collector's item? Maybe.

Our journey was almost like a great vacation, and yet I couldn't help feeling a little nervous about what to expect when we got to the end of the journey. Incidentally, they held an open table tennis tournament on the boat. I won the tournament since I was a very good table tennis player, and I received a gift voucher for twenty-five pounds (approximately $36.00) to spend at the ship's gift shop.

The trip on the ocean took almost six days, and what was very interesting for me was that just about two hours from New York harbor a small speed boat came across the water. A ladder was lowered from the side of the ship, and a civilian carrying a large briefcase climbed up the ladder from the speed boat and came on board. The speed boat immediately took off. The ship's captain explained on the PA system that a ship's pilot was on board to take over and guide us through the channel for a safe docking at New York harbor. Seems like I'm always learning something.

We eventually landed at New York harbor, and I will never forget my first view of the Statute of Liberty. What a grand sight. I remember first learning about it in my early elementary school classes in England. The Queen Elizabeth seemed to sail close by it. It's such a huge structure, and it means so much to the U.S.A. It is a sort of symbol of freedom.

We proceeded through American customs this time, and it seemed to take hours to get through it but in actual fact it took just under two hours. When we left England, it was overcast and rainy and about sixty degrees. On this day, June 3, 1953, it was a hot New York at ninety-eight degrees. We had a one and a half hour layover and then we got on the train to Chicago where we changed on to another train which took us into Portland. When we arrived in Chicago it was a steaming hot one hundred and four degrees. Remember we were not used to this type of weather since the hottest I can ever remember was about eighty-four degrees. The three of us felt very uncomfortable, but we just toughed it out and boarded the Chicago-based train bound for Seattle stopping for us at Portland, Oregon.

It was a very eventful journey for us since we were seeing towns and countryside that we had only seen in movies or read about in magazines. I can well remember the train pulling into Sun Valley and seeing young boys and girls carrying skis getting off of the train. You just don't see that in England, at least not in Manchester, unless someone has produced a snow mountain over there. I don't know exactly why, but thoughts of Sonya Henjie went through my mind seeing all of this. Remember her in Sun Valley? I think she was the star in the movie made there.

Eventually tired, rather hungry, and with very little of our cash allowance remaining, we arrived in Portland, Oregon, at the Union Station where nearly all the families were waiting for our arrival. The reason a few were not there was because they just couldn't get away from their work, but we would catch up with them during that same evening. It was on June 5, 1953, that we pulled in to Union Station, and although it was a nice day, it was a much more comfortable temperature than Chicago since it was between eighty and eighty-five degrees.

The American side of the family had arranged for us to stay with my wife's younger brother, Harry, his wife, Sylvia, and their daughter, Janet, who was about our son David's age, until we were able to settle down. The evening of our arrival all the families came to Harry's house to meet us, and it was confusing for me since there seemed to be so many of them. Of course it would be easier to know them as time went by.

The first few days in Portland were extremely rough for the three of us, especially our six-year-old son. We were just, to put it bluntly, plain homesick. However, we kept hoping that it would wear off after awhile, but it didn't. As a matter of fact it got much worse before it got better.

It seems that just before we arrived in Portland the family's large business began having problems and it was a difficult time for them. Consequently, the job I had envisioned for myself failed to materialize, and I found myself out on the streets literally unemployed and looking for a job. After about two and one half weeks of searching, since I wanted to stay away from upholstering, I finally took on a job at an army surplus store. The owner was the same age as myself, thirty-five, and was an American ex-Air Force waist gunner. The only other person working with him, that I could tell, was his mother, an elderly lady in her seventies who just sat by the cash register and watched the main floor. It was a huge building, five floors, containing mostly GI surplus merchandise, and everything was spread out with no organized layout.

It was very difficult for me at first, mainly because I had to learn not only the merchandise, but all the many different American names and words for everything. I'm a very quick learner, however, and after a couple of months I had a very good grasp on things in general. I was on the main floor selling, and I would also help unload huge trucks which were sometimes full of very heavy equipment. I also cleaned up the store and set up displays. In general I just did whatever it took to help sales. My boss would sometimes go off for days at a time on buying trips, leaving his mother and myself to take care of the business. Having been in business I was able to handle it very well. The surplus business was getting bigger and better, and I liked to think I had a little something to do with it since I was working very hard to try to improve the business. We eventually took on some extra help. The boss got his brother-in-law to work with me, and we also took on a part-time female secretary. This job was more challenging than I'd ever imagined.

Meanwhile I had been getting lots of mail from my brothers, and they also mailed some newspapers since they all knew I enjoyed reading the sports sections. In one of these papers an item caught my eye. It was about an ex-Fly Weight Boxing Champion of the World named Rinty Monaghan, and he was making a public appearance to open a new arena. The name was familiar to me, and I can clearly recall why. Rinty was Irish and born in Belfast.

The year was 1943, and I was on leave from North Ireland. I was heading back to Ireland on a boat from Stranraer in Scotland. We had just set sail, and I began to walk around the boat even though it was evening. I thought I heard someone moaning as if in pain. I looked around, and in one of the corners of the bays sitting on the deck with his back up against the side of the boat was this young teenager who looked to be no more than about fourteen to sixteen years old. I was to learn later, however, that he was twenty-two years old about that time. I had my flashlight on my equipment belt and had a good look to see what the problem was. His face was a mess. One eye was almost completely shut, the other eye was slightly discolored, and his lips were all puffed up. He told me he was a boxer and that he was returning to his home in Belfast having fought the previous night in a town called Newcastle which is northeast country. He was hungry and cold. I didn't have a blanket, and the boat certainly didn't cater to passengers, especially troops since it was war time and their job was just to transport the troops. However, at Stranraer that afternoon, prior to boarding, all service men were given rations for the long trip which consisted of one meat sandwich, one candy bar, and two ginger snap biscuits. I immediately knew what I had to do to help this young boxer. I took the meat out of the sandwich and had him apply it to his eye. I then gave him half my candy bar, a biscuit, and a drink of the cold water I had in my canteen. I saw to it that he was comfortable, but then I had to leave him since I had to report to the administration office. I never did see him again during the journey since it was a rather big boat. I learned later that he had won that fight.

The years went by and it was 1946, just before the end of the war with Germany. I was in my wife's home in Liverpool having the evening off duty at the

Army School, and I noticed in the local paper that Rinty Monaghan from Belfast would be fighting an opponent whose name I can't remember for the Flyweight Championship of the World in Liverpool Stadium the following week. I told my wife how I met him, and she said, "You enjoy boxing, why don't we go to the fight to see him in action?"

The following week I was able to get that evening off, and along with my wife I went to the stadium. What a great fight it turned out to be. I couldn't believe this was the same kid I met on the boat. He looked bigger and very fit. He won a fifteen-round decision and the World Title. I told my wife, Rose, that I would try to get to see him in his dressing room after the fight. Meanwhile, here he was with the championship belt around his waist singing a good old Irish song in the center of the ring. He was really something, this kid, and he was a terrific singer.

I made my way to where the fighters dressed, and there were all kinds of security guards there. My wife waited a little distance off to the side, and I explained to one of the main guards who I wanted to see. He began to tell me it just wasn't possible, but as luck would have it one of Rinty's handlers overheard me. The handler came up to me, and I told him who I was and why I was there. He went into the champ's dressing room and in no time flat he was out again telling the guard it was all right for me to come by. I had no sooner entered the dressing room when Rinty stepped out of the shower, having about dried off, and almost smothered me in his grasp. He kept telling all his handlers around him that, "This is the feller that took care of me after that hard fight in Newcastle." I didn't think he would remember me after three years. He asked to meet my wife after he slipped on a robe. We had a nice but short talk and finally said our good-byes. He really was a great kid.

Reminiscing of my years in the British Army, I can still recall being issued a Lee Enfield 303 Rifle MKI with the long bayonet and open sights. The rifle weighed over seven pounds. It felt like a ton of bricks when I first handled it. I was given instructions by the platoon sergeant to "Treat your rifle like a close friend and for goodness sakes never ever let it get lost!" I really worked my rifle over during the next few weeks. I constantly polished the action and cleaned the barrel bore. It got so that I felt the rifle was part of me. Although it was a single shot bolt action, I got to the point when I was at the army school that I could fire from a prone position at a target one or two hundred yards away, get off between twenty-five or thirty shots in a minute, and be somewhere around the target. Not bad for a kid who had never handled a rifle before the war. All guns were banned in England except for use by the military forces or police. I'll have a word on that subject later on. Anyway, my old rifle, serial #A91827, was scrapped and replaced by a much lighter rifle, still a

Lee Enfield 303 but MK4. This issue had a much shorter and more pointed bayonet, and the bayonet could be used separately as a hand weapon in close combat. It also had aperture sights for more accuracy instead of the old open sights. So much for my old rifle, which was like losing one's best friend, but sometimes changes are for the better. The newly issued rifle turned out to be just that and more.

I don't know if I mentioned this previously, but forgive me if I have. Going into the army I thought, "Well, here goes my football (soccer) and cricket days," but I was wrong about that. The army put out several representative teams in both sports. The teams often played against the Navy, the Air Force, and teams from the local towns. Most teams were made up consisting of two, three, or sometimes more professionals who were now in the service. I got lucky and was selected to play on one of the army teams, not only in soccer and cricket, but also in field hockey which I picked up in the army. In field hockey I played right wing, which was my playing position in soccer too. I really felt good about all of this. I became a fairly good field hockey player.

This brings to mind a time when I was a full corporal in Northern Ireland and along with my platoon sergeant I was in charge of a platoon (thirty-six men) training new recruits. We had this one skinny-looking dark-haired kid who was having trouble knowing his left from his right, so I had to take him one-on-one for extra instructions. His name was Eddie Wainwright, and he was from Liverpool. Since I had been in and around soccer before the war, the name rang a bell for me, yet I couldn't bring myself to believe that this awkward kid could be the same one who played left wing for Everton, a Division One team from Liverpool. I asked him, and it turned out that he was one and the same. He even played for England a couple of times before going down with an injury. I got to play on the same team in an army inter-company game, and it was almost impossible to believe that this was the kid from our platoon who didn't know one foot from the other. He was such a brilliant player, and he was fast, like quicksand. He eventually became a much better soldier and was shipped out overseas. I never did remember him getting back after the war.

I got to see literally thousands of recruits pass through the training depot in which I served at Palace Barracks, Northern Ireland. These young kids were from all walks of life, and at first looking at them coming up the hill into the main gates you couldn't help thinking how little like soldiers most of them looked. Yet after a few weeks of rigid training the change in most of them was simply amazing, and they went out to serve their country with so much pride. It gave me much personal satisfaction.

Sometimes it was a little amusing for me to see friends I'd left behind coming in for recruit training. They all seemed to realize I had a job to do, and we never had any problems of familiarity. NCO's were not allowed to fraternize with private soldiers. I doubt if that has changed even in these modern times. Yes, I could probably write a book on my army memoirs alone, but maybe another time. So much then for the army days. Now, again, I must get back to my story.

It was 1956, and I was getting very used to the type of business in which I worked and meeting many different people from all walks of life. I also still missed England, my dad, and my brothers and sisters. My wife urged me to take a trip home by myself since it would be very expensive for all three of us. I had two weeks holiday coming to me, so I took an extra week and went home for three weeks. I went by train from Portland to Vancouver, B.C. Then I took another train to Quebec via Montreal and boarded a ship to Southhampton (England) the day after arriving in Quebec. I was able to look around the city of Quebec, and I recalled its history with General Wolfe which we learned as kids in school. I never ever dreamed that one day I would get to see where the saga of General Wolfe took place. Since French was a language most English children learned in elementary school, I was able to converse with people in Quebec.

We sailed from Quebec and passed Newfoundland. On the way we got to see a huge iceberg even though it was a long distance from the ship. Having docked after a nice five days on board, I got through customs and then rented a car and drove on the motorway from London to Manchester. It was good to see the family, and before I knew it the three weeks had gone by. Once again it was time to say good-bye until we meet again. Little did I know, it would be the last time I would see my dad and it would be thirty years before I got to see my brothers and sisters again. Well, it was almost thirty years.

I drove the rented car back to London (which took nearly three hours) and arranged to return to Portland by plane. I got on the plane at Heathrow airport in London and landed in Chicago where we changed planes for Portland. Before taking off from Chicago the stewardess made the announcement that there were three nuns who had to make Seattle by that evening. If she could get three people to give up their seats, they would each receive $200.00 and then catch a plane that was due to leave five hours later. I gave up my seat along with two other passengers, believing that someone at the airport would tell my wife I would be on the next plane. The plane on which I gave up my seat crashed just a short distance out of Chicago, and though the casualties were few, there were some serious injuries. When I got to Portland, my wife and some of her family were at the airport and couldn't understand what had happened since they were not informed about my delay. I was lucky, and I honestly felt that someone up there was looking after me. After all of this it was back to my job at the surplus store, and this time I felt much better about it.

One day shortly after I had been back about two or three weeks, my employer came up to me and asked me if I would care to go with him for a workout lifting weights. Lifting weights was something I had only heard about but with which I had never come in contact. My soccer training was mainly exercises like present-day aerobics and ball control, ball heading, and chesting, and of course shooting corner kicks, penalties, and on-goal shots. Anyway, I readily agreed to go, and I clearly remember the first time I went. It was in the evening after we closed the store and it was winter. The roads were icy, it was snowing lightly, and it was very cold. My employer drove us to a large home on the southeast side of Portland, and we went down to the basement of the house. It was a fairly large place with lots of free weights, a squat rack, a bench for bench press, sit-up boards, etc. The owner of the home with this unique basement gym was George Pavlich who, with his wife, Eleanor; his two boys, Paul and Walter; and a girl named Melinda, lived in the house above the basement. After being introduced to George and about half a dozen other people working out there, my employer gave me a careful introduction and a beginner's workout of about forty-five minutes. When I was through and ready to leave, he told me I'd feel a little sore the next morning but not to worry. He also told me that if I liked working out, I could come back two days after and work out on a steadily increasing weight program three times a week. He also told me to be more careful about what I ate since working so hard getting in shape and not eating correctly would just be wasting time. That's been almost thirty-eight years ago, and I'll never forget that very first workout. It seemed to change my whole way of living. I have to thank my wife, Rose, and my son, David, for being so supportive of me doing this all these years, and I'm still doing it.

I should mention just for the record that George Pavlich was a National Junior Champion power lifter, and most of the ten guys working out were champions in their own weight class. I was sort of the new kid on the block at thirty-seven years old. Gosh, I thought I was an old man in America, but boy was I ever wrong. It eventually became a good part of my life since I was working out three times a week. Although I was the lightest weight in the gym, I was able to keep up. We really were a competitive bunch, and after just a year I entered my first power lifting contest. It was a dead lift competition in the 148-pound class, and being only 125 pounds, I was up against heavier lifters. However on this particular night I got lucky and won first place with a 400-pound lift. Later on I did lift 435 pounds, but it was during training and so it only mattered to me personally.

After a couple more years of heavy lifting, I decided to start on lighter weights and go into body building. This meant lots of sit-ups, push-ups, jogging, calisthenics, and many reps with the weights using lighter weights on the basic power lifts. I soon was able to do thousands of sit-ups without a break, and I actually did get carried away one time and performed 10,500 sit-ups in exactly four hours. This feat made the pages of a muscle magazine along with a picture of myself doing sit-ups. Meanwhile I was starting to look more like a body builder, and I was talking into entering a Pacific Coast Mr. Past 40 Physique Contest. I knew I had no chance, but I surprised myself by coming in fourth. I received a nice big trophy for my efforts.

Our basement gym closed down. George Pavlich and his wife Eleanor saw their children growing up fast, and they thought it was just not a good idea to have all these guys going up and down the stairs. Reluctantly George had to say "No more!" He told me to go over to his close friend Sam Loprinzi's gym in southeast Portland. Sam, himself an All-American Physique Champion, was in those days, along with his brothers, Gus, Joe, and Phil and cousins, Dave, Tony and Gus, the pioneer, if you will, of weight training and body building in Oregon. I won some more trophies working out at Sam's, and to this day I am still working out there three times a week. I thoroughly recommend weight lifting to men and women, and believe me, some of the women are very good.

Meanwhile back at the surplus store, I was taking more control of the business since my employer was often gone for days at a time. I gradually started making up my own ads for insertion in the local paper. Soon our total sales started to climb, and I asked my employer if he would mind having my wife work part-time on the sales floor. He agreed and it turned out for the best. My wife, Rose, loves people and she also loves shoes. She sort of took over in the shoe department. My son, David, who was now about thirteen years old, came in the store one time and helped out.

We were going along real good in the surplus store, and I kept up my workouts after work. Sometimes I did not get home until ten o'clock, so those were long days for me as I generally left home before seven o'clock in the morning. I liked what I was doing, but one day my boss came up to me to tell me that he had taken a full partner into his business and we were going into the wholesale business as well as retail. It was at this point that I knew I would never get any further in the store since I had some hopes of maybe one day being offered the chance of a small part of the business. It was not to be, however, and I even found myself having to put more hours in and work that much harder once the partnership began.

It was just a few months previous to this that I recall reading in the Oregon Journal that a disc jockey contest was being run by the KPOJ radio station. Before even being looked at you were to submit an application and resume of experience. Deep down I guess I was still hoping for a spot in show business, so I sent in my application and just forgot all about it until about a month later. A representative for KPOJ called me to invite me to the station for a personal interview. They talked to me and finally asked me if I could do a twenty minute disc jockey show. I of course said, "yes," but I said that I would like to use my own records which were all English entertainers and new issues that my brother and show business friends had sent me.

As best as I can recall, there were two other young men and a young girl besides myself who were to spin records for twenty minutes each. I was the last one to go on the air and I was eager and ready to go. I had brought along four records of entertainers who I personally knew from back home, and I was able to give the listeners some interesting information on each of them, having done my homework well. I can still remember the host DJ for KPOJ that day. He was a young, energetic man named Rod Louden who later did some wrestling announcing. As I was spinning my records, I could hear his call board ringing and lighting up, and he gave me a thumbs up sign, so I knew it was going well. I learned soon afterwards that I had placed first, and I was asked to return for a full thirty-minute program at a later date. By the way, first place carried with it many prizes of good merchandise, including a complete set of World Book Encyclopedias which I still have and use constantly.

After my return visit to KPOJ, I learned there was a DJ spot open at another prominent Portland radio station. I auditioned for the job hoping to get into show business again. I thought I'd done well, but I was told they couldn't consider me because my English accent was a little too thick. So my hopes went out the window even though shortly after that I did a spot with another DJ at the now-defunct Amatos Supper Club in downtown Portland.

Well here I was once again, back at the surplus store and as you American's often say, "working my tail off"! It just didn't get any easier although I was able to handle the work very efficiently.

The years went by, and my son was at Lincoln High School. He had just starting his freshman year. The year was 1962, and I had been at the surplus store over ten years now, with never a day off. I came down with a kidney infection. I was hospitalized for a few days and had a recurrence shortly after. Finally, after a few days off, I was back to feeling good again. However, the day before I was going to return to work, I decided to look in on my employer and advise him that I would be returning to work along with my wife who had taken off work to be with me. My boss was very nice and very sympathetic, but he said he could not accept my wife coming back to work. He said he didn't want to pay both of us for being off work if I got sick again. I may be wrong, but I really didn't think I deserved what I was hearing, and my wife was with me at the time. What he was saying in a guarded way was that he did not want my wife to return to work. Naturally there was nothing I could say or wanted to say, but right there and then I made up my mind that I would start making plans to do something about my future. But for the time being, I would return to my job and do the best I could just as I always tried to do.

Meanwhile, the secretary of the surplus store advised my wife that she had worked long enough to be eligible for unemployment benefits. My wife applied and eventually received her first payment check and it turned out to be a little more than she was making part-time at the surplus store. What a way to get a raise.

I knew at this time I would not be working much longer at the surplus store. I'd already been there almost eleven years and in view of what had happened, I felt that I ought to be thinking of moving on to bigger and better things. After a couple of months drawing her unemployment pay, my wife, who is a very smart sales person, got herself a full-time job with a discount shoe store. At her new job she was paid more than double the salary she made at the surplus store.

It was now mid-1963, and my wife had worked at the shoe store for nearly a year. She loved selling shoes, especially ladies shoes, and she would often sell six to twelve pairs to a customer. Meanwhile, I had plugged along on my job, but I was not as happy on the job as I had been for so many years. I was getting myself ready to get away from there, but before I leave off on this part of my life's journey, I would like to recall an incident that happened to me a long time back. Since I am recalling my story completely from memory, I sometimes must go back in time because I forgot to mention something or other, so please bear with me.

Anyway, I had only been in the U.S.A. a few week and the surplus store in which I worked was located on S.W. 1st Avenue in Portland. Located right behind us on Front Street was the Oregon Journal newspaper building which covered a complete block.

One day at the store a young man approached me and introduced himself as a columnist at the Journal. He asked if I'd be interested in writing a piece for his column making a comparison between living in the U.S.A. and living in England. Rather reluctantly I agreed, and I finally came up with a rough draft for his scrutiny. It dealt mainly with the two things that stood out so vividly as far as I was concerned: gun control and health care. Remember this was 1953. I also dealt with sports on a lesser note, saying that the U.S.A. was so far ahead of England, which I thought was due mainly to having the benefit of a population thirty times larger. I finished off with saying that the U.S.A. was one of the best, if not the best, country in the world and people ought not to take the country for granted and be thankful for being an American. Now I don't know if I wrote it forty years too soon or came down too hard on the two main points, but the article was turned down. I still have the original copy, and I sometimes look at it. I still feel it's even more applicable now than it was then. Gun control and health care are both hot issues today.

It was the middle of 1963 when my wife and I decided to take a chance. We were both the same age, forty-five years old, and thought it was time we tried to open up our own business. We decided we would open a discount family shoe store, an area in which we both had expertise. I decided the best way to go would be for us to locate a low-cost rented building, begin with a low budget stock, and let my wife run it at the beginning along with a part-time helper and my son helping out after school and on weekends. First things first, however, and our first job was to find a suitable location. We searched around for some time before deciding on a vacated old building in a low rent area of northeastern Portland. It had been a pharmacy and it was a corner location. You might say we started from scratch since there were hardly any other stores around us. We did have a doctor and a dentist in the same block which made it more comfortable.

I still recall taking my wife along in our station wagon, driving very early one Sunday morning to an appointment we had with a discount shoe store in Tacoma, Washington. We arrived there around nine o'clock, had a quick cup of coffee, and went on to meet with our contact. Our negotiations took us about three hours, during which time we had purchased somewhere around three hundred or three hundred and fifty pairs of assorted ladies and mens shoes and had them loaded in our wagon and ready for the trip back. When we reached Portland we unloaded at the store we rented and worked until late evening setting out the shoes in some order so that we could be ready for selling the following morning. The selling was now my wife's job, and I can tell you that opening a store from scratch, even with a small local ad in the paper, is far being a cake walk. As a matter of fact, that very first week's sales were so bad I wouldn't have blamed my wife if she would have said, "This is hopeless!" But then again, both my wife and myself are very hard workers, and we certainly do not give up on anything very easily. Our son is also like his parents.

As for myself, I carried on working at the surplus store for a couple of reasons. One being that I thought it made good sense to ensure that we had at least one paycheck coming in each week and the other that it would be wise to see how we made out in the first year of business.

In relation to all of this, I would like to tell you of an incident that happened to me at the surplus store during our first year of business at the shoe store in the northeast. I was just finishing off a large amount of camping gear sales to a customer and he asked me how my wife was doing and where her store was located since she had served him a few times at the surplus store. All I could really tell him was that it was tough getting started, I could only give him the street number since it was almost impossible to give accurate directions from where I worked at the shoe store, and I also didn't feel comfortable doing that. It just so happened that the new partner overheard what was going on and later approached me. His first works were, "Are you in the habit of directing our customers to your wife's shoe store?" I just sort of ignored his comments, but I was resolved more than ever not to spend much more time working in that store. I'd just about had enough, and I had very little to show for almost eleven years of hard work, along with accepting all the responsibility given to me and being an extremely honest person. As my boss said to me when I eventually gave my notice to quit a few months later, "You realize of course that you are not indispensable." I agreed with his remark and said so at the time. I really meant what I said because I've always felt that no matter how good a person may be at what they are or what they do, there is someone somewhere who will always be or do it better. However, I must say without being facetious that they never did find someone to effectively do my work, and they tried any number of people. I'm not saying it was because of my leaving their store, but after I left their business began a steady decline. Maybe it was just a coincidence, but a few years later they were out of business.

As for me, I had gone over to join my wife and run the shoe store. It was 1964 and though there had been a slight steady increase in sales that first year, it was a long way off from being good enough. I decided to take to the road and go searching for contacts to purchase job lots of overrides or distressed stocks of shoes and also to submit bids on a couple of bankrupt shoe stores. My travels took me as far as Hollywood, California; Roseburg; Klamath Falls; Albany; Seattle; and even Montana. I was very fortunate in making contact with some nice business people. I was able to purchase, by this route, a fairly large assorted inventory, with the main emphasis on ladies well-known brands of shoes. You name it, we had them. We were also lucky enough to be the high bidder on a Lake Grove shoe store complete with al the accessories, and so now we had our shoe store well stocked with an all-around good inventory.

The next step for us was that we worked out a quarter-page ad for the Sunday Oregonian, the Oregon Journal, and the Portland Reporter. I worked on the ad for hours with input from my wife, my son, and a wonderful Oregonian salesperson named Wes. I wish now that I'd kept a copy of the first ad since it worked so very well for us. It was headed in a banner-like heading: SPECTACU-LAR SHOE SALE. We had the space divided in boxes, each box with a picture of the shoe and the discount price. Then, of course, the days and hours of the sale, the length of the sale, and the location was listed. Our store was really mobbed that first day, but learning from my experience at the surplus store, I had anticipated something like that and hired extra help. Some of the girls who worked for us are now doctors, nurses, and executive officers, and as I always told them, "Once you learn to sell shoes you are able to do whatever you set your mind to." I still say selling shoes is such a great experience, and it is no longer the butt of jokes for comedians as it used to be. I know of many movie and television stars and some high level executives who started off in life selling shoes.

As the years went by things gradually got better for us. In 1968 we purchased our very first home in the U.S.A. It was a rather modest, three-bedroom, ranch-style home with a single garage and just one bathroom. It was close to our store in the Rose City district on the northeast side and just a ten-minute drive to work. It was our very own home, and we took such good care of it. We went on to live there twenty-one years.

My son David had graduated from Lincoln High, and he was a freshman at Southern Oregon College in Ashland. He had to decide between a medical or law degree, and he finally chose the latter. We sure missed his help at the store since he was one heck of a worker and he was very good with children. After a year at Ashland he decided to come back to Portland, and he graduated from college at Portland State. He decided to take a year off before going to law school at Lewis and Clark and he worked again at our store for the year. After a year he began law school at Lewis and Clark, and even though his work load was heavy with tons of studying involved, he still helped us out on weekends when we needed him most. He finally graduated from law school in 1974. It had not been easy for him since he had put a lot of time in helping us out at the store. He made a decision not to pursue his law career since we really needed him at the store, but we did not make the decision for him.

My son gradually began to take on more responsibility in the store, and he began doing some purchasing. At this time I should mention that about six or seven years earlier the Nike athletic shoes were the real hot item in the business. It was impossible to connect with the Nike athletic shoe people, then trading as Blue Ribbon Sports, to purchase from them. We were initially turned down since the demand was so big they could barely keep their regular retailers happy. Phil Knight, a one-time Oregon track miler, was the man in charge. I, of course, knew of him but had never spoken to him. One day I was in the shoe store and I was thinking of how nice it would be if we could latch on with Nike athletic shoes. Our phone rang constantly with people asking if we carried the Nike athletic shoe, and we felt so bad about telling people we didn't carry the shoe. So who should walk into our store but my good friend and brother of Sam, Joe Loprinzi. Guess what shoe he wanted? You guessed right if you said the Nike athletic shoe. I told Joe how I'd tried and was turned down. Joe knew Phil Knight very well since he was Athletic Director at the MAC Club and Mr. Knight worked out there. He suggested I call him and to let him know about Joe suggested I call.

A couple of days later I was finally able to make contact with Mr. Knight. I explained that we were a family shoe store in retail and had at least four or six high schools all within close proximity. I told him that we were snowed under with calls for Nike athletic shoes and we felt terrible having to tell them we just didn't carry that brand. Being extremely sports-oriented myself made it even worse for me. Mr. Knight was very nice and listened to all I had to say. We finished our conversation with my explaining to him that since there was no other Nike athletic shoe retailer within a couple of miles of our store we ought to be given consideration. He told me he would give the matter some thought and asked me to call him back in a couple of weeks. He was and still is a class gentlemen. I did call back, and I was very surprised and happy when he agreed to supply us, as he put it, "on a limited basis" since their production was so far behind in orders. He wished me good luck on our future business relationship and we left it at that. This began a very good business venture for us when we latched on with Blue Ribbon Sports. We would eventually end up being one of Nike athletic shoe's best independent retail stores. We felt like a part of the Nike athletic shoe family.

I well recall driving in our station wagon to the Nike athletic shoe ware-house to pick up the cartons of shoes which we urgently needed and seeing all of the employees working and looking very happy at their work. I can't say I was surprised since the Nike athletic shoe people are a class act with a super guy at the head of the company. My relations with the company were always the best, and I'll always have good memories of them. Not incidentally, by any means, but Nike athletic shoes also manufacturers a great line of shoes. Sorry if I sound like a Nike athletic shoe salesman, but since this is a biography of my life, I just like to say whatever I'm feeling or have felt.

I have to tell you about a time when, after being in the U.S.A. just over a year and it was 1954, I was given a one week holiday from my job at the surplus store. We had an old but rather big four-door passenger 1945 Dodge which we bought after about three months on my job. Anyway, we decided to take a chance and go to Santa Cruz and then to Santa Monica. My wife and I were both thirty-six years old and my son was seven years old at the time. Without too much thinking about whether we could make it, the three of us took off. It was in July and it had been a very hot summer. I can still remember lots of things that happened along the way.

I remember we went by way of Klamath Falls where the engine of the car overheated. After pulling into a service station and getting the thermostat fixed, we carried on into Redding where the temperature was a burning hot one hundred eleven degrees. We pulled into a public park with an outdoor pool and I went for a swim while my wife and son relaxed at the pool side. After a swim, I laid down on a Sunday newspaper which had been spread out on the grass, and all three of us fell asleep since had been going since leaving Portland. When I awoke my wife took one look at me and began laughing her head off. It seemed that I had a full page print of the Sunday Oregonian on my back. It must have looked weird, so I jumped in the pool again and got cleaned up after I got out. What an experience that turned out to be.

Soon we were on our way again having eaten and feeling refreshed. We stopped again after a few more hours of driving somewhere near Sacramento at a local park, and I could hear music coming from somewhere. We made our way to from where it was coming and parked the wagon in the shade. The sun was still very hot and strong although it was late afternoon. I'd never heard music with a sound like that before, and we lingered a while to listen and enjoy the music since it sounded so very good. I later asked one of the young men standing around what kind of music was playing, and that was when I first heard the term "Country and Western Music." I always had a good ear for music and for recognizing talent. I told my wife that one day this kind of music would catch on big in this country, and eventually it turned out to do just that.

We had a good time in California, especially in Santa Monica, which had a beautiful beach. We also went to the MGM Studios on a tour and saw quite a few movie stars while we were there. We went to a baseball game and it was, if I re- member correctly, at Chavez Ravine Stadium between the Los Angeles Angels and New York Yankees. Our son wanted to see Mickey Mantle since he had heard so much about him at his school. We got to see him play, and it turned out to be a great sunny day and a good game. Mickey played great too.

Finally, before ending our stay in sunny California, we went to watch horse racing at Holywood Park, which I'd only seen on the movies in England. It's a beautiful sight to see. It is very picturesque and extremely colorful. My boy had his tiny camera with him and took some nice pictures of the horses and jockeys. Sad to say, though, the pictures all turned out perfectly, but they have somehow disappeared these past few years. It's really a pity because he had taken one photograph of the great jockey Willie Shoemaker. As we were leaving the racetrack, I can still remember David asking, "Dad, do you think you can one day buy me a racehorse?" What a dreamer, I thought at the time. As events were to prove later on, he was right on the mark.

We finally make it back to Portland with just one minor incident which turned out to be a punctured tire. We had a great time and it was a time all three of us would always remember. I vowed, however, that if ever I returned to California, it would have to be in a much better car than the old Dodge.

I must apologize to my readers for sometimes going back in time to recall certain episodes of my life, but I feel obliged to speak about them as they enter my mind. It's just a little difficult going back forty years in time.

The year was 1974, and our business was doing quite well. The work was hard but we enjoyed it, and we enjoyed our customers along with the children who were always nice to have in the store. They were a good part of our business, and we got along so well with them. Now our supply of Nike athletic shoes became more plentiful since we were doing such a good job selling them. We went into selling Nike T-shirts, shorts, bags, headbands, wrist bands, sweatshirts, caps, and sweatsuits. Our relationships with the Nike athletic store factory were really first class. I can recall a time in our shoe store when the Nike athletic shoe factory sent one of their public relations men out to our store to give some sort of input on our sales.

He was a big giant of a man who stood well over seven feet tall and weighed maybe two hundred-fifty pounds or better. His name was Darryl Imhoff, an ex-Trailblazer basketball player. At the time he dropped in on us we happened to have a store full of people all wanting to purchase Nike athletic shoes. He introduced himself to me. We exchanged some small talk for just a few minutes, and I left him to attend to business.

After staying for about fifteen minutes or so, during which time the traffic in the store was as busy a every, he came to me. If I can remember correctly, he said something like, "Well, Barney, it's obvious that you guys don't need me to bolster your sales. You already have a very nice business. Just keep on as you are doing." He left and we never got to see him again in our store. He was sort of a very gentle giant of a man, and he was very likeable.

During our many years of business, and especially in the latter year, we had many celebrities patronize our store. To mention all their names would be just too much, but they came from all branches of sports. Writers from the sports media; basketball players from the Portland Buckaroos; track stars from the University of Oregon, Oregon State, Washington, and Washington State; also professional boxers and wrestlers. Indeed there was some talk of the late Steve Prefontaine coming to our store, but his tragic fatal car accident put an end to that. He was at one time an important figure in the Nike organization. What a fine young athlete he was for Oregon.

I've often been asked by many people, including people in the industry, why we were able to succeed in such a competitive business. There really was no simple answer for that, but my own reasoning is that we were able to discount all of our shoes. In addition we were always doing our best for the customers, and we ran a very happy store. We were well known for giving Tootsie Roll candies not only to the children but our adult customers too. We really enjoyed our work and our customers, and I believe they liked us too. It was a case, you might say, of mutual admiration.

Lots of college athletes came into our store, and we enjoyed talking with them. It was also nice to be able to be of service to some of the high school cheerleaders, and I still can remember the Grant High School cheerleading team putting on a mini-routine for us right inside the store. We were so pleased with the performance we rewarded each of them with Nike headbands and wrist bands.

I believe it was in the fall of 1974 that my son began to sound me out about purchasing a Thoroughbred race horse for our enjoyment since it seemed that all of us worked long hours and had very little time for recreation. He thought it would be a nice break for us away from business. At first I wasn't very keen on the idea of going into something about which we knew absolutely nothing, but eventually I agreed. I vowed to myself, however, that I would get to know something about the horse industry first.

My first step was to place a phone call to the secretary of racing at the Longacres Race Track in Renton, Washington. He turned out to be a very nice young man, and he was very helpful. His name was Ralph Vacca, and he gave me some do's and don'ts of the business. He advised me to visit a local horse ranch and talk with the owners. The farm we went to was in McMinnville, Oregon, and was owned by Mr. and Mrs. Clarence Bernard. They showed us around, and they were very helpful. They were really a nice couple.

Our next step was to attend the annual yearling sale at Longacres. Yearlings are one-year-old babies with no racing experience whatsoever. At the sale, Ralph Vacca introduced us to one of the top agents in the country, Mr. Rollin Baugh, who, along with his mother, owned an agency in Los Angeles called California Thoroughbreeders Association. What a personality he was and still is today. Mr. Baugh was a strikingly tall, handsome guy well over six feet-plus, and he had a nicely shaped shaven head. He helped us make our first purchase at the sale. It was a rather inexpensive dark bay colt, and we named him Rodabar because of our names—we used the first few letters of Rose, David, and Barney. The colt raced at Portland Meadows and Longacres. Rodabar wasn't a great horse, but he was a hard runner. We eventually sold him and broke even on the deal. We had gained some valuable experience with Rodabar and a couple of other inexpensive horses with which we were fortunate to again avoid any losses, but we didn't achieve any gains either.

We were learning fast, however, and decided to go for a better horse, meaning one with good breeding. We had learned that the best horses are generally Kentucky bred and the yearling sales are held in September at Keeneland in Lexington, Kentucky. Ralph Vacca advised us to go to Lexington and try to pick up a reasonably priced horse at the auction sales. In order to ensure a purchase of a healthy horse, he contacted a good young Kentucky veterinarian, Dr. Richard Miller, to meet me at the Lexington airport and help us with our purchase.

Meanwhile, my son David had spent all of his spare time studying the sales books containing over one thousand horses, and he got a good line on the breeding. He finally came up with a list of six horses in preferred order. Armed with this list and knowing anything we bought would at least not be damaged goods, I made my way to Portland airport and boarded a Delta Air Lines flight for Kentucky via Chicago. This was my first time ever on this airline, and I can tell you I've used it many times since. They treat all their coach passengers with first-class service. I really enjoyed the flight.

After many hours of flying and a good mile walk in Chicago's airport to change fights and also to readjust to the time change, I finally arrived in Lexington where Dr. Miller was waiting for me. He was truly a very nice young man in his early thirties, and like most Kentucky people, Dr. Miller was very friendly. We drove to his home in Lexington where I was to reside for the next four days. During that first evening at his home, be briefed me on what to do and what to expect at the sales.

The following morning Dr. Miller and I drove to Keeneland with its vast spectacular parking grounds. The sales building itself is a huge circular structure, and the horses are led into the sales ring from the colorful barns located a distance away from the sales paddock. The horses are inspected by prospective bidders, and the doctor and I went along seeking out the six horses my son had selected. Buyers came from all over the world.

We finally got through inspecting the horses, and on the first day of the sale we never even got to bid on our first or second choose because the bidding began too high. However on the second day we were able to buy our number three choice. He was a fine looking chestnut colt, and he stood pretty tall with excellent confirmation. He was all ours for what was then a reasonable price.

The following two days of my trip were spent arranging transportation to take the colt to Portland, arranging insurance, and having Dr. Miller give the colt the appropriate shots and medication for travel. I arranged for the colt to be shipped to J.D. Taylor in Orchards, Washington, where he would be boarded and eventually broken by J.D. himself. All went well, and I thoroughly enjoyed the rest of my visit. It's no wonder they call Kentucky the Land of the Bluegrass. Sure the grass is green, but there are times it seems when it has a blue tint to it. There are horse farms everywhere, and you can see those freshly painted white fences all over the place. I made many friends there since they are such a friendly crowd, especially those in the horse industry. I'll never forget Mr. and Mrs. Ben Walden, of Deerborn Farm, who had owned the horse we purchased, coming over to me to wish me good luck and tell me I had bought a truly fine colt. How right they turned out to be. I have good memories of my friendship with Pope McClean, owner of Crestwood Farms, and Tom Caldwell, chief auctioneer at Keeneland. I met up again with agent Rollin Baugh at the sales, and we had a nice get-together. I also remember a young farm manager of Three Chimneys Farm who was very highly thought of in the business, Danny Rosenberg. His younger brother Michael lives here in Portland, Oregon, and he is a good friend of mine.

The colt shipped very well and arrived in good shape at the J.D. Taylor Farm. He remained there for the next three months being broken. Then he was transported to Portland Meadows for winter training in readiness for the opening in late spring of 1975 at Longacres. All proceeded well with the colt, and we engaged the services of one of the northwest's top trainers, Norbert "Nub" Norton. The colt was at the barns in Portland Meadows. We had him registered in the name of D.B.'s Dream—the first letters of David and Barney. He trained well, and Nub Norton said he would be a good colt one day.

His first race was at Longacres. It was a maiden race for two-years-olds. He was fifth in a field of twelve horses. The very next week we ran him back in a Stakes Race for two-years-old juveniles, and he ran a great mile race to win over a good field of horses. He won one more race after that, finishing a good 1975 with three races and two of them were big wins. Not a bad way to end his two-year season.

In 1976 he won a couple more nice races at Longacres then shipped to Exhibition Park in Vancouver B.C. where he won both the Canadian Derby Trial and the Canadian Vancouver, B.C., Derby the following week. He was really at the top of his game, and we were quietly thinking, Could he be Kentucky Derby quality? We felt the best way to find out was to ship him to Southern California and try his luck against the big boys. Our trainer thought he was just a shade below the very top flight, but nevertheless we went ahead. It was a major, major mistake. He ran in a $100,000 Charles Strub Stakes at Santa Anita and was hurt coming out of the gate, finished near the back of the pack. He never did recover fully after that. We eventually had to let him go in a low-price claiming race, but we have so many good memories of D.B.'s Dream.

I can remember the many quality times I spent with him on visits to his stall in the barn area of Portland Meadows during his first few months as a two-year-old in training. He got to a point where he could sense me coming from a short distance away. He was a very playful colt, and until he got hurt he was in excellent physical condition. I've watched owners who see their horses win, and they enter the winner's circle for so many pictures, trophies, and lots of congratulatory handshakes that it make you think that they are the ones who won the race. I would never lose sight of the fact that the plaudits belonged to our horse only and we just happened to be the lucky owners. Yes, horses are truly great athletes.

After losing D.B.'s Dream, we purchased another horse, and he was a dark bay colt. We named him D.B.'s Pride. He raced well for us. He would have gone on to be a great horse, but he developed bad knees and we had to let him go. He did well for us, so we didn't lose anything owning him.

We didn't succeed in finding another horse to match the quality of D.B.'s Dream, so we decided not to pursue it any further. Now we just enjoy watching the races on television, or once in a great while we will go to the race track if we are on vacation and meet up with old friends. We were fortunate enough to have our horses race at Santa Anita, Hollywood Park, Golden Gate Bay Meadows, Exhibition Park, and, of course, Portland Meadows. It was a great experience.

On looking back at the experience we had with our horses, I would have to say that it was really great except that we didn't or couldn't devote as much time to them as we would have liked because of our shoe business. We enjoyed every minute of it, and we certainly have only the best memories. There are so many very fine people in the thoroughbred industry.

It was 1979, and though I was working out as diligently as ever, I had given up competing in contests. I'll leave that side of it to the much younger crowd. However, hardly a day went by that I didn't do some form of exercise. I went to Loprinzi's Gym on Monday, Wednesday, and Friday. I swam at the U.S.A. Club on Tuesday and Thursday. That left Saturday and Sunday when I worked out in a small gym I set up at home. I did lifts or exercises that I didn't do at my regular gym. I also had a good quality treadmill at home that my whole family used and really enjoyed. Working out is truly great, and it gives you a good feeling. If you've never tried it, I would suggest you do. Remember you are never too old to begin, but it's wise to get your physician's okay before you do.

Things were going along fairly well with our business. I was able to go to my workouts in the early morning knowing the business was in good hands with my wife Rose, my son David, and a good work crew taking excellent care of things.

We decided to make some kind of plans for our future since we felt we were keeping our son from following his career in law. He was now a very essential part of the business. I discussed what was on my mind with my son, telling him that we were thinking of perhaps retiring. I asked if he would care to carry on the business by himself. Of course I knew that the only reason he had stayed with us when he graduated from law school was to make it easier for his mom and dad, but as he said, "Now, soon it will have to be my time." Do you know what? I couldn't agree more.

What to do about the business? Now I knew this was going to be a major problem, or so I thought. I do not recall ever mentioning to anyone that we were trying to get out of the business. It was such a good business, and we were still fairly young, so most people, especially our customers, just wouldn't believe us.

We just carried on business as usual even though our son had indicated to us that he had plans for his law degree in the very near future. Time went by without anything different happening except that one day I decided to run a tiny ad in the paper under "Business for Sale" to see what kind of a reaction we would get. Well, we got reaction all right. We received lots of replies through the mail box. We got some of the weirdest replies of which you can think. Mainly what most of the people wanted was a business without paying for it. How they could even send letters like that is beyond me, but anything is possible I suppose. Anyway, we just didn't get any legitimate prospective buyers. So much for advertising to sell a business in the newspaper. I guess selling a business is much different than selling shoes through a newspaper ad.

We were content to roll along and conduct business as usual, and things were just as busy as ever, especially at Easter, back-to-school time, Christmas, Thanksgiving, and New Year's. We just didn't worry too much about selling the business since there was no real emergency, and our son agreed to stay with us until we were ready to go. The only other way to dispose of our business other than selling it would be to sell the stock off slowly until there wasn't too much left, but that is easier said than done. It is especially difficult when you have lots of customers who want your products. In any case, we really had not tried very hard to sell the business, so I just thought I'd wait a while and then really concentrate on trying to sell.

However, it was to be almost one year later that things began to happen for us. I think it was in October 1980. We had been fairly busy that day, and as it got a little quieter we were able to take a break for some hot tea. Just then a fairly young couple came in the store asking to speak to me. It seems they were a married couple who owned four shoe stores. They had been watching our store for some length of time, and they liked what they had seen, especially the steady flow of customers, which is always an indication of a fairly successful retail operation. They indicated to us they would be interested in purchasing our store if we were prepared to sell and if a fair deal to both sides could be worked out. They seemed to be a very nice couple. They told us they had other stores, and their plan was to operate shoe stores in various locations in Portland and the outlying suburbs. My first reaction was to talk with my wife and son and discuss what had transpired. I told the young couple I would certainly give the matter a lot of consideration. I asked them to call me back in about two weeks at which time I would probably either accept or reject their very fair offer.

After talking with my family, we all three agreed that since our son wanted to go on with a law career, since getting a bonafide buyer for our business might not be that easy, and since they were such nice people, we would accept their offer if and when they called back.

Sure enough, almost two weeks to the day, the couple called back and we set up a meeting at our attorney's office. Papers were drawn up and both sides were given all the correct legal information for purchasing and selling a business. After we had taken a complete physical inventory of everything in the store, it was back again to the attorney's office for the signing and taking over of the business. It was all done very neat and very tidy, and for both sides it was a pleasant selling and buying of a good business.

The only regret I had was that they didn't want us to spread the word to or customers that the store was to be sold. They felt that in view of our excellent relationship with our customers they may resent new ownership after twenty-one years of being there for them. I really wasn't too happy about this part of the deal, but things had been going so smoothly I just didn't want to do anything that might upset anyone. So what I suggested and what they agreed to was to let my son, David, stay on for a week with the new owners, and maybe that way some of our customers wouldn't feel too bad.

It came about that on the first week of the new year 1981, the store began operation with the new owners, with the same employees and my son being there for them. As for my wife and I, we were officially retired. We had many things of which to take care immediately in the way of paperwork and official documents. It's amazing when one reaches the age of retirement all that needs to be done, but it's pleasant business and people are always there to help you.

Although the takeover had been completed without any problems, some of the customers kept inquiring as to what had happened ut us, and I felt more than a little guilty at not being ale to tell them we were on our way out. We had hundreds of loyal and regular customers who had always been so very nice to us. Even nowadays when my wife and I are out somewhere shopping or just walking along, we nearly always meet up with one of our customers, and they always seem so happy to stop and talk to us. We feel the same way about them too.

Once we had most of our affairs in order after leaving the store, our thoughts turned to my family and my wife's sister back home. We began to think that perhaps it was time for us to take a trip to England. After all, we had not been back in almost thirty years.

First of all we had to find out what our son was going to do since he indicated to us his desire to use his law degree. He had worked very hard with us at the shoe store since earning his law degree, and he thought he would take about three months off before seeking a position in law. We were able to talk him into accompanying us on our trip to England, and since the family hadn't seen him since he was almost six years old, we thought it was a great idea.

So it was in the June 1982 supposedly summer weather that we took off from Portland's airport for London's, Heathrow airport via Seattle and the polar route. We were also going to England to attend our nephew Graeme's wedding to Janet. I remember that at the time we left we had been having ninety-five to one hundred degree temperatures, and the day we left was ninety-eight degrees and hot. After a fifteen or sixteen hour flight we got to Heathrow, and wouldn't you know, it was barely fifty degrees, drizzling rain, and chilly. We hadn't brought any warm clothing, and we all felt cold.

We wanted to get to Manchester as quickly as we could, so we rented a small car. A small car in England means really small. The three of us just about made it with our luggage, which fortunately we had kept to a minimum. I must tell you that the dashboard of most cars in England are very sparse compared to what they have on them over here. They are more simple I suppose. Anyway, we drove on the motorway express, and most of the way cars were travelling at one hundred miles per hour, but our car doing sixty or seventy miles per hour didn't seem capable of too much more. We really didn't care to go much faster anyway.

Now for those of you who have never driven the motorways in England, I might, if I may, tell you that the roads are fairly wide with generally three lanes, sometimes four, and of course the steering columns on English cars are on the right side which is opposite of American cars. In England you drive on the left side of the road. It really doesn't take long to get used to it.

Now thirty years ago the trip from London to Manchester by road would be a three and a half hour minimum drive. Nowadays with the expressway it takes just two and a half hours, which is just about the time we took even with a fifteen minute stop for petrol (gas) and a snack. Approximately every fifty miles along the motorway they have what they call service centers which consist of a gas station, restrooms, and a snack buffet. At the buffet they have a fair choice of snacks including fish and chips. So one need not go hungry if you have the money to spend on food.

When we finally got to Manchester it was late evening, around nine o'clock, and we were a little later than expected because of a one and a half hour late plane arrival. Anyway, most of the family got to meet us that same evening, and it was quite a reunion. Rose and I stayed with my middle sister, Sadie, and her husband, Les. Our son David stayed at his married cousin's home abut one mile away which was close enough for us to get together during the next few days while we were in Manchester.

I promised my wife and son that we would all go to spend a full day at the Old Trafford Cricket Ground to watch Lancashire (county) play. Cricket, next to soccer, is the best loved sport in England. I must explain that most county cricket games last two days. Each team of eleven players plays two innings each. Sometimes if one team is very much on top, then the match could end in less than two days. I will tell you, however, that when countries like England, Australia, New Zealand, and India play each other in what are called Test Matches, they generally last five days, but there again it depends on how quickly an inning is completed so it could be much less. Test Matches are like the all-star games in the U.S.A. and consequently the matches take much longer than the ordinary county games.

It's not been my intention to go into the rules of cricket with you since that would obviously take far too long, but like baseball, once you get to know the rules of the game, it becomes very interesting to watch. When we were living in England, we would often spend a full day at the game. The matches always started at eleven o'clock in the morning and went on all day until seven o'clock in the evening with a break for lunch at one-thirty and a break for tea at four-thirty. It was always a great time for us. However, the slightest rain would always stop and postpone play.

Anyway, sad to say, we never even got close to a cricket ground. During the whole three weeks in England it rained, mostly that fine drizzle for which Manchester is noted. We had a good time with the family. Since most of our family is in show business in one form or another, we had lots of entertainment going to shows, concerts, and dances. One of our very close friends was the number one pop star in Great Britain when we left England. He was just a young boy barely twenty-one years old. His name was Frankie Vaughn. He had been over in the U.S.A. to make a movie with Marilyn Monroe called Let's Make Love. We had gone to Hollywood to catch up with him, but they had wrapped up the film a couple of days early so we missed each other. I knew I might get to see him when I went to London later on to visit my youngest sister.

Meanwhile, it kept on raining in Manchester so our activities were mainly limited to indoor visits during the days. In the evenings we went to see some of the family perform wherever they were booked to appear. I remember one place where my nephew's group The Lemon Tree was playing. It was a very select hotel for a dinner and dance, and they had a nice health club, so I got to get a workout in too, which for me is always a plus.

After a couple of weeks in England it was time to bid farewell to all of the family in Manchester and go on to London where my youngest sister, Sonia, lives with her husband, Alec. Sonia and Alec have a boy and two girls, all married and all with children of their own. In addition to that I have one nephew who also lives in London, and he is married to a French girl. They have two children.

We stayed with my sister for the last week of our vacation, and still the rain kept pouring down. We just felt cold all the time even though we had all been given extra sweatshirts and sweaters from the family. I had hoped to get to see horse racing at one of the tracks in and around the London area, but at the time we were in London all the underground railways were shut down because of a strike. In London when that happens there is complete chaos. Cars are travelling bumper to bumper. The buses are all overloaded and just go right on by you at the bus stop. It's just impossible to make any plans and be sure of getting where you want to go. As a matter of fact, when we eventually left London's Heathrow airport our plane was to depart at 4:30 p.m. To make sure we were able to cover the ten-mile drive to Heathrow we left my sister's home at 10:00 a.m. We did not arrive at the airport until about one o'clock.

Anyway, our visit to London was quality time, especially when it was time spent with family. It's simply amazing what changes take place in thirty years. I was hard pressed to find my way around Manchester even though I'd live there thirty-five years.

My friend Frankie Vaughan was supposed to appear at a huge outdoor theater near Hendon, which was about twenty-five miles away from where we were staying with my sister. He was supposed to perform a huge benefit concert for handicapped children. Naturally, the weather got worse the day we had planned to go see him and the benefit was canceled until a later date. We didn't get to see him at all during the trip, and I really wanted to get together with Frankie and his lovely wife, Stella. They are so very nice and both are so very humble. I might mention that just last year (1993) Frankie was given the O.B.E. by her majesty, Queen Elizabeth. It's the Order of the British Empire and it is given for outstanding service performed by a British Subject for the good of the country. So now whenever I write to him I make sure I give him the full title he deserves, Frankie Vaughn O.B.E.

The rain continued to fall the entire time we were in London, and the only consolation we had was that we were able to watch World Cup Soccer on television. Everything in Great Britain is high priced, especially food.

At this point, I thought some of you would be interested in knowing a little about Great Britain:

Great Britain	*consists of England, Scotland, and Wales.*
United Kingdom (UK)	*consists of Great Britain and Northern Ireland.*
British Commonwealth	*consists of all of the above plus the British Colonies and Dominions.*
British Isles	*United Kingdom plus Eire (Ireland), Isle of Man, Herbrides, Orkney, Shetland, plus many tiny minor islands and inlets.*
Great Britain's Population	*approximately 49.5 million or about 1/3 of the population of the U.S.A. which is a land area thirty times larger than Great Britain.*
British Empire/ Great Britain	*andothers giving allegiance to the crown along with colonies,protectorates, and mandates.*
Monarch (The Crown)	*the Royal Title of the Ruler of all of the above is:*

Queen Elizabeth II by Grace of God. Queen of this realm and of her other realms and territories. Head of the Commonwealth, Defender of the faith.

The Queen does not have ruling power, but she has much influence. The Minister of the Cabinet is responsible for all acts carried out in the Crown's name.

Incidentally, the Commonwealth is made up as follows: Great Britain, Canada, Australia, New Zealand, India, Pakistan, and Ceylon.

The British judicial system is based on common law.
It is based on two main principles:

   1. A person is innocent until proven guilty;
   2. A person has a right to trial before a jury twelve of equals.
England is a kingdom joined with Wales, Scotland, and North Ireland to form the United

Kingdom of Great Britain and North Ireland. No country had a greater influence on modern history than England.

The width of England at its maximum is 320 miles; its length is 360 miles.

The population of: England is approximately 40 million;
Northern Ireland is approximately 1.5 million;
Scotland is approximately 5 million;
Wales is approximately 3 million.

I hope the information I've provided helps you a little more with your understanding of England, Great Britain, the British Isles, United Kingdom, the British Empire, and the Commonwealth. Please forgive me if I seem to have rattled on, but it's sometimes helpful to have some idea of the logistics of countries friendly with the U.S.A.

Now I must get back to London and the last few days of our visit. We still had almost three full days left before departing for our permanent home in Oregon. I decided that the three of us would take off in the rented car and head for Wales using roads which were not too congested. It took us much longer this way, but at least we avoided heavy traffic since an overheated car would be a distinct possibility. I will tell you that Wales is a country just a little smaller than the state of New Jersey. It is located on the extreme west coast of England.

The Welsh name for the country is Cymru which means "Fellow Countrymen." As for the Welsh people, they have their own language, literature, and traditions. They also have a great national pride. Nothing will stir you as much as being at a Welsh national rugby or soccer match and listening to one hundred thousand voices singing the Welsh National Anthem in their native language. The English title of their anthem is "Land of My Fathers," and how well the Welsh people sing. It is also a land of poetry as well as music.

Our trip was to take us to the Isle of Anglesey which lies just off the northwestern corner of Wales and on which I was stationed for two years after the coventry bombing and clean up. I can never forget being in a town called Bangor, and our unit marched in full equipment about four miles to a railroad station with the longest name of any other station I've ever known: Llanfairpwllgwyngagerychwyrndrabwllllandysillagagagoch, The name means, "Church of Saint Mary in a hollow of white hazel, near to a rapid whirlpool and to St. Tysilio's Church close by a red cave." I got so that I was able to say the name of the station fairly well. How about that Jonathan (Nicholas). Most locals and the post office used the abbreviated term calling it "LLANFAIR P.G." That is much less of a mouthful, don't you think?

Anglesey is separated from the mainland by a narrow channel named the Menai Strait. The Menai Suspension Bridge joins Anglesey with the mainland.

The two main industries in Wales are coal mining and metal product such as cooper, zinc, tin, and nickel. We visited Fishguard where I'd been stationed during WWII. It really hadn't changed as much as I expected after so many years. After a nice visit we began our long drive back to London. We stopped for a snack at Chester, a small historical old Roman town where I had finished my army service. During all of this time the rain hardly ever ceased. We finally made it safely back to my sister's home in London. Except for the dismal weather, it had been a very enjoyable side trip.

Most people visiting Europe from the U.S.A. will generally include London in their itinerary. There is not much wrong with that except my advice would be to not spend too much time there. The beauty of Great Britain lies in the rugged mountainous valleys and streams of Wales. There are many castles with moats still intact, and many of the old Roman walls are still standing. I would also recommend a trip to Scotland.

Scotland is a land surrounded by water except in the south where the Cheviot Hills met the English border. It lies between the North Atlantic Ocean and the North Sea.

The products of Scotland are internationally well known, such as powerful clydesdale horses, shetland ponies, and Scottish wool and tweeds. Incidentally, shortbread and Scotch whisky are other well-known products. The game of golf originated in Scotland. In the highlands of Scotland the rapid rivers are used to produce electric power. The largest hydroelectric plant was built here in about 1950. It is still the largest in the United Kingdom. It is located on the western shore of the famous Loch (Lake) Lomond.

The language spoken in Scotland is English, but it is generally spoken with an accentuated brogue. With all its deep history, it's a county worth visiting. It's great to go up into the highlands with its fields of purple heather.

A visit to the United Kingdom would not be complete without going to Ireland. First go to Northern Ireland, which has a small population of 1.5 million and an area 85 miles in length and 110 miles in width. The people are called "Ulstermen." They manufacturer mainly ships, linens, wool, rope, twine, cigarettes, and whisky.

A governor is appointed by the Queen, but the governor is more of a symbol than a ruler. The country's affairs are conducted by the Parliament of Northern Ireland. The country conducts most of its own affairs except for major decisions such as peace or war. The capital is Belfast, and English is the only language spoken in Northern Ireland. The southern part of Ireland, a republic called Eire, is separate from Northern Ireland. Eire takes up four-fifths of the whole of Ireland, and its dimensions are 275 miles in length and 174 miles in width. It is located west of England in the Atlantic and separated from England by the Irish Sea. Eire's population is roughly about 3 million and its river Shannon is the longest in the British Isles. The languages taught in all schools here are both English and Gaelic. Nearly all of its trade is with Great Britain, mainly exporting all types of food. The government is called the Dail Eirann (council), and the main political party is called Fianna Fail. The president of the council is the prime minister who has the ruling power.

Just a few closing words about England. If you do visit and the weather cooperates, you simply must go up to the beautiful Lake District and Stratford upon Avon, the home of William Shakespeare. Seeing the sights in and around London is surely very nice, but the real beauty of England is found going up into the Yorkshire Moors and the other places of scenic beauty I've already intimated.

I hope I've been helpful in your having a little better knowledge of the United Kingdom and for what to look and expect when you visit.

And now back to my original story. Time was up for us in London, and I said a sad farewell to my sister and all the rest of the family living there. We cleared customs with not much delay and boarded our flight for Chicago, where we changed flights and proceeded back to the Portland airport.

Our flight was without mishaps of any kind, but on landing at Chicago we were told our flight to Portland was delayed an hour and a half, and that would entail a four and a half hour wait for us. That's a long wait in any airport, and all we could do was sit and read or just watch people. I don't know how most of you feel, but I'm not a great lover of O'Hare Airport. Those of you who have experienced a few hour layover at an airport will understand how boring and what a drag it really is. Finally, after going through half a dozen different newspapers, a couple of cups of coffee, and lots of conversation between ourselves, our flight was called for boarding.

It felt good just to get seated on that plane. Anyway, this was Chicago's airport, and if you are familiar with it then you can believe me when I tell you that when it was almost take-off time the voice of the flight captain on the PA said, "We are taxiing in preparation for take off and have been informed we are ninth in line, so we may be a little late. Sorry, folks, it's just a busy day here."

After almost an hour delay we eventually were in the air and on our way. We arrived in Portland, having once again to readjust our watches. We picked up our luggage and stepped out of Portland's airport into bright, lively sunshine and ninety-degree temperatures. After three weeks of solid rain, this was such a welcome relief, and we were happy to be back again. We took a cab home since at that time we lived only ten minutes from the airport.

I don't know if you experience the same feelings as I do, but it seems to me that any time we take a trip for any length of time and get back to our house it always seems to look so very clean and neat and warm looking. Do you ever feel that way after a trip?

It really took all three of us a week or so to get our act together. My wife and I were still in our first year of retirement and just trying to get used to it. As for my son David, it was time for him to begin searching for a beginning to his law career. I think most newly graduated lawyers who have just passed the bar exam will probably tell you that finding a good place to start is not always that easy.

David took about four and a half months after returning back from England before he was able to latch on to something, but it turned out to be a very good and helpful for his knowledge of criminal law which is what he had decided upon.

One of Portland's most prominent judges in the judicial system, Judge Donald Londer, agreed to let my son work in his courtroom as his temporary law clerk. Judge Londer, at the time of this writing, is the presiding judge in Multnomah County Court. What a truly great person he is, and he is also one of our very best judges. Portland indeed has a fine team of judges.

Anyway, my son stayed with Judge Londer about a year, and in that year he told me he learned more about criminal law than he did during his entire time at law school. I guess you just can't beat hands-on experience, but it's also true that Judge Londer taught my son whenever he could. Today, with his own practice, David will often relate to me how he follows the law just the way Judge Londer would. Sounds like he had an excellent teacher.

As for my wife and I are enjoying our retirement, well, myself, I still do all the things I've always done, like working out, swimming, walking, and involving myself a little more than I used to with my place of religious worship. Being Jewish, of course I go to my synagogue as often as I can. I used to go when we were active in the shoe store, but now that we are done I find myself being able to attend more often. I have been a member of the congregation called Kesser Israel (Crown of Israel) for many years.

I was also elected to be vice president of the congregation. My wife Rose enjoys doing housework, and she also gets together with her three sisters at least once a week. She also enjoys walking and working out on the treadmill.

All in all I would say that retirement can be the best part of one's life. It's all a matter of how one approaches it. It's a good idea to find some special project with which to go and do other things on the side. Sure it's nice to sit down with a good book or watch a good television show, but one should not make that a large part of one's life, but rather as a time to relax after exercising or working or whatever.

My wife does not drive a car, and one of her enjoyments is to go by charter bus to Reno. She likes to walk around and see the bright lit-up signs, and she also enjoys playing the nickel machines. As for me, going to Reno takes me away from my daily regimen of exercising at the gym, swimming at the club, and attending my congregation. I also attend another congregation during the week at Shaari Torah, a traditional synagogue in northwest Portland. My own synagogue is an orthodox congregation in southwest Portland. As far as Reno is concerned, I go because I know how much work is involved in housekeeping and my wife deserves the break. I'm not much of a gambler I'm afraid. I do enjoy, however, going to one of Reno's sports books and placing a very small wager on a baseball, football, or basketball game. Then I watch the game on television while enjoying a cup of coffee. Both of us also enjoy going to the shows in Reno.

Talking about going to shows! I've been around them enough both here and in England to know a good one when I see one, and I have to tell you that I've seen shows in Reno in some of the casinos with no cover charge or very little that were so much better than the regular high-priced shows. Some of the talent in the small clubs or casinos is surprisingly top quality.

We had never been to Las Vegas until last year when our son bought us a trip to there. It included tickets for the Holyfield-Riddick Bowe Heavyweight Championship of the World fight. We had a great time and saw an exciting fight, which Bowe won. This was their first fight. Bowe lost the return fight, but we didn't see that one.

Although we had great accommodations, we enjoyed the trip, and the weather cooperated too, my wife and I both agreed that we feel more at home in Reno. Maybe it's because Las Vegas is so much bigger. Anyway, I have no particular desire to go back to Las Vegas.

The Year was 1991, and we had just begun the new year. I recall thinking to myself that it had been almost ten years since we went back to our homeland. After talking it over with my wife, we decided we would take a trip back again sometime in July. Eventually we purchased plane tickets after looking around for the best way to go. We wanted to go to Manchester from Portland rather than to into Heathrow airport in London. That was the only way we could go by way of Chicago. We looked forward to our trip all during the winter months. As luck would have it we didn't have too bad of a winter that year. Anyway, winter went by with nothing much out of the ordinary happening.

As I'm writing this, I have the television turned on and it's January 17, 1994. There has been a fairly strong earthquake in the Los Angeles area resulting in a few deaths; many injuries; and of buildings, homes, and even freeways badly damaged. The reason I mention this right now is because I happen to be talking of a future visit back to England and can't help thinking how far removed the people of England are from anything remotely resembling an earthquake. When anything like this happens over here, such as today's earthquake, the one in San Francisco a couple of years back, or the Mt. St. Helen's volcano, then I always get calls from my family in England to inquire if we are okay.

In the spring of 1991 the weather was great. We decided to take a trip to visit a friend of ours in Los Alamos, California. Our friend Joe Tevis has a thoroughbred race horse farm called Hidden Valley Ranch. It's a beautiful spot with very large acreage, and he boards, breaks, and trains horses. It's not a very pleasant trip as far as driving from Portland to Los Alamos, so we decided to go by Greyhound bus. I'm sure that many of you have never travelled by Greyhound. I can tell you that having taken quite a few trips with them, not only is it very reasonable, but they are nearly always right on their scheduled times. Also a bus trip is one of the better ways to see this great country. They go through most of the small towns and villages along the way.

We left the Portland bus station at 9:00 p.m. on a Sunday, and we arrived in the town of Santa Maria at 6:30 p.m. Monday. Our host, Joe Tevis, having driven his pick-up the twenty-five miles, was there to meet us. Joe is a fairly young man in his early forties, and he lives on the ranch with his wife and three boys and a girl. We were able to have a very nice visit, and the weather, as usual in Los Alamos, was very dry and warm. After a couple of days it was time for our return, and Joe drove us back to the depot. We had a two-hour wait which was by design since we wanted to go around Santa Maria before boarding the bus for home.

Santa Maria is a beautiful town. It is very colorful and very clean, and it has a nice shopping center. It seemed like no time at all before we were making our way back to the bus depot. The bus as usual arrived right on time, and finally we were on our way back to Portland, Oregon. It's a very enjoyable and scenic trip, especially going through the very small historical Spanish towns in California. Of course you also travel throughout the night, and most times you are able to get some sleep. Of course there are the times when the bus stops along the journey for meal or snack breaks. All in all it's a very nice trip, especially when someone else is doing the driving.

During the late spring, my wife and I drove up to the beach at Seaside just for the day. We always enjoy that. We did that a few times during the spring of 1991. Meanwhile, we had slowly been making preparations for our visit back to England. We were to be gone for a period of three and a half weeks. That's really not a very long time when one is overseas, but it's about as long as we care to be away from our normal way of life. Those of you who have been gone for any similar length of time from your home will know what I mean.

It was the beginning of July 1991 and we were booked on an American Airlines flight direct to Manchester via Chicago. The weather in Portland the day of our take-off was just as it was ten years before when we made our last trip to England. It was actually ninety-eight degrees at 11:45 a.m. take-off time, and the plane left on time. It was one of those wide-bodied 747's with plenty of leg room and nice, fairly wide aisles. It was a very smooth flight to Chicago, the food they served was very good, and the service was excellent. I can still recall the movie they showed in flight. It was Chariots of Fire which my wife and I had not previously seen. All in all we had a good time before we finally touched down in Chicago where we were to change planes after a one and a half hour wait. However, it was business as usual at Chicago's airport where our wait turned out to be almost three hours. Seems they have a hard time staying on schedule at O'Hare Airport.

Once again, after a dragged-out waiting period, we were on board for the final leg of our trip that would take us straight into Ringway Airport in Manchester. This of course was the longer flight. The flight to Chicago took about four and a half hours, but the last part of our trip took over ten hours. Once again we were in the air, but this time we were in a plane which was not quite as big. Still it turned out to be a good flight, and after landing we picked up our luggage and proceeded to go through customs. Let me tell you, nowadays the customs inspectors in England are very thorough and rightly so.

Having cleared customs, we then sought out our families who were on the other side of the customs barriers waiting to pick us up. It was so good to meet up again. I think it's a wonderful thing when families get together.

Once again we were to stay with my oldest sister although we would be away for days at a time during the three and a half weeks. I have to tell you that upon our arrival at Ringway Airport the weather was…you guessed it…raining. I just couldn't believe our bad luck with the weather. Here it was July and summer time, and the weather was wet and fairly cold. It didn't change much throughout the time we were over there, but we were determined to make the best of it no matter what. This trip we had our sweaters with us.

It took us a couple of days before we settled in and got to meet all of our families. My wife and I went to the City Center to do some sightseeing and a little shopping. Everything over there is very high priced. We stopped at one of the luncheonettes at a department store called Lewis's. They were in business when we emigrated to the United States. We ordered two cups of coffee and two very small scones. We were charged almost ten pounds. That's approximately fifteen dollars.

On looking back I think I should have questioned the cashier on that amount. Another custom, if you can call it that, is that most cafes tell you there are no free refills on your coffee. It's sort of hard to get used to that. Do you suppose we are badly spoiled here in the United States? No, I don't think so.

My younger brother, Sonny, the show business entrepreneur, owns a caravan (mobile home) in Blackpool which is a northwest seaside town and one of the most popular towns with the British people. The site where the caravan sits is about two miles from the North Sea. The caravan is a two-bedroom with a bath, shower, toilet, and a large living/dining room with a separate kitchen. The length of it is about forty-five feet, and it occupies a large piece of ground. We, along with my brother and his wife, Pamela, arranged to go there for a long weekend. We left Manchester early Friday morning, and we planned on staying until Monday afternoon. It's only an hour and a half to Blackpool by road. Anyway, we packed our gear and food for the trip and took off. Just as it was on our 1981 trip, the rain continued to come down non-stop. As we got closer to Blackpool the wind started to kick up very strongly.

We eventually arrived at the RV site, and it was our first taste of life in a caravan in England. Do you know what? It was very nice, very warm, very roomy, and so very comfortable. It was just as well since because of the bad weather we spent most of the weekend in the caravan.

I should mention at this point that one of the main reasons for our going to Blackpool was to have a reunion with my dear friend Frankie Vaughn and his lovely wife Stella. It had been thirty-six years since we last got together and longer than that since we last saw him perform. I'd like to explain, if I may, that Blackpool has some wonderful tourist and vacation attractions. Its main feature is the Blackpool tower which can be seen within a radius of ten miles and further at certain points. It is built like the Eiffel Tower. It is a very high structure with a speed elevator running through its center. The ground level is very large and it has a grand ballroom with a restaurant and shops. The top of the tower has some shops and a nice hallway. Bear in mind that this tower is more than one hundred years old, and it is as good now as when it was first constructed. There are three piers jutting out from the promenade to the North Sea. Each pier is almost a half mile in length, and they all have restaurants, shops, rentals, etc. Each pier has a large concert auditorium where top-rated shows take place. They are named according to location—North Pier, South Pier, and Central Pier. My friend Frankie had contracted for the summer season to perform on the Central Pier, headlining the show, and changing his supporting cast every couple of weeks. His following is so large that they sell out almost every performance.

We had called him ahead of time, and he reserved seats for us. He also arranged to meet with us right after the show on Saturday night. The weather continued its steady diet of rain, and the wind started to kick in. There are so many open-air vendors in Blackpool that it was almost impossible for them to operate in weather like that. We all spent most of our time in the caravan where it was warm and dry and we also had television. However, the television programs in England leave much to be desired. I guess over here in the States we are used to the very best of everything.

Well here it was Saturday evening and time to take off for the show on the Central Pier. We all packed into my brother's small compact car with just enough room for the four of us. Parking is rarely a problem over there since there are far fewer cars per household. Having parked the car, we proceeded to walk along the pier towards the auditorium. I must tell you that on this particular night it wasn't so much an experience, it was an adventure. The rain was pelting down, the wind was howling, and the waves from the sea came over the sides of the pier, making it almost treacherous to be out walking on the pier on such a night. The wind was so strong it was difficult to hold your head up and still walk a straight course. Deck chairs and tables used by people just for lounging or drinking during the day flew all over the place. However, eventually we made it to the auditorium, and I was surprised to see how crowded it was.

We were led to our seats by an usher, and our seats were among the best in the house. Looking around I couldn't help noticing how very few seats were not taken on such a nasty evening.

The show got started, and my friend was at the top of his form. He was at the time just in his fifties, and he moved around the stage a lot during his show. His voice over the years grew richer if anything, and it sounded very good. The remainder of the show consisted of other acts, some of whom I knew because of my nephew, Brian, the leader of The Lemon Tree.

During the show, Frankie pointed us out to his audience, which surprised me, but it was nice of him to do that. The show itself lasted two and a half hours. It was an excellent show.

We had been told to wait in a side lounge to meet with Frankie after the show. Meanwhile in the large lobby just below us there were probably two or three hundred people lined up waiting to meet Frankie and obtain his autograph. He had a great rapport with his fans and went out of his way for them.

About twenty minutes or so after the show, Frankie and his wife Stella joined us. Considering we had not seen each other for thirty-six years, it was a very nice reunion. He looked just as good as ever, maybe a few pounds heavier, but other than that the years had been very kind to him. He still had a great head of jet black hair with just a spot of grey here and there. We talked for about half an hour, but I felt a little guilty about all the people below waiting patiently and probably feeling cold. We agreed to say our good-byes with a promise from Frankie and Stella that they would come over to the States one summer and be our guests for as long as they could stay. We really had a very enjoyable evening, and it was good to see them both again.

When we left the auditorium the weather was, if anything, worse than when we arrived, and we sort of staggered along the pier until we reached the promenade where it was a little less stormy. What a night.

Every year in the month of September the town of Blackpool puts on an Illumination Extravaganza. All the buses, trams, piers, and towers are lit up with thousands of colorful lights and various designs, and the whole length of the promenade is brightly lit up. As my wife once remarked when she first went to Reno, "The lights remind me of Blackpool."

Anyway, on this particular Saturday evening they had switched on the Illumination lights for a full evening's test, and instead of going back to the caravan, we drove along the lengthy promenade. It was an amazing sight to see all the thousands of different colored lights and the different pictures depicted by them. However, due to the stormy weather, a lot of the lights were not lit up, and many of them were swinging wildly all over the place. Eventually our tour of the lights came to an end, and we made our way back to the caravan.

It was so nice and warm in the caravan, and we were well protected from the awful weather going on outdoors. It was past midnight but Pamela brewed a large pot of tea and made some nice sandwiches. Since the television was closed down for the night we just sat around and talked until well after one o'clock in the morning, and finally we went to bed.

The sleeping quarters were just great and getting to sleep was no problem. My wife and I are early risers, and we were awake by six o'clock. Having showered and dressed, we were both ready to go for the three-mile walk to the local village. It was still raining, but just lightly. There's only one small shop that opens on a Sunday, and we purchased a Sunday paper. We were on our way back when my brother Sonny came along in his car and we rode back with him.

My sister in London, Sonia, and her husband, Alec, drove from London to Blackpool, a three and a half hour drive, since she wanted to spend some time with us. My nephew Brian and his girl vocalist also came down for the afternoon, but they had to be back in Buxton for an evening show. Buxton is a small town approximately thirty miles from Manchester.

They all showed up even though it was a bad day to be out driving. Anyway, we all had a great time and finally it was just the four of us left.

We enjoyed a very nice dinner, watched a television show, and got an early night's sleep since we were going back the following day.

On the way back to Manchester on Monday morning it actually ceased raining for awhile, but the rain resumed by the time we reached Manchester. Regardless of the foul weather we had ourselves a great time over the weekend with many fond memories. I was so happy to have seen my friends again after so many years.

Before going any further with my life's history, I would like to intrude, if I may, with something that is current.

Today as I write it is Wednesday, January 26, 1994, and last night on national television President Clinton gave his State of the Union Address to the nation. The reason I bring this up now is because he spoke about gun control and health care in very similar terms to the article I had written forty years ago for the Oregon Journal which never got to be printed. Remember my mentioning it at the beginning of this book? Without going too deeply into it since I'm definitely not into politics, I'll just briefly give you my thoughts on these two very important issues;

(1) Health Care

Nearly every country in the world except South Africa and the U.S.A. have some form of national health care. You can talk to a dozen people in this country and ask them who is their health care provider, and more than likely you will get twelve different answers and invariably they are never very sure of how much coverage they do have. Most of them will tell you, "Oh, yes, we have coverage for at least 80 percent of all our medical bills." It's the other 20 percent that can really take its toll. You can also be canceled anytime. Let me put it to you this way. Take your average couple who works steady for many years and is able to put something away for their eventual retirement. Then one of them or sometimes both of them get sick and it's a treatable illness. Then comes the avalanche of high-priced medical bills. Sure their insurance covers a good deal of it, but it's the balance that this couple has to pay that cleans them out completely and then some. It seems a shame that this kind of thing can happen, but it does. That's where national health would be so beneficial to all. Sure the logistics have to be worked out for such a program to go forward, but isn't that the job of the people in the government? I think national health will come about in the not too distant future, and then everyone can go about with their daily lives not having to worry about paying any bills in the event they get sick. Anyway, that's the way I wrote about it when I first came to the U.S.A.

(2) Gun, Control and Crime

Since these two topics are somewhat related I will address them together.

Some people have the notion that guns do not kill people. Having spent my almost seven years in WWII firing rifles and guns most of those years, I can say without any hesitation whatsoever that guns do kill people. If you have any doubts about this statement, pick up your morning newspaper or listen to your national or local television newscasts, and you will become a believer that guns do kill.

Something needed to be done long ago in this country to control or even ban guns. I hope the president can get congress to move quickly on this, but I feel that just banning assault weapons is really not enough. Are we saying that it's all right if you use a semi-automatic or single shot weapon? I know a complete ban of all guns, except for the military and law enforcement officers, may be a long way off, but if you stop to think about it, wouldn't it be great if it ever happened here?

In regard to crime in the country, I think the president was right on with most of his remarks: more police, stiffer sentences, and three time losers receive life with no parole. That briefly is what was said, but to add to all that, it would be good for everyone if all the courts in the nation speed up a little. Also, the avenue of appeals seems to be endless, and there are times when a case does not come up for trial until years after the event. I'll leave this topic by relating to you what my son, David, who is a criminal attorney, once said to me when I asked him his feelings with regard to justice in the American courts.

He told me that when it is a trial by jury, the jury is made up of people from all walks of life, and an onlooker in the court may wonder what qualifies them to judge someone. However, he told me that eventually when it's all said and done, they always seem to come up with the right verdict.

When it's a trial by a judge, he tells me that all judges are extremely fair and impartial and their verdicts are always judicially correct. So much then for these topics in relation to what I had written many years ago. Please forgive me for the long intrusion, but I just wanted to get it out while it was still on my mind.

Now I return to the town of my birth, and since I didn't get to see some of my old friends during the last trip, I was determined not to miss out on it again. The very first one I sought out was the employer for whom I worked when I was conscripted for WWII. I was very surprised and happy to see him looking so well and happily retired having sold his business. We had a very nice long chat over tea and biscuits and we recalled many happy times. Of the close friends with whom I used to hang out when I was single, I only located two of them. One was married and settled in Capetown, South Africa, and another one regrettably passed on.

Ny nephew Graeme told me that most of my old soccer team was scattered or in other towns, and so I didn't try to connect with them. I did the next best thing, and that was to see my own team, Manchester City, play Sheffield Wednesday in a home game at Maine Road. I'd play on this pitch as a schoolboy in a Cup Final in which we were beaten 3–1. For once just the thrill of seeing the ground (pitch) again was almost enough. As for the game itself, the crowd of 42,000 was very vociferous with their singing chants, but it all makes for good sports. Both teams responded to the large crowd by playing some excellent football (soccer). Manchester City went ahead and led by two goals to nil, but back came Sheffield in the second half, helped by John Harkes, the American International, with two goals of their own. The game ended in a 2–2 draw.

Getting away from the city ground you take your life in your hands, especially if you are driving. Walking from the ground is just as treacherous. The drivers take hairline chances. It's safer on the motorway driving eighty miles an hour.

Unfortunately that was the only football game I got to see since I spent time with my wife seeking out some of her old girlfriends, which is the way it should be. She got to see quite a number of them, and she also called some of them when they lived a distance away.

It was time now for us to go to Liverpool to spend a couple of days with my wife's sister who, as previously mentioned, was the only one of her family left in England.

Graeme had some business to take care of close to Liverpool so we rode with him. It used to be just a few years back that driving from Manchester to Liverpool took about an hour and fifteen minutes, but now they have this express motorway which takes just about thirty-five minutes doing a steady fifty-five or sixty kilometers per hour.

Liverpool is the third largest city in England and is, of course, a port with daily sailing to far off countries. The city also has a beautiful cathedral and a very large university. I've often been asked what is the difference if any between a town or a city. Speaking from an English point of view, a city is a very large area of land with a large community that has its own cathedral. As an example, City of Manchester, City of Liverpool, and City of London. A town is a smaller area of land and a smaller community with no cathedral. As an example, Huddersfield, Grimsby, and Walsall.

The definition of a town in the U.S.A. is slightly different. The word town means a community of closely clustered dwellings and other buildings in which the people live and work. It could be large or small, but in the U.S.A. we use the word town to refer to any municipal unit that is larger than a village but smaller than a city. We have here cities like Portland, Eugene, and Medford. Towns are places like Woodburn and Tualatin. Perhaps this helps clear up a question you always wanted to ask but just couldn't bring yourself to do so.

Anyway, my wife and I, along with our driver and nephew Graeme, arrived at my wife's sister's home, and Graeme took off to attend to business with a promise to pick us up the following afternoon to return to Manchester.

My wife's sister, Sadie, lives in a nice home in the Queens Drive District, a suburb of Liverpool. Her husband is deceased, and she had two girls. One daughter is married and living in Ontario, Canada, and the other is single working and living in London. My sister-in-law has a rather poor history of health, suffering mainly from arthritis which keeps her home. The government helps her with meals and housekeeping, plus of course the government pays 100 percent of her medical care and costs.

Since the three of us had not been together for ten years, we had much about which to talk. Since we were staying overnight, my wife began to prepare a hot dinner for the evening and she did some housework. We also decided to go to the local supermarket and purchase some food to stock up for her.

I must tell you how the supermarkets in England compare with ours in the United States. In England the supermarkets are most always very large buildings, but generally they are rather plain without the fancy front facades that we see in the States. They are more like huge barns in England. They are never brightly lit, but the lighting is adequate enough to see everything. Stocks are displayed well enough but not as huge as the displays we see over here. One other thing that is very noticeable is that all of the cashiers sit on chairs at their cash registers and they are seldom rushed to check out. You do your own packaging and they have only one type of plastic sack. While all this is not quite as efficient or elaborate as we have in the States, it seems to work very well for the British people. The one thing I've heard talking to many people, however, is the complaint about the cost of living being so high they just manage to live without saving anything. Be that as it may, if one were to go to any seaside resort in England on a nice summer day you will find thousands of people on the beaches basking in the sun.

Having made all of our purchases, we began to make our way back to the house. We were walking and both of us had a sack full of groceries to carry. We didn't have too far to walk, just about half a mile. One the way back we came across a large open air pub with a front courtyard where a band was playing and a girl's drill team was performing with precision marching. It was a fairly dry day for a change, so we stopped for almost an hour and enjoyed the music and unusual marching routines.

That evening we enjoyed a wonderful fish dinner that my wife prepared, and I know her sister enjoyed it very much. We both slept well that night since we had been moving around non-stop for over two weeks in England.

We rose fairly early in the morning, and after a quick breakfast of tea and toast, my wife and I took a bus to the city center. It's always nice and relaxing early in the morning before the crowds converge to do their shopping or plain gawking. After ten years not too much had changed, but later on we walked down to the Liverpool Pier Head. Things had changed dramatically since we were last there. It seems that the authorities had somehow or another located long underground tunnels beneath the dockside buildings, and they opened up small specialty shops, cafes, barber shops, and even pubs in these tunnels. This reminded me of going from one carriage to another on a very long train. A tour of these shopping tunnels is a must for any tourist. In addition to all of this, a large square with ample seating all around had been constructed and there was a large military band concert later on in the day. England is famous for its military band concerts, one of its best being the Annual Aldershot Tatoo.

My wife decided it was time for us to return to her sister's, and since it was way past lunchtime we departed by bus for our journey back. After a light lunch and some more conversation, my nephew Graeme arrived and it was time to say Ta Ta (good-bye) to my sister-in-law.

Needless to say that though the weather had been dull and overcast all day it started to rain again during the drive back to Manchester. The rain continued on and off for the rest of our stay in England. Seems to me we get better weather than that in Oregon during the winter.

We only had a few days left before leaving for the States, but there were still many things I wanted to do.

I had not been back to Old Trafford, the ground of the Manchester United F.C., since 1953. As a youth, when not playing on my own team, I would always go there if I was fortunate enough to catch them playing. They have always been a great team, and some of you may still recall the tragic event of the late 1950s when a plane carrying the entire United Team and its entourage crashed on a flight to Munich. Almost the whole team perished, and its great manager, Matt Busby, survived with severe injuries from which he recovered to manage again. However, as I write I am sad to say that Sir Matt Busby passed away last week at age eighty-four, and all of soccer throughout Europe paid homage to this great man who I saw play many times. What a great player he was. He was a multi-capped Scottish International, and his legacy is stamped on the brilliant type of soccer played by his beloved Manchester United. They are, as of this day, January 30, 1994, a precision-type team at the head of the Premier League in English football, and the team will go on to win all kinds of championships and trophies this season.

I just wanted to talk a little about seating accommodations before we leave this subject. Old Trafford has undergone many changes these past few years, and now they have covered stands almost all the way around the ground. These stands do not go all the way down to ground level, and below the stands are the open terracing with steps leading from the top of the stands all the way down to the level of the playing pitch. Seating is available under the stands, but those who pay general admission all stand on the terracing which has steel barriers every half a dozen or so steps to protect the crowd from being crushed. Can you imaging standing for over two hours at a pro-football game here in the U.S.A. This gives you some idea of how much they love their soccer in England.

Not too far away from the soccer ground is the Lancashire County Cricket Ground also in the Old Trafford area. It is on this ground where all the big important matches are played. I spent many summer days as a young boy watching Lancashire play, and many times I saw England play a five-day game versus another cricket country. I can well remember my wife and I just after I got out of the army spending a full day at a cricket game and leaving at seven o'clock in the evening to go to the Belle Vue Speedway and watch the motorcycle races. Belle Vue itself is a very huge complex like a small Disneyland, and it has one of the largest animal zoos in England. It also has a vast rugby ground where the Belle Vue Rangers play. They are a pro team in the top division. We would leave home for the cricket matches at nine o'clock in the morning and it would be well after midnight when we returned home. That's a full day any way you look at it, but boy did we have great times. Do I miss all of that? Well, of course I do, but the many friends and pleasures we have here in the States more than compensate for that. I should mention that Old Trafford, Belle Vue, and the home in which we lived in Manchester are all within a radius of about eight miles.

We returned to my sister's and had just a couple more days remaining before leaving for our home in Oregon. The phone kept ringing very often with some member of the family asking to take us out to dinner or inviting us to attend one of their shows. As for myself, I began to long for a good workout, and I was able to get my nephew Brian in between one of his performances to take me to one of the big gyms in Manchester for a quick hour and a half workout and a half hour swim. This gym was called the Wishing Well, and lots of show business people worked out there. We had a good workout.

An unusual thing happened to me while working out at the Wishing Well and perhaps it's worth relating. I was wearing my Loprinzi's Gym sweatshirt and never even gave it a thought since my mind is always on my workout. It's a dangerous practice to let your mind wander when lifting weights. Anyway, someone called to me. I approached him. The man was maybe just a wee bit younger than me, and he wanted to know about my sweatshirt and where I lived. To cut to the real story, it seems that he had been on a three-month visit to the States in early 1949–1950. During his visit he had seen Sam Loprinzi take first place in a small man's division of Mr. America. Our world really is getting smaller, or is it that our modes of transportation are getting so much better and faster? Anyway, I gave him an update on Sam Loprinzi and what he was doing. Of course when you get right down to it, Sam was the one who really pioneered weight training and body building in the state of Oregon, and although he is now retired, the gym on Southeast Division bearing his name is still in full operation with owners Ed and Jan Kenworthy, two very nice people, as I have said previously. I still work out at Sam's.

There were still many things we had planned to do before leaving England, but we knew we just wouldn't have enough time to do it all. One place we just had to visit was the Bury Open Air Market. Bury is a very small town six miles from where we were staying. My sister, Sadie; her husband, Leslie; and my wife and I all jammed into the tiny car Les drove, and we were on our way to Bury. It's a town where they produce a lot of toffee (candy), and there are also a couple of medium-size cotton miles. The people are mostly blue collar workers, very warm and friendly, and they speak with a little different accent than the Mancunians (Manchester). It's a fact that in England, especially in the Country of Lancashire, you will hear different accents every ten miles or so. Anyway, it was a day with mostly intermittent rain showers.

It was, I believe, a Thursday, and the market was just packed with people walking around. Most of the women carried shopping bags or canvas hold-alls for their purchases. The markets have both indoor and outdoor stalls, and that is the pattern for most all markets in England—even Petticoate Lane in London which is known internationally.

Wherever you go and whatever you purchase there are ques lined up to be waited upon. I might explain that queing in England is a holdover from WWII. As a matter of fact, one of the most popular songs written and sang in WWII was called simply "Queing." I've never forgotten the song performed many times on the air and stage by my brother, Sonny. The opening verse goes like this:

Queing, queing, that's what Britain's doing.
It's enough to drive one crazy.
Waiting for an hour or more,
Half of them are wondering just what they're waiting for,
And they'll be queing, queing, etc.
It was quite a hit.

We made a few purchases of different toffees that are only found there such as Nutall's Homemade Mintoes, Victory V Lozenges, and Rose's Famous Chocolates. Also Eccles Cakes which are like a crispy sort of tea cakes with lots of currants inside. Scones can be purchased in many different varieties.

We stopped at one of the small cafes for a cup of tea and some scones. We waited about half an hour, and as we were served buffet style, we were told refills would be extra. I never did find anyone offering free refills.

Listening to the spiel of a market person selling their wares is very entertaining. They really are very good at what they do, and the British public love it. We were at the Bury market over four hours, and the time went by so very quickly. By the time we got back to my sister's home, we were all a little tired and a lot happy.

Talking about food brings to mind some of the meals one has in England that are not common here in the U.S.A. For example, a breakfast in England that is popular is bangers (sausages) and eggs, poached eggs on toast, or just toast and assorted jams (not jelly). A popular evening menu can include fish and chips (french fries), eggs, and chips or welsh rarebit (grilled cheese on toast).

I can tell you one thing about food. If you ever make the trip to England and happen to be in London in the Golders Green District you should be sure to visit Bloom's Restaurant. It's a kosher restaurant with very large dining rooms, and it has a spacious deli section. They also have take-out service. We enjoyed taking out fish and chips. One of their tastiest meals is a pickled meat sandwich with rye bread, sour pickled cucumber, fish and chips, and Russian lemon tea. It is all fairly reasonably priced, and the food is excellent.

We used up our last couple of days in England visiting old friends. Some of our friends have moved to other towns, and a few had passed away. On the evening before we departed, most of the family had a get together, and we were able to say our good-byes once again. After they had all left it was time for us to pack, and somehow or another it always seems to take less time when packing to return home than packing to begin a long journey.

On the morning we left for Ringway Airport it had stopped raining. Wouldn't you just know it. Now that we were headed home the weather got better. Oh well, there was plenty of nice sunny and warm weather waiting for us in Oregon. When we arrived at the airport, we were informed that our flight to Chicago was delayed three and a half hours. Fortunately, one of my nephews, Clive, and his wife, Louise, along with their three children, live just a stone's throw from the airport, so along with some of the family who came to see us off we made our way back to their home. It didn't take long for Louise to make coffee and cakes for everyone, and it turned out to be a very pleasant couple of hours.

We made our way back to the airport, and this time there were no more delays. After the family had taken lots of pictures, and with lots of hugging and some tears, we finally boarded our plane.

The flight was a good one, and since we were tired from having been on the go for almost four weeks, we were able to sleep most of the way. We finally arrived in Chicago's O'Hare Airport, and wouldn't you just know it, they had been having torrential rain for almost two days prior to our arrival. There had been some flooding at the airport, and they were operating on emergency power. All flights were delayed and some were even cut.

We were driven to the customs shed and cleared for further flight quicker than usual. We had to wait a full three hours for our plane to Portland. Eventually we were in flight, on our way home, and feeling thankful that we were able to make it safely.

It felt good to be back in the U.S.A. Those of you who have never ventured outside of the U.S.A. may not be able to appreciate as much this wonderful country in which you live. As you may hear so many international travelers say, we had a great time, but it was so good to be back.

We finished the summer of 1991 staying put in Oregon. We did manage a couple of day trips to Seaside, a trip to San Francisco, and a four-day trip to Reno. The rest of the year went by rather quietly, but on the whole it was a very nice year.

The year 1992 began with my son and I deciding to purchase a high–tech treadmill, and having done so I have to tell you that it's been an excellent investment. It is really good for one's well being. I often go on the treadmill, most times for an hour, and I use that time to organize all the many things I want to do either that very day or on some future date. Best of all I can get some good exercise at the same time. Most times I have my little radio for company. My family uses the treadmill too.

At the beginning of the year it was announced that there would be a fight for the heavyweight championship of the world between the boxers Evander Holyfield (the champion) and Riddick Bowe (the challenger). Our son David got us a package deal for air fare and tickets to the fight, including hotel accommodations for two nights. It was to be held in Las Vegas at the Thomas–Mack Convention Center complex, which is where the University of Las Vegas Nevada basketball team plays its home games. I remember most everything about this trip. We had a great flight from Portland to Las Vegas, and we were accommodated at the beautiful Riviera Hotel and Casino. We were transported to the fight by Riviera's own charter bus with escorts. If the fight was not a sell out it must have come awfully close since I couldn't see too many vacant seats. What I did see was lots of television, movie, and sports celebrities. There were just so many of them, and my wife got a kick out of that.

In my time I've seen a myriad of fights, but this was the first heavyweight title fight I have seen, and what a thriller it turned out to be. It really was in actual fact one of the best fights I'd seen. Bowe won a decision on points after twelve gruelling rounds, taking the title away from a truly game Holyfield. This was Riddick Bowe's night to celebrate a great victory.

Coming away from the Thomas–Mack Convention Center that night was wild to say the least, and it wouldn't have been difficult for people to become separated from each other. I almost lost my wife in the crowd as we were trying for the large main exit doors. I just lost touch with her, but only because she had spotted Shaun O'Grady, the young eloquent boxing analyst on TV's Boxing Tuesday Night Fight. There they were hugging each other, and I finally got her attention to keep on moving. She had seen him and gone over to tell him how much she enjoyed his comments on TV, and Shaun, being very gracious and respectful, had responded. Shaun O'Grady was the Lightweight Champion of the World just a few years back. Thank you, Shaun, for being so nice to my wife.

It reminds me of another time in Reno when I thought I'd lost her but this time she had just wandered away to talk. We had watched the show at John Ascugas' Nugget in Sparks Reno and, as I recall, the main attraction that evening was country singer Freddy Fender. One of the other acts which literally stole the show were three French brothers doing some unusual and amazing acrobatic routines.

Anyway, after the show we sort of drifted around the casino, and that is when Rose decided to go to the ladies room. After about fifteen minutes and no sign of her returning I began looking for her. I soon found her talking and gesturing with one of the young French acrobats. My wife (bless her) really loves talking and helping people. When I asked her why she talked to him she said, "I recognized him and told him how good they were and asked him how they were able to do all those things." Anyway, she said he was awfully nice to her but he didn't understand English very well. So much for my wife's detours.

We were finally able to get back to our charter bus after the fight, and we were back at the Riviera in about thirty minutes. It was really a great night, and we enjoyed every minute of it.

When we got back we freshened up a little and went downstairs to the snack bar for some toast and coffee. Later on we watched Magic Johnson and a couple of other celebrities who had been to the fight hosting a blackjack table.

One of the things I liked about Las Vegas was the very long walks my wife and I were able to take all the way along the strip. They were right in the middle of constructing Treasure Island and the massive new MGM Hotel and Casino. Even Reno has some new buildings under construction. I guess gambling does have its way of forging ahead. When one stops to think about the millions of dollars being spent on these projects then one certainly begins to wonder about it.

I have to say that though my wife and I prefer Reno to Vegas, we did have a great time in Las Vegas on this trip. We were always curious to see it, and having done so we feel content.

When we got back to Portland we resumed our everyday routines almost as if we had never been away. It's not like that however after a trip to England. It seems to take weeks to get back down to earth as it were.

I've often heard people discussing their way of life after retirement. So many of them are into the game of golf for their recreation, and they don't seem too eager to pursue other avenues of using their time for the benefit of their health. I've always impressed on anyone interested in working out that there are no guarantees when you work out, but at least you will never have to regret not working out should your health fail. That's only my opinion of course.

After we returned from Las Vegas I was once again back to my normal program of daily routine. I thought that perhaps you may possibly be interested on how my weeks go.

On Mondays, Wednesdays, and Fridays, I'm awake by a quarter after four. I shave, shower, and change into sweats. I devote fifteen minutes to daily prayers, then by about ten 'til five I'm on I–5 North to the Loprinzi Gym, getting there just before five-thirty. I park the car and walk or jog, returning in time for the gym to open at six o'clock. I do a good, fairly rounded one hour and forty-five minute work out (no stopping), shower, change to street clothes, get back on the freeway to Tualatin, and return home by eight forty-five depending on traffic.

I generally have a round of toast and tea for breakfast. If my wife goes to Portland to have lunch with her sisters or just goes shopping by herself, she takes the bus which stops right outside our house. As for myself, my son generally has some work for me to do such as filing papers, picking up documents at the courthouse, or even going to different jails. I get many letters from home, about an average of three a week, and I like to answer them as soon as I can.

I also put in one hour on the treadmill. My congregation has me oversee affairs at the synagogue's cemetery, and that generally entails driving to East Portland at least once every other week to be sure the grounds are taken care of well.

It's generally late afternoon, four or five o'clock, by the time I get through providing things go fairly smoothly. The evening is my time for relaxing. We don't go out too much in the evenings except in the summer. So there you have it, my Monday, Wednesday, and Friday routine.

On Tuesdays and Thursdays I wake at the same time as I do on the other weekdays. I take the freeway to Portland and stop off at Winchells for coffee and read the morning paper. Then I'm off to the NW Shaari Torah Synagogue for daily morning prayers and finish around eight o'clock. From there I cross two freeways to drive to the U.S.A. Olympic Club on SE 82nd where I swim a few laps for about twenty or thirty minutes, shower, sauna, change, and head for home where I'm generally back by ten or ten-fifteen. Before having breakfast I do a one-hour routine of sit-ups and push-ups, leg exercises, a couple of bench press routines, and some waist trimming exercises.

I have my light breakfast of toast and tea, write a letter or two, and help my wife do some housework, though I'm not very good at it. Then, if there is nothing else going, I get on the treadmill for one hour. My wife (bless her) is now up to forty minutes on the treadmill. That's not too bad no matter how you look at it. So that for me is a typical Tuesday and Wednesday.

Saturday of course is the Jewish Sabbath. I rise a little later than I do on weekdays, generally around five-thirty. I only wash when getting up and change into sweats. I do my one hour of exercise as I do on Tuesday and Thursday, and then I shower and change. I drive to the local 7-11 store and pick up an Oregonian. I have my tea and toast, read the sports page of the paper, and switch on the television to channel 54 to watch my beloved English soccer. It's a funny feeling being so far away and watching a game being played in your hometown.

By nine o'clock my wife and I leave for the synagogue in Southwest Portland. The services are generally over by eleven-thirty or twelve o'clock. Sometimes we stay in Portland after the services and go to one of the malls and enjoy a cup of coffee. Incidentally, we don't even stock coffee at home. Being English we are mainly tea drinkers. We normally return home by two or three o'clock in the afternoon, and then it's an hour on the treadmill once again.

On Sunday I am awake between five and five-thirty, wash, shave, and put on the sweats for the one hour of exercises. I shower, change into street clothes, drive into Portland, stop off at Winchells for coffee, and read the Sunday paper. Then it's off to the Northwest synagogue for the daily prayers which begin at eight-thirty. Services are over by nine o'clock and I generally drive across town to my own synagogue in southwest Portland just to check up on things. On most Sundays I'm generally back home by ten-thirty. I have my light breakfast, and after a brief rest my wife and I generally drive to Portland to do some browsing and some shopping. Sometimes we stop by Nordstrom's downtown to have coffee and a relaxed chat. Most times we are back home by about four o'clock. We both do our treadmill before dinner. The rest of the evening is spent reading, writing, or just enjoying some television, generally sports programs.

So there you have it. Just a normal week in my life, as if anyone really cared, but I thought perhaps some of you might be interested.

During the winter months of 1992 we didn't stray too far from home. Other than a quick three day trip to Reno we were more or less around the vicinity of our home.

The year 1993 came soon enough, and sad to say it was rather tragic for me. My young brother, Sonny, called me one evening to inform me that our good friend Frankie Vaughn had suffered a heart attack and was undergoing surgery. I was really shocked because he had performed so well and looked so good when we last saw him in Blackpool. I do remember saying to him, "You work much too hard on stage, so keep working out." This is exactly what I meant earlier in this biography when I said that working out is not an absolute guarantee but it can never harm you. As of the date of this writing, February 6, 1994, Frankie is fully recovered and performing as well as ever. Could it be that the workouts helped in his recovery? I'm inclined to think that they did. Anyway, it's good to hear he has recovered, and hopefully we will get together in England this summer.

I have to tell you about something rather nice that happened in mid-1993. My wife Rose likes to go shopping for groceries, and since she does not drive I always take her wherever she wants to go. One of the places she enjoys shopping is the Sheridan Fruit Market on the east side. Before I go any further I might mention that when we moved from our Northeast home to Tualatin we found that we didn't have room enough for a twenty-five year old radio and record player console cabinet that we had purchased from K-mart. We had used it constantly since I have a fairly large record collection. About 60 percent of the records are English records. Since the console was rather the worse for wear, and because of the shortage of space, I decided to give it away. Now this brings me back to what I was saying about Sheridan Market.

We generally go there on a Friday morning after I've returned from my regular workout, and we would be at the market around about nine-forty or ten o'clock. Just one block north of the market is a Salvation Army outlet that opens up at ten o'clock on certain days if they have enough merchandise. There always seems to be quite a few people waiting for them to open up. My wife was well aware of how sorry I felt about giving away the console cabinet and how lost I felt being unable to play any of my records. We had been looking to purchase another one now that we found we had enough room, but it seemed a lost cause since they had long ago ceased manufacturing them.

Just on a whim my wife decided we should slip into the Salvation Army and see if they had one of these console cabinets. We were inside and people were milling all over the place, but I didn't see anything resembling one. My wife doesn't give up easily, and she had wandered away into a far corner of a side room where she spotted what looked like a console cabinet buried underneath a load of small appliances. She got my attention and I looked it over as best I could. I doubted if it would even play if it was hooked up since there were loose cords protruding from the back panel. One of the helpers heard my doubtful comments and came over. By putting a couple of leads together we got the radio part to operate, and it had a great sound. As for the record player part of it, it was anybody's guess if it would operate or not.

I asked the person in charge the price he was asking for it, and when he told me eight dollars I was shocked. However, to transport it back to Tualatin was not possible in our small compact car. We asked him if he would hold it for us until noon so we could have someone look at it and then pay for it and transport it away from there. My wife came up with the idea of calling a very dear friend of ours, Mike Dernbach, who lives with his lovely wife, Margaret, on the northeast side just a few minutes drive from the Salvation Army.

We called Mike on the phone. He not only agreed to pick it up with his truck and pay for it but also to take it to his home, look it over, and get everything working and clean up the cabinet which is pecan wood. It was very heavy to haul being very solid. Mike is a retired lieutenant of the Portland Fire Department, and two of his daughters worked for our shoe store while going to high school and just like their dad they were both excellent workers.

Mike got back to us after almost three weeks to tell us he was on his way to our house with the console all finished and ready to be hooked up. When he arrived I helped him carry it in, and that thing was very heavy. I didn't think we were going to make it but we did. We got it hooked up and everything worked perfectly. It appeared to be almost new since all the attachments were still sealed. It even had the price tag on the warranty, and the price was $414.00. I hate to think what it would cost to manufacture now a days. It has to be a least twenty or thirty years old.

Anyway, I can now once again listen to some entertainers, many of whom I know. I have a recording of England's Billy Cotton and his band when they first introduced to the British people the song generally associated with Merv Griffin. It's an original first press of "I've Got a Lovely Bunch of Coconuts." Also, I have one of a young singer in the sixties era named Lee Lawrence who was the son of a famous Jewish Cantor from Manchester. Lee was also an old school chum of mine, and his real name was Leon Sirroto. He was the lead singer for the well-known Stanley Black Orchestra. I also have a few early albums of the singer Vera Lynn, who happens to be not only a great singer but she has the clearest word pronunciation of any singer I've ever heard. She also was honored by H.M. Queen Elizabeth. Vera Lynn really is a true lady.

I can vaguely recall an incident that happened a couple of years before WWII. Perhaps it was 1936. My friend Jack Gore and I went to see one of our ex–school mates perform in a variety–revue show in a town called Bolton about twelve miles from Manchester. His name was Larry Jason and he was a very unusual impressionist. He was pretty good, and since it was a Saturday night and the show was being wrapped up, the whole cast was having a get–away party. Larry invited us to come along so, as he put it, "You two can at least get to see some of the chorus girls close up." Of course we were both probably barely sixteen years old at that time so you might say as far as boy meets girl goes, we were a non-factor. There was this one girl there who was very quiet, rather dark-skinned, and fairly attractive. She was being bothered constantly by these three boys from the show trying to hit on her. It was well past midnight, I think, so their intentions were not entirely honorable. Finally, this young girl spoke to one of the other girls and they both left together, safely I presume. That girl I learned later was Vera Lynn. It's no wonder that she became the idol of the British troops in WWII. Very Lynn is a classy lady.

Naturally, I also have a stack of Frankie Vaughn recordings. One other very special recording I have was made by a young Jewish Dutchman from Holland. His name was Leo Fuld, and he recorded this melody just a few weeks after Israel was declared a state. The words tell of the Jewish people oppressed in communist countries having no place to go. Of course the song comes to a happy ending now that they are able to at least hope to finally make their home in Israel. It's a great song by a very talented singer, and it's titled "Tell Me Where Can I Go."

I just wished I could spend some time spinning those records for you. One thing I could promise you, you've probably never heard some of these artists and tunes and you'd really be entertained. Anyway, we have to thank Mike Dernbach for giving us back an almost brand new console. I say "giving" because the final note is that he wouldn't let us even pay for the whole thing including his refinishing. That's the kind of friend he is, and he's always doing favors for us. It is hard to find friends like Mike and Margaret.

It wasn't too long before the 1993 winter holidays were upon us. We observe Thanksgiving Day in our own quiet way, and it was just the three of us having dinner together, that is my wife and I along with our son, David. Shortly after Thanksgiving came the Jewish holiday of Chanukah which we have all enjoyed. Chanukah is always a very happy time for all of us. We also enjoy the wonderful holidays of Christmas and New Year's with our non-Jewish friends. Of course our Jewish New Year came in September before Thanksgiving, so we were able to enjoy the best of both worlds as it were. I remember when I was in the army I would always do guard duty or Sergeant of the Day so that I could give someone the opportunity to be with their loved ones if possible at Christmas and New Year. It was no great sacrifice. I was just happy to do it.

Well now here we are in the first days of the New Year, 1994. This is the year of the 1994 World Soccer Cup and also the Winter Olympics.

I can promise you all that the American people will have a lot more interest and knowledge of the game of soccer after the World Cup games are completed. Soccer is by far the largest spectator sport in the world and it is played in this country at the elementary, middle, high school, and of course college levels. The American team is made up mostly of very young players. This team may not win the World Cup, but I can assure you they will give a very good account of themselves. I'm looking forward to seeing them. Like all my fellow countrymen in England, I was shocked when England was eliminated in the qualifying games. Watch out for the Team USA four or five years from now. They will be very good.

And now some thoughts about the upcoming Olympics. I would be remiss if I failed to mention the sad state of affairs in ladies figure skating because of the Nancy Kerrigan-Tonya Harding case that, at the time of this writing, February 7, 1994, is being considered for adjudication by the various figure skating and Olympic committees. Not being sure what the outcome will be, I can just say that whatever decision is eventually made it will be fair and impartial in the judicial system in this great country. The U.S.A. will be well represented in Norway, and I hope they can come away with one or two gold medals.

The Summer Olympics of 1996 will be held in Atlanta, and as I write preparations are going ahead to prepare for all the events and accommodations for all the participating athletes. The American team will win its fair share of medals in Atlanta two years from now.

In about four months we will be going back to the land of our birth to once again reunite with my brothers, sisters, and all the nieces and nephews, and my wife will re-unite with her sister and her niece.

I've frequently, over the many years we have lived in this country, been asked the question, "How come you have never become an American citizen?" This is to my mind a very fair question since we do live here and have made a fair living in this country. My wife, my son, and myself are all British citizens with British passports, and to answer the question one has to be truly honest about it. Speaking for my family and myself I really believe that one should always remain and be proud of being a citizen of the land of their birth. Personally speaking I just don't think that by studying a little American history and then answering a few simple questions relating to it that you then become an American citizen. Remember I did say this was just my personal opinion and I'm sure there are many of you who will disagree with me. I can respect that, but be that as it may I firmly believe once an Englishman, always an Englishman.

When we go to any sporting event and they happen to play our national anthem "God Save The Queen" we sort of have a longing to be back home. On the other hand during our last visit to England at a Lemon Tree show my nephew Brian had the band play "The Star Spangled-Banner" especially for us and our feelings were exactly the same, we found ourselves wishing to be back in the U.S.A. We experience sort of mixed-up feelings. I hope you can understand my feelings on this issue.

Talking about citizenship reminds me of a time, I think it was 1976, when our son had graduated from law school and was allowed to take the bar exam. After passing it he became eligible for military service even though he was a British citizen. No complaints on that score. Living in this country one should be ready and willing to serve, which our son was. So it was that in 1976 he was inducted into the army and based at Ft. Lewis, Washington, for recruit training.

We drove up to Ft. Lewis a couple of times. We had been invited by the base commander to visit. The way they treat visitors at Ft. Lewis is extremely first class, and all the staff there were so ready and willing to help everyone. In addition to all of this, they also had a large buffet table laid out with refreshments of all kinds. We actually enjoyed our trips to Ft. Lewis.

Meanwhile, back out our shoe store a couple of tall, stern-looking men came in one morning and immediately showed us their credentials and identified themselves as F.B.I. agents. They proceeded to tell us that our son, being a lawyer, was being considered to complete his tour of duty in the army serving in a branch of the F.B.I. They also questioned a couple of close friends of ours. It was sort of a background check.

However, nothing much happened since our son was released by the army. He was released because his flat feet just couldn't stand up to the vigorous training, and after five months he was back again in the shoe store. We also learned that he was turned down by the F.B.I. when they realized he was not an American citizen.

Currently our son has his own practice, and his office is on the southeast side of Portland. Since retiring from our business we have had a few opportunities to go to Multnomah County Court and also Washington County Court to listen to our son in court, and he even surprised us. He is an excellent trial lawyer. I don't feel too guilty saying this since I've heard other attorneys saying the same thing about him.

We are now right in the middle of the winter of 1994. So far it's been a very mild winter to say the least, but we still have a few weeks left. Looking back it's hard to believe that we have lived in this great country thirty-nine years. This means we have lived longer in the U.S.A. than we did in England.

From now until late June we will be getting a few things together that we can take for the children when we go back to England. Also we both have to maintain our good health, and that brings up the health care situation I promised to comment on earlier in this book.

If I were to select twelve people and ask each one individually what type of health care they now have, I would almost guarantee you that they each would have a different carrier or different types of health care. On further questioning most of them would not be too sure of exactly how far their coverage extends. Oh I know many of you will read this and say to yourselves, "Well I'm fully covered. I know." Still I keep hearing about people who have had major health problems, and even though they were covered they have had to fork out hefty sums of money.

I stand to be corrected if I'm wrong, but I believe that almost every country except the U.S.A. and South Africa have a system national health care, and contrary to whatever tales you may have heard, the countries with national health care are doing very well. The people in those countries can go about their daily lives knowing that if they do get sick they will not have to use their hard earned savings to get well again.

Just as an example, take an average married couple with two children. Both parents have worked for, shall we say, twenty years with little or no health problems, and collectively they have been able to save a tidy sum of money for their future retirement. Things are going well for them when suddenly one of the parents or one of the children is suddenly a victim of a major illness requiring constant medical care and attention including a lengthy stay of hospitalization.

The odds for being fully covered 100 percent for this type of illness I can assure you would not be good. All of the money saved for retirement could be used up in a very short time. My contention is that people in this country should not get sick worrying about getting sick. This is just too good a country to carry on this way. How many of you go to a pharmacy and pay those exorbitant fees for your prescriptions? It just shouldn't have to be that way at all. I'm not saying we should adopt Hillary Clinton's health care program cart blanc, but at least let's take a good long look at it and act as soon as possible one way or another.

Well I've said my piece on this issue. I just hope I've not offended anyone, but if I have then I sincerely apologize for that. All I care about is that we all should be able to enjoy life without having to worry about medical bills of any kind whatsoever, and everyone in this country deserves the same coverage. Every individual, however, should learn to take care of his or her body at a young age. It will pay dividends.

On a more personal note, I had to visit my dentist this morning for my twice a year check up. During my visit the dentist and I talked about old times for a few minutes. We go back about thirty-eight years together. I can still recall when I first started working out in George Pavlich's basement and this young high school kid, I believe he was from Washington High, asked me to do a couple of different exercises with him. Although he wasn't my full-time workout partner we did curls and squats together. He really was a dedicated young man.

One evening I got down to the basement gym and we got together. I mentioned I was having a severe toothache, and he said that he was hoping to become a dentist. He said that he would take care of my teeth if he ever became a dentist. Well, to get to the point of this story, he became a very good dentist. Of course he has me for a patient, and he takes good care of me. His name is Dr. Anthony Service and he works out regularly at the Multnomah Athletic Club. He is also an avid marathon runner. He has his clinic on the northeast side of Portland. If you ever see three tall good looking guys in sweats running east along Fremont towards Rocky Butte, then you are seeing the three dentists and close friends—Dr. Anthony Service, Dr. Jerry Wrench, and Dr. Lee Wheeler. Nice going, fellas!

Today is a Thursday in mid-February and a typically normal one for me, although it is a little on the slow side. Just to give you some idea of what I mean, this is how it went:

I was awake at four-thirty in the morning and heading north on I-5 by five o'clock after having showered and dressed. I got into Portland just a little after five-thirty. I picked up an Oregonian newspaper and stopped for a cup of coffee. I read my newspaper and finished my coffee, and by six-thirty I was on my way to the synagogue for daily prayers. By eight o'clock I was driving over the freeways to the U.S.A. Athletic Club opposite Madison High School on S.E. 82nd. I then swam laps for about half an hour or so, showered, changed again, and drove back to Tualatin and home by a quarter past ten.

I then went upstairs to my little gym where I did a solid forty-five minute routine of sit-ups, push-ups, leg raises, leg extensions, and a couple of bench presses using fairly light weights (I consider Thursday my off day).

After working out, I had breakfast, or you might call it lunch since it was after noon. Breakfast consisted of a slice of wheat toast and a cup of tea. Then along with my wife I drove once again to downtown Portland where I picked up a replacement contact for my son from his optician. Then I had to deliver some documents for my son to a judge's chambers.

The judge was Judge Koch and his secretary was someone we knew very well since she was Judge Casciato's secretary for some time. We had a nice visit with her. Her name is Loren, and she is such a very sweet person. Judge Anthony Casciato is a close friend of ours who is retired, but he does some pro temp work when called upon. He is one of the most respected and loved persons in Portland, and he has a lovely wife too.

We completed our messages in Portland and got back to Tualatin after three o'clock. We did a few odd jobs around the house to help my wife out. It's now five o'clock and I'll write for half an hour or so and then relax for the rest of the evening. I hope I didn't bore you with all that, but it's truly how I spent my day and for me it was one of my slower days. I really do enjoy my evenings after a busy day. I should also mention that I do an hour on my treadmill during the day.

There is so much controversy surrounding Oregon and Portland in particular nowadays. First it was the Bob Packwood situation and now the Tonya Harding story, but be that as it may the population of Oregon keeps growing. Here in Tualatin alone the population has increased from 12,600 to just over 17,000 in less than two and a half years. It also appears to be that many people are moving here from California. Probably it is because they feel it is a lot safer in Oregon. We really do have one of the most beautiful states in the country.

It's not quite into the month of March and yet we are having fairly spring-like weather. This is very much in sharp contrast to the weather back east, especially in New York where they are knee deep in three feet of snow right now with fairly low temperatures to go along with it. Back home in England my family tells me they are having one of their worst winters in years—ice, snow, fog, cold, and wet. In other words, their weather is miserable and people there go around looking and indeed feeling rather depressed. I know exactly how they feel when the weather is so depressing.

There is much turmoil in the world today, especially with the fighting going on in Sarajevo, the capital of Bosnia. It is so sad to see the killing of civilians on television, especially the small children. Here at home we have our earthquakes and floods plus heavy snowfalls to contend with.

However, far from all the news is negative. During the last few years we have seen tremendous breakthroughs in medical science. There have been different types of transplants, vast strides in heart surgery and the battle against certain types of cancer, and now there is talk of a possible cure for Malaria, a disease which my brother, David, contracted serving with the 8th Army in WWII and to which he finally succumbed after years of suffering.

Another good piece of news comes out of the land of my birth, and it's a project that has been on the table for a long, long time. It's concerning the building of a tunnel from England to France. In order to familiarize my readers with the project perhaps a little information is in order at this point.

The English Channel is an arm of the sea separating England from France. It is one of the world's most important waterways being 350 miles long and varying in width from 100 miles to 21 miles at its narrowest point between Dover, England, and Calais, France. I have crossed this channel many times, and I can tell you it can be very rough because the currents of the North Sea and the Atlantic Ocean meet in the channel. As a matter of fact, during WWII it was only the rough waters of the English Channel that kept the German armies from invading England in 1940-41. A few years later, however, the Allied armies succeed in landing troops on the beaches in Normandy (France), commanded by U.S. Army General Dwight Eisenhower.

Plans had been made at various times prior to WWII to build to tunnel connecting England and France under the English Channel. Both countries strongly objected to such plans chiefly because they were afraid enemy armies might use such a tunnel for an invasion. So it was that just a few years after the end of WWII that once again the subject of the tunnel was brought up, and eventually the idea gained the support of both countries.

What may be considered to be one of the finest feats of engineering in the world, the English Channel Tunnel, which at this point in time is on the verge of completion, will be open for public use sometime in June or July of 1994. It will indeed be a very historic occasion, and I hope it will be open during our contemplated visit around that time.

The details of transportation are still a little vague, but I can give you some of the information passed on to me from people who have some knowledge of this tremendous project.

There will be separate modes of transport. Eurostar is the rail service that will carry passengers via the tunnel linking Great Britain, France, and Belgium. The trains run at fairly high speeds and the stretch of tunnel will probably take thirty to forty minutes. Le Shuttle is the train that will carry freight or vehicles with their drivers between England and France. Cars and trucks will not be able to drive straight through the tunnel. They will be required to pull off of the M20 motorway on the English side of the A16 autoroute on the French side.

Le Shuttle will carry as many as one hundred eighty vehicles and their passengers up to four times an hour every day of the year twenty-four hours a day. The complete length of the tunnel is thirty-one miles, and it is operated by a French-English company called Eurotunnel.

Cars and trucks, when entering the tunnel either on the English or French side, will be able to drive their vehicles straight on to Le Shuttle and remain in their vehicles until the completion of the journey.

As of this time there are still many details to be worked out mainly dealing with the cost of tickets for each type of passenger or vehicle. What little I have learned so far is the price of a round trip from England to France for a car or van (no limit on riders) will be approximately two to four hundred dollars depending on the time of year, excursion fares, etc. The price for straight passenger train fare is not yet available.

Sorry I can't be of more help than this, but I will pass on any further information to you should I get knowledge of it later. Anyway, if you are planning a trip to Europe and you wish to go to Belgium or Paris from London, then you best bet is the English Channel Tunnel from London to France and then by rail or car to Paris or Belgium. I hope some of this information has been of some help to you or at least proved to be interesting. It's just a great work of engineering and it has been a dream of the English people for decades.

Today being Wednesday I got back from my workout in Portland and after breakfast my wife asked me to take her shopping for groceries. So we drove back to Portland and did our shopping there. My wife, bless her, has this thing about always making sure there is more than enough food in the house. I'm afraid this stems from the day we first arrived in Portland, Oregon. We had travelled a long way, we all three of us were so very tired, very hungry, and practically broke. We arrived in Union Station around noon or thereabouts, and it was late evening before we even saw any food or drink. It seemed that everyone was showing us what they had over here and how good it was, and since nobody suggested anything in the way of even a hot drink I decided to take my wife and son to a small cafe. I was glad I did. I'm not faulting anyone. I thought then that perhaps that's the way they do things in America, but I learned later on that its not that way with everyone.

My family and I become good friends with the girl who worked with me at the surplus store. Her name is Ida Hiromura and her husband is Yuji Hiromura. Whenever we visit their home in southeast Portland the first thing Ida does is to set a table with tea and cakes and cookies. That's how it's always been for us back home whenever people visited us or we visited them.

Incidentally, I would feel a little remiss if I didn't tell you about Mrs. Hiromura's wonderful parents who are both deceased. In those first two or three years after we first came to this country they would invite us to their very modest home on East Burnside where they had some acreage and grew lots of vegetables and strawberries. They would always send us home with a supply of veggies and strawberries. What lovely people they were, and even today we remain firm friends with all of their children.

George Nakamura, the father, was an avid fisherman. He would always send us a huge piece of red salmon on every Jewish holiday, and we'll always remember him for taking our son, David, fishing and helping him reel one in his first time out. Mrs. Nakamura spent her last few years in a nursing home, she couldn't speak English, so I went to the library, took out a Japanese language book, and taught myself as much as I could. We would go visit her and I'd go through all the phrases I'd learned. She would understand me, but after exhausting all of my knowledge I was all through. She was a great lady and she understood what I'd been trying to do. We really got along great. We really miss George Nakamura and his wife.

Gosh! I believe I was telling you that we had gone shopping for food, and before I knew it I was into all this other stuff. But I'm writing this as it comes into my head, and I'm trying not to hold back on anything. To sum up what I've been trying to say, however, my wife made a promise to herself that our family (we three) would never be short of food again. Actually there was no excuse for our poor welcome.

While on the subject of our plight on the day of our arrival into Portland in June of 1953, I'd like to go a step further and tell you what happened the first day after our arrival. I remember being awake early, feeling a little nervous but eager, and ready to go meet my sponsor (my wife's uncle) who was the president of this large furniture, electrical, hardware, appliance, and sporting goods store. They were both retail and wholesale.

My wife's two brothers and three sisters were already working there and they had been since they landed in America. Anyway, on my arrival at the company store one of my wife's sisters ushered me to the main office upstairs, first taking me through a large room where about a dozen or so office girls on each side of the room were typing away or rapping away on typewriters and calculators. My feelings on seeing this was that hopefully I'd be given a good job which is all I really wanted to get me started.

I was led into what seemed like a very large conference room. There was a long table in the center with chairs on either side. Seated at the head of the table was a man who looked so much like my wife's father that he had to be my sponsor. My wife's sister introduced me to him in these exact words, "This is your long-lost nephew from England." I'd much rather have introduced myself since I enjoy keeping a low profile. I'm not normally an attention getter. He was the president of the company and he had three or four brothers with him in this business. In addition to the president there were a few people seated on either side of the conference table.

I was now alone since my wife's sister had rushed out of the room having introduced me to my wife's uncle. His very first words to me were, if I remember correctly and I'm sure I do, "There's nothing for you here since we don't have any openings." Then he proceeded to tell me to go downstairs and talk to one of his so-called managers in the warehouse and he would perhaps be able to advise me about a job. I couldn't really believe I was not being offered a job since this was my sponsor who had signed an affidavit promising me a position where I would not become a burden to the state. I felt so deflated and guilty about leaving my country and having this happen to me. It just didn't seem fair. To top that off I did go to the person in charge of the warehouse, and to put it bluntly he finished some small conversation with me by putting his arm around my shoulder like a friend some-times does. He said, "You know we have a newspaper in this city called the Orego-nian which you should purchase. Look in the want ads and there are lots of jobs to be had." I just told him very quietly but firmly that I didn't need to come over seven thousand miles to hear this kind of advice, and I left it at that.

Now I had to go to the home in which we were staying and relate to my wife what had happened. She was naturally shocked and very upset when I told her, but she kept telling me not to worry and things will work out for us. The words of my friend, Jack Gores' father, kept going around in my head. When I first told him we were emigrating to the U.S.A. he was surprised and said, "Barney, over here you have a nice loaf of bread and now you go to America looking for crumbs?" I had answered that I wasn't expecting too much, but all I needed was a job and I was sure I'd get that. Now I wasn't sure about anything, I couldn't help thinking about the mess I'd made not only for myself but for my lovely wife and six-year-old son. I vowed I'd stop feeling sorry for myself, and I didn't wish to make trouble for my sponsor which I could so very easily have done since he was legally bound to provide for the three of us. That's just not my style however, and after about two and a half weeks I got the job with the surplus store.

I thought from here on in things just had to get better, but I was about to receive another shocker. My wife's young brother in whose house we were staying had come over from Liverpool to Manchester to live with us for three months be-fore to going to the states with his dad. He asked me if I could find him a job for three months so he could maybe save a little for going away. Being on very friendly terms with my ex-employer I got him a job being a general sort of help around the upholstering factory. He was being paid three pounds ten shillings a week, which in those days was a very fair wage. He would give my wife half of his wages to save for him, but he always ended up each week by getting back much more than he gave her. Our own business was doing well, and I didn't mind my wife giving him whatever he needed. At that time the room above the drapery shop where my brother and I worked was not big enough hardly for the two of us, otherwise I could have given my young brother-in-law a job with us. He was a real nice kid and he and I became good friends. I missed him when he left for America.

However, I must get back on track. As soon as I got the job in the surplus store we began looking to rent a place of our own. We were fortunate to find an old three-bedroom house in the Fulton Park district off Barbur Boulevard, and the rent was thirty-five dollars a month. Now it was time to move away from the house in which we had been staying for just under three weeks. Not thinking anything special, but just out of courtesy, as my brother–in–law and his wife were standing together to see us go I asked them how much they wanted for us living there. I never dreamt they would even entertain such an idea. You could have knocked me over with a feather duster when my wife's brother said, "How about eighty dollars!" and his wife said, and I quote, "No, babe, sixty dollars will be enough." That they would even charge us absolutely floored me, but I paid it and kept my thoughts to myself. Remember that my wife's brother had lived with us in England for over three months and the thought of even taking a penny off him never entered my mind. I was more concerned with making sure he always had enough pocket money. I never thought I'd get this off my chest, but now that I have it feels pretty good. At the same time, however, I would like it to be known that we have tried to put all this behind us, I just wanted the readers to know what an awful beginning we had in this country.

While still on the subject of family and relatives, I would like to tell you of an incident that happened after I'd been working at the surplus store for about three months. I had sold a man a GI-type foot locker and we went to the cash register. The man gave me the $8.95. I rang him up and started writing his receipt. He then told me the foot locker was for his son who would refund him the purchase, but he asked if I could make him a receipt for $12.95 since, according to his own words, he was entitled to make a profit. I flatly refused to do this and he got very upset. He asked to talk to my employer, which he did, but he didn't fare any better. He eventually left with the foot locker and his receipt for $8.95. I couldn't imagine a father making a profit off his son. My faith in America was really shaken at this point, but eventually I met so many very nice American people, I also met nice people from the other countries.

Having so much family back in Europe means that I get mail from England every week and today was no exception. Among the mail from England was one letter I had been waiting for, giving me some additional official information regarding the tunnel, or should I say tunnels, thirty feet below the bed of the English Channel.

The official name is The Channel Tunnel. There are three tunnels that run parallel with each other, each thirty-one miles long. The center tunnel is for service only, such as trucks, vans, etc. and it has a double track. The tunnels at each side of the service tunnel are for passenger cars and they are a single track rail.

Official opening by H.M. Queen and President Mitterand: May 6th, 1994.
Passenger toll fee: 280 pounds sterling, approximately $420. Per car round trip.
Total building cost: 10 billion pounds, approximately 14.5 billion dollars.

There is to be an inauguration walk through at the official opening using the center service tunnel, and this will be the one and only time walkers will be allowed.

I hope the extra information gives you somewhat of a clearer picture of this amazing piece of modern engineering. By the way, the normal journey time is thirty-five minutes from platform to platform with twenty-six minutes of this time being under the channel. The overall time for the entrance to the exit of the terminal is just under one hour.

I can assure you that May 6, 1994, will take it's rightful place in history for the people of Britain and France.

The month of March is just a couple of days away and still no signs of real winter weather. Soon it will be spring and the outlook of people everywhere is upbeat. We are right in the middle of the Winter Olympics, and everyone seems to be anxious to have the Harding-Kerrigan issues resolved both in skating and whatever else may be determined to be proper.

I'm writing here at the local Tualatin library, having to pick up a book I ordered almost three months ago. The book is called Decider by Dick Francis. Dick is an ex-champion steeplechase jockey from Great Britain, and he is a very successful author, writing mostly stories of fiction dealing with race horses, both steeplechase and flat racing. He generally divides his time among England, Florida, and the Caribbean. I have read most of his books and they are mostly always excellent, but his last two or three have not been up to his usual standard. His main fault is that he introduces too many different characters in the first ten pages, utterly confusing his readers.

Anyway, the librarian here tells me she has read this latest one and it's more like his usual Dick Francis standard of writing. I hope so since I fully intend to enjoy this book on the charter bus ride to Reno which my wife and I will be taking this coming Sunday. We will be returning to Tualatin Wednesday evening.

I can remember not too long ago when we went to Reno and I always drove there, until my wife talked me into going on one of these bus trips to Reno and Lake Tahoe. Actually I'm glad we did now that I've tried it a few times. Some people tell me they love to drive to places like Los Angeles and Reno and they are able to relax while driving. Perhaps it's just me, but I can't seem to fully relax while driving. I find that I have to be on the alert all of the time while driving. I do my best to be calm, but I just can't be fully relaxed.

In any event it's just nice for me to sit back read a good book or the Sunday Oregonian and leave the driving to a very experienced and safe bus driver. One gets to see so much on a trip to Reno that is almost impossible to see when you are driving your car. Anyway, it's a trip my wife always looks forward to since it's also a break from her regular everyday housework chores. I sort of enjoy it too, except that I miss my regular gym workouts.

When I first began to write this book I never even gave any thought to a title for it. To be quite truthful I never even thought I'd get to the point where it even entered my mind. But my friend Michael, who talked me into this and has been brave enough to read the many pages I've already written, asked me just yesterday if I'd really given my book a title not simply because I really couldn't be sure if it would ever reach the publisher. My thinking once again was, Why in the world would anyone be interested in the story of my life? My young friend, however, assured me that I would be pleasantly surprised. So here I sit, writing and thinking about an appropriate title for this book.

Just about the time prior to our leaving England for the U.S.A. in 1953, one of the biggest hits on the English Telly was a young comedian named Harry Korris. Along with a couple of sidekicks he had a weekly one-hour show, and he had a tremendous viewing audience. The opening theme song for the show was titled "We Three We're All Alone." It was a very catchy tune, and one could hear it either in the work place or just out on the street. The opening verse went something like this:

> We three we're all alone,
> We're not even company
> Old Enoch, Ramstbottom, and me.

Even on the long journey to the U.S.A. the tune kept running through my head, and after the horrible first few weeks in Portland I began to feel how appropriate the words of the song were as they applied to my wife, my son, and myself. This then brings me to the title on the cover of this book except to change one word, using it in the past tense, to read: We Three Were All Alone.

We may have been surrounded by relatives, it's true, but the fact remains that I was literally unemployed for the very first time in my life. We were without food in a way, and we were almost without funds. My wife and I are not the kind of people to ask for anything, and since help was not forthcoming we knew we were in for a very rough time. With that in mind I took the very first authentic job I could get.

This of course was the job at the war surplus store, and I promised myself I would work so very hard at it that eventually I would be offered some chance of becoming a part of the business. I've already related why it didn't come about, but at least the job, even with it's meager salary, was sufficient to help us survive. Later, many years later as a matter of fact, my salary was raised a few times and eventually we were able to save quite a bit.

I must apologize for carrying on a little more than I had intended when all I really wished to do was to tell you how the title of this book came about.

Since this is a book about my life, it would be appropriate at this time to talk about some of the many good people who help take care of my life. Naturally the first and most important one is my dear wife, Rose. However, when it comes down to the medical part of it, that's when one has to be under the care of professionals.

When we first came into the country and I worked at the army surplus, one of our regular customers was a German doctor with a downtown office practice. His name was Dr. Julius Frahm. I say was because he retired many years ago to live in Hawaii where he passed away four years ago.

He was very good to me and my family, and once he drove all the way from his Wilsonville farm to our northeast Portland home when our son David had severe stomach pains. He was able to medicate him and the pains eventually went away. We had kept in touch with each other even after he ceased to be our family doctor.

While we were at the shoe store, we had to be sure we had a family doctor. We didn't need to look too far since Dr. James Thorup was in the same block as we were. He was a man in his seventies with lots of experience. We didn't need his services often, but it was comforting to know he was just next door to us. He eventually passed away when he was about eighty-two.

After Dr. Thorup passed away we were once again without a family doctor, but then we got real lucky. One day a lady came into the shoe store when it was not real busy since we were not yet selling Nike athletic shoes. Anyway, she kept browsing around the store. My wife spoke to the woman and from what I can remember she told Rose she was feeling a little under the weather. My wife made her a cup of hot tea which this lady enjoyed. Then she told my wife her name was Miriam Duncan and that her husband was Dr. David Duncan, with an office practice just three blocks away. Rose told her we were without a family doctor, and she arranged for her husband to take care of our family. Thus began a friendship with the Duncans, in addition to being our doctor, which has endured over thirty years. Although the doctor retired four years ago, we have remained very good friends and we visit each other's homes frequently. They are both very special people to us. They have three wonderful sons who are all married, and we know the families well.

One of the sons, the middle one, was Dr. Angus Duncan. He was a brilliant young cardiologist to whom I had been going for an annual treadmill test and cardiovascular work up for about ten years since his dad, our family doctor, said it was a good idea to do it.

*Me at tender age of 1. Dressed in
sister's Polish handmedowns.
Manchester 1919.*

*Doing our laundry. The one in the middle is me.
Fishguard, Wales 1941.*

My dear parents. Manchester 1936.

My brother Sonny and his wife Pam as a duo.
Manchester 1943.

WW II *1943.*

The complete staff of western command weapon training school Altcar rifle ranges.
That's me, center row, fourth in from right. Our CO is on front, dead center,
lost right arm on a commando raid.
Liverpool, England 1944.

*David our five year old
in front of our home in his school uniform.
Prestwich, England 1952.*

*1st place for best abdominals
Mr. Past 50 Pacific Coast.
1970.*

*After 1 year of weight training,
that's me on extreme right. The others are all trophy winners.
From L to R, Bob Hopkins, George Pavlich and Harry Shleifer. 1955.*

...Doing my 10,500 situps. 1971.

That's me in 2nd position. Mr. Past 50 Pacific Coast. 1971.

David at work in B&R Shoe Store.

D-B's Dream gets his first win at Gold Gate California 1976.

My two nephews-Graeme extreme left, Brian third from left. 1988.

*My brother Sonny with our dear friend and one of England's most popular singers,
Frankie Vaughn. Blackpool, England 1993.*

*Pictured above with Neil Fairbrother Lancashire County
and England's Brilliant Cricket Player.
Manchester 1995.*

Departing Ringway Airport. Rose, myself and Brother Sonny.
England 1995.

Manchester City F.C. Coach Alan Ball with my wife Rose and me.
July 1995.

Unfortunately Angus passed away rather suddenly while jogging on the beach in Hawaii where he was on a short vacation from his very busy practice. We were in shock when we first heard the news, and personally speaking I had lost someone who was such a good friend and health care provider for me. What an exceptionally clever and humble person he was, and he was still so very young at the age of forty-eight when he died. He was just like his parents. They are all good people.

A family came into our shoe store one time and said they had been recommended to us by customers of ours, Nancy and Jim Blair. The husband, a young man in his very early thirties, was a fine six-feet three-inches tall with good posture, but he was sitting in one of the chairs sort of slumped down. We got to talking and he told me he was a doctor just finishing his internship. He had just undergone surgery on his shoulder, which was the reason he couldn't sit up straight. He was a nice, personable young man and he was really good looking. They came in many times after that. Dr. Angus Duncan was still very much alive at this time, but he was so overloaded with patients that he had decided to take on a partner in his practice.

He talked to me knowing that I knew this young doctor, whose name incidentally is Dr. John Wilson, and he asked me what I could tell him about him since he was considering him as an associate. I told him that he and his family had been recommended to our store, and having known him about a year now, everything I knew about him was exceptionally good. I told Dr. Duncan that if he was as good as a doctor as he was a person, his choice couldn't be better.

Angus and Dr. Wilson began an association that was to last just a few months because of the sad tragedy that befell Angus. It was indeed a sad time all around for his family, friends, Dr. Wilson, and all of the nurses and office staff.

Dr. Wilson took over the responsibility of caring for all of Dr. Angus Duncan's patients, and though it was a heavy load for him he handled it superbly. He is indeed an excellent cardiologist and his patients seem to know that. I go to him for my annual treadmill test. I enjoy talking sports with him. Being still a young man, he still plays some pick-up basketball.

Now regarding our health care, our main health care physician (family doctor) is Dr. Clell Clifton who practices in a southeast Portland clinic. We have indeed been very fortunate to have such wonderful doctors to care for us, and Dr. Clifton is no exception. He is such a very humble person with a vast amount of medical experience. It's so very comforting to know that we will have the best possible care should anyone in our family get sick. Let's keep a positive attitude.

Today is a Friday. It's raining some which is normal for this time of the year, but it's not cold. This coming Sunday my wife and I will be taking off for Reno for a few days and we will be returning home Wednesday evening.

Remember me telling you earlier how nowadays we go to Reno by a charter bus with about forty people? That's how we will travel this Sunday if all goes well. It's really a very pleasant and relaxing trip.

I've often been asked what my thoughts are on the subject of working out at one of your regular gyms as compared to working out in your homemade gym. It takes a little more than a few words to answer that question but I'll try.

First of all, and speaking for myself, the idea of fixing up a small gym at home serves a very useful purpose. It's good to know you can work out at home when the weather gets so bad in the winter that you can't make it to the gym. There may be some days when the regular gym is closed, and there may be the rare times when you just can't make it to the gym.

In addition to all of this there are the many friendships one makes at a gym. When you work out at a gym at least three times a week and see a lot of the same faces over the years, it's only natural that you get to know each other on a very friendly basis.

One of my closest friends in Loprinzi's Gym is a person I've worked out with and jogged with, and we also swim together. He is a Roman Catholic parish priest and he was affiliated with Assumption Church here in Portland for eighteen years. He is now in semi-retirement and he fills in on a regular basis. We have worked out together for over thirty years.

His name is Father Pio Ridi (I call him P.R.) and he is a wonderful and humorous person. He's also a very good singer, and they tell me it's a pleasure to attend mass when he is conducting it. He is also the only naturally blonde Italian I have ever seen. We are together quite a lot, and we phone each other every once in a while too. I mention his name because he is truly a remarkable individual possessing exceptional stamina. As good a swimmer as I am, he is even better and it's that way in his workouts too.

He still talks with a thick accent and I tell him he talks kind of funny. I guess I do too, and he tells me the same thing. As one person in the gym hearing us talk said to us, "You know, you both talk funny." Anyway, we remain to this day real good friends.

Of course there are many others I classify as friends due to my working out over the last thirty-eight years. Just to mention a few there is John Ross who boasts about being exactly ten years older than Father Ridi and I. There's also Tony Loprinzi and another Italian who I've always known as just plain Tony. Then there is Chris Mayther, a giant of a man who oversees and instructs at the gym. There are many, many other whose faces I know but I do not know all of their names. As you can tell, then, I'm all for working out at a regular gym whenever it is possible. I'm sure that by this time you are all beginning to get the message that I am a firm believer in exercise and a sensible way of eating. I really don't care to use the word diet too much since it can conjure up people who are dangerously thin and below their natural weight. Yes, I think it is sensible to eat good foods such as vegetables, fruit, fish, potatoes, and bread every so often, but put nothing on them. It's really not that difficult to cut out the chocolates, cakes, fried foods, etc. Moderation I guess is the key word.

I've been in and round the body building and weight training business for over forty years, and I'm constantly being questioned by students at the gyms where I happen to be working out on all different aspects of exercises and weight training. One of the most common questions I'm often asked is, "What advice would you have for both young people and senior citizens relating to body conditioning?" This is a very good and indeed a very fair question.

I will deal first of all with young teenagers, both boys and girls. I would remind them to take very good care of their bodies. You are only given the one body to take you through life, and it is up to you to take care of it. If you don't drink or smoke, then don't start. If you do, then certainly try to put a stop to it. Smoking definitely has no health value whatsoever and it could prove very harmful. Alcohol on the other hand may be a little less dangerous. It should be avoided, however, if at all possible even though some medial reports tell us that if taken very moderately it will do little harm.

I would also suggest to my young friends to pay some attention to the calibre of food they put into their bodies. I am referring mainly to high calorie foods such as pastries, candies, potato chips, and all types of fried foods. The main thing, however, is to take on an exercise program and perhaps combine it with some sport and try to stay with this type of program. This would all be much better of course if it is performed under some kind of supervision where your progress and weight can be checked and regulated.

As I've said before, a good way to start such a program is to enroll at a well-established and reputable health club. If you young folks do this, I feel sure you'll never regret it.

Now for our senior citizens. In this respect I'm focusing on men and women over the age of fifty-five when perhaps many of you have started retirement.

If you both smoke and drink, then I would advise that you gradually cut down on both and perhaps make a serious effort to stop. You will feel so much better if you do. If you have not been working at a job where you are constantly on the move, then chances are that your cardiovascular condition needs to be upgraded. This of course means getting yourself on to a steady exercise program. Before you do this, however, you should consult with your primary care physician and he will then inform you of what you can or cannot do.

Having been given the green light to go ahead then, as with my advise to the young people, find a gym with a solid reputation. Preferably find one that has individual instruction. If you do all of this and stay with the exercise program, then before many months have passed you will feel very good about yourself. You will even take pride in your body. Even the food you eat will taste so much better, just as long as you do not over indulge.

All of this then is my answer to the popular question I've often been asked.

On a slightly different note, I can well remember going back in time some thirty or forty years ago when people would poke fun at my weight lifting. When I'd be running outdoors people driving by would lower their windows and yell out with some degrading remarks.

As for many coaches in all types of sports, the very mention of weight lifting did nothing but upset them. They were very much opposed to the idea of including it in their various conditioning programs, thinking it would do nothing but produce musclebound athletes. How very wrong they all turned out to be. Now, every amateur and professional sport encompasses weight rooms, and indeed all athletes are encouraged to take up weight lifting. Almost, one might say, a compete turnaround.

There are so many times that I look back on my life and think about the various triumphs and losses along the way. I must admit in all candidness that the losses outweigh the gains by far.

Winning has never come easily, at least not for me. One great advantage I've always had ever since I can remember is stamina, and that's always played a big part in the success I have had in the arena of sports.

I well remember the time when I won my first amateur boxing bout, and my brother Joey treated me to an ice cream cone victory celebration. During my teenage soccer days I'd always treat myself to some candy or chocolate after a good win. During the past two decades, whenever our big horse D.B.'s Dream won one of his big races, whether in California, Canada, or Washington, we were happy celebrating during the journey home. The few wins I enjoyed during my days of competing in weight lifting and body building were always a good reason for celebrating.

However the losses, of which there were very many, I learned to accept and I tried very hard to be a good loser. I have never been angry about losing just as long as I knew that I or my horses had done our best.

Do not misunderstand me. I've never been one to enjoy losing, and I have tried whenever possible to come back another time and win. I just don't care to see a very angry loser.

Which brings me to the point I'm trying to convey. Do not ever be afraid to show your happiness and celebrate any victory, but at the same time try to show some class and be a good loser. In this game of life there will always be winners and losers.

So much for my health lecture, which I can assure you would be much longer if I was really talked into giving one. I'll finish on this subject with some words of wisdom that have been posted on the wall of Loprinzi's Gym ever since I can remember. It goes something like this, "What a shame it really is for any person to have to go through life without knowing the strength and beauty of which their body is capable." What an inspiration for wanting to workout.

Sunday, February 28, 1994

It's a quarter after seven in the morning and my wife and I are on a charter bus just entering Interstate 5 southbound for Reno. My young friend Michael, who encouraged me to write this biography, suggested that I should take my readers along with me via my writing pad and pen, and that is exactly what I'll try to do.

It's a fairly nice morning and there is not much traffic on I-5. The bus is a fairly new one, and it's nice and warm and roomy. The seating on the bus is only about 75 percent full since they will pick up the remainder of the passengers along the way at designated points.

It's very relaxing to just sit here and look out the window. We are just pulling into Woodburn. We will pick up some more travellers and be on our way again in a minute or two. Most of these charter tours are very organized.

I picked up a Sunday Oregonian just before leaving the house, and I look forward to reading all the sports, especially about the conclusion of the Winter Olympics and our own Portland Trailblazers. These Sunday editions are getting bigger and heavier as time goes by. Could it be just my imagination?

The people on the bus seem to be a very cheerful group. There's quite a few young people in the group on this trip. I enjoy listening to other people talking, and it's rather surprising the things you can learn by talking to different people.

We are now approaching Salem where they will pick up the remainder of the group and the bus will be full. I understand from the hostess on this trip that our breakfast stop will be at a McDonalds in Eugene where we will stop for one hour. I think I'll rest my pen for now and catch up on all the news, especially the sports.

I'm back once again after having a light breakfast and reading the newspaper. It's now just after eleven o'clock and the sun is starting to peep through occasionally. It really has turned out to be a fine day for sightseeing while riding the bus.

We are just passing through the town of Oakridge, which is just a small community. Soon we will be going through the Willamette Pass, and I expect we will see some snow since it's about five thousand feet above sea level. It's very interesting just to look out and see all the different types of farms and houses. These are things you don't see if you are driving.

Now we have just gone through the pass and past the Willamette Ski Lodge and ski area. There is snow all around—on the hills, on the trees, and certainly there is about a foot of snow on the ground. But right now it is not snowing. The beautiful Odell Lake is off to the right of us and it looks so very clear. In just about two hours or better we will be in Klamath Falls and we will take a one-hour stop for lunch. I guess my wife is tired since she has been asleep this past hour or so.

I look at some of these isolated farm houses along the way and can't help wondering what they do to bring in their groceries and such since some of them are a long distance from a town or even a village. They probably purchase enough supplies for a long period of time.

It's now two o'clock and we are just leaving Klamath Falls after lunch, which for us consisted of dry toast, coffee, and a banana. The weather here is very mild for this time of the year, and since we are still in the state of Oregon it would seem that Oregon could have an early spring.

They played a few games of bingo along the way. My wife won eight dollars which should buy her a lot of nickels in Reno. The bus is pulling out now and we are on our way once again. There will be a couple more stops along the way of brief periods, and our estimated time of arrival in Reno is for seven-thirty. We will be staying at the Colonial Hotel Casino which has very nice rooms, but most of the hotels in Reno are very nice.

I guess I must have dozed off, because the next thing I know the bus stopping at the California Border Agricultural Inspection Center where an inspector boards the bus to enquire if anyone is bringing fruit of any sort into California. They are, I suppose, afraid of contamination.

It is at this point that we encounter snow again. There is about six inches on the ground, but again it isn't snowing or even raining. If anyone ever tells you it never snows in California, well here's my testimony that it certainly does. However this is the northern border of California, and southern California, such as Los Angeles or San Diego, is an entirely sunnier and warmer climate with little or no chance of snow.

The rest of the journey is fairly uneventful. Soon we see the well-lit lights of Reno, and we are in Reno by twenty minutes after seven. Good timing I would say.

After getting into our hotel room, changing, and taking a shower, we are ready to spend a leisurely evening on the town. We will go to one of the casino snack bars and have some coffee with a muffin. After that we watch a Rod Stewart-type of show which isn't too bad. It is now eleven o'clock, and being our first night after an all day travel, we make our way back to our hotel for a relatively, for Reno, early night. We must have been really tired since we were both asleep in no time, and stayed that way until six-thirty the next morning.

Monday, February 29, 1994

We leave the hotel at eight forty-five for the first of our casino stops. We spend three hours at each casino where we receive a cash bonus of four to six dollars and a coupon for drinks, free plays, etc. There are no basketball games or hockey games until early evening, so I just read the sports papers or watch television and my wife sometimes wanders off for fifteen minutes or so to play the nickel machines.

The first casino didn't produce a profit, but on the very next casino we visited my wife won ten quarters with her first spin of the machine. We came away from there about four dollars to the good. I surmise you guessed by now that we are not exactly high rollers.

At the last casino of the day my wife said she broke even, whatever that means. Meanwhile I have placed a five-dollar bet on the Chicago Bulls to win by nine points tonight. I'll be watching the game on television and it will probably carry on until about ten o'clock.

I'm now here at your hotel for a shower and a change, and I will go into one of the casino sports bar to watch my team trying to win for me. I will join you again a little later. Hope you are enjoying this Reno trip so far. It's almost a record temperature here in the high sixties with a chance of hitting over seventy degrees tomorrow. It is not too bad for this time of the year, and it is a beautiful sunny day with a clear blue sky.

I guess I'll be going to bed a little out of pocket tonight, my team did not even get close. However my wife, playing around with nickels and a few quarters, managed to finish up about seven dollars ahead on the day. It's really been a great day. We finished up the evening by watching a couple of great acts of Circus Circus, and in my book both acts, one a family of high flying acrobats and the other a brother and sister bicycle performance, were good enough for a Barnum and Bailey circus. Anyway, it's just after midnight and it's back to the hotel and to sleep.

Tuesday, March 1, 1994

It's a beautiful Reno morning. The sun is already up above a clear blue sky with not even a trace of cloud. It's predicted to be a warm and sunny day with temperatures into the low seventies.

My wife and I are here at the Cal-Neva Club having coffee after a nice long walk. It's nice to be out walking early in the morning when the air is so nice and fresh and really invigorating. Besides which walking is so very good for you.

Soon we will walk back to our hotel since we will be leaving at eight forty-five for Boomtown. This is a casino that resides in an isolated spot, and yet it seems to be a very busy club. They give us a cash bonus of about three dollars plus a free buffet for either breakfast or lunch, and it's generally very nice.

The club here in Cal-Neva is not very busy yet but soon it will be. It really is one of the most popular casinos in Reno, and they really cater to their patrons. It is time for our early morning coffee.

It's now about eight o'clock and time to take a casual walk back to the hotel to get ready for the start of our last day here of casino hopping.

We are here in Boomtown which lies in a type of valley surrounded by snow capped hills. It's really a very pretty scenic view. Although it's still early morning, there are lots of people here and they all seem to be having a good time.

Just as a matter of interest, Boomtown began as a small trucker's stop many years ago. It has gradually grown over the years. A new addition costing millions of dollars has been added on this past year and it is in the form of a huge playground, sort of like a miniature Disneyland. Boomtown is situated just seven miles west of Reno in the tiny town of Verdi, California. In this very small community the folks take a great deal of pride in the land and the Nevada way of life.

The lunch buffet, by the way, was excellent. We had plain lettuce and tomatoes with fresh baked buns, fresh fruit, and coffee. Naturally there was much more to be had, but I guess we just are not big on eating out. They really do a good job of taking care of visitors to this lovely facility.

It's now noon and we are aboard our bus again, bound for our next three-hour casino stop at the Nugget in Sparks, Reno. It's just about a twenty minute drive from here. The sun is really starting to feel much warmer now. Short sleeves are in order, so we can discard the coats we wore earlier early this morning. By the way, I forgot to mention that Boomtown has opened a large new complex on the outskirts of Las Vegas.

We are now in Sparks, Reno, at the famous John Ascugas Nugget. They have just built a brand new sports book facility. After looking around a while I placed a two dollar bet on a horse called Just a Lord, and it won very easily. My wife collected eight dollars and twenty cents on the ticket and that will be it for me. Now I'm a winner. I'll just sit back and relax while watching some sports on television. My wife will probably play some machines, or sometimes she enjoys just talking to people.

The Nugget is such a dazzling complex. It is very luxurious with expensive chandeliers all over the place. It is a bit too rich for my blood, but most people seem to be used to it and just take it in stride. We spent the remainder of our time here just looking around at all the remodeling they seem to have done.

Here we are back on our tour bus for the last casino stop of the trip to a club called Baldinis. It's located somewhere between Sparks and Reno. It sure didn't take more than a few minutes to get here. There's also a lot of construction going on here. They too are expanding the existing casino. I truly never realized gambling casinos were doing that much business. It just goes to show how much I know about the industry.

Baldinis is a relatively small club compared to all the others we have visited, but they are certainly as busy as any of the others. They have a unique way of rewarding poker players who get good hands by giving them six packs of Pepsi or beer which they can trade in for merchandise or take home if they wish. The more six packs the better the trade-in merchandise. They win cash too of course.

Oops! My wife just came back from playing, she has won 160 nickels and she is cashing them in. Smart girl. Why give it back when it's so hard to come by?

The time seems to have gone by quickly and we will be leaving here in less than an hour. Instead of going back to the hotel, the bus will stop in downtown Reno so people can stay in town for dinner. I think we will go back to our hotel for a shower, a change, and to rest up a little before our last evening on the town. I will stop writing for now and perhaps resume later.

It's just after eleven o'clock and we are now back in our hotels. We are getting our bags packed for our journey home tomorrow morning. We leave here at a quarter after seven and we will be up at five o'clock tomorrow morning.

We really had a very enjoyable evening. We even won a few dollars on a couple of basketball games. We came home about twenty-two dollars richer, so all in all I would say we made a few dollars this trip. Not much from a gambler's point of view, but it is more than enough for us since we had a good time to go along with it.

So now we will watch a little late television, and I'm sure we will be asleep around midnight or shortly thereafter. Good night to you all. Hope to be back again with you tomorrow morning.

Wednesday, March 2, 1992

Good Morning!

It's a great Wednesday morning, and my wife and I were up at five o'clock since we will be going back to Oregon, leaving the hotel at seven-thirty.

We took a brisk morning walk, had a nice drink of hot coffee, and went back to our hotel for a final check of our luggage and personal effects before we handed in our room keys and boarded the bus.

We finally were on our return journey. After just about half an hour we made a stop at a place called Bordertown which, as it's name implies, is the borderline between Nevada and California. They have a huge liquor store and restaurant along with some slot machines. Our stop will enable people on the bus to either recoup some losses or go even deeper in the hole.

I can hardly believe this, but my wife re-boarded the bus and told me she just won ten dollars on a quarter machine. All in all she has done well on this trip. I'd say we both came out of Reno in good shape. Listening to the people conversing on the bus it would seem to me that there were very few winners, but they all seem to be very happy.

It's now a quarter after eleven and we are stopped at a very small village called Likely. Our bus is parked in front of a small cafe appropriately named the Likely Cafe. This is in Modoc County, California. This tiny cafe is noted by most tourists for its wonderful homemade ice cream. We don't eat ice cream, but I enjoy watching people having a great time doing that very thing.

Now it's time to get back on the bus once more, and this time we will go straight through to Klamath Falls which will take just a little over two hours.

We made Klamath Falls right on time, pulling in at 1:30 p.m. The weather, though still fairly warm, was starting to cloud up. Rose and I had a couple of plain buns we had picked up in Boomtown, and along with a cup of coffee and some cherry tomatoes we had brought along, we did just fine for lunch.

It's two-thirty and once more we journey on, headed for the town of Oakridge. We have gone about thirty miles and the weather has changed. We seem to have left the warm sunny weather behind us, and we are now running into lots of rain. There's snow on the ground, but most of it has turned into slush.

Most of the people on the bus are fast asleep. We are due in Oakridge for a half hour coffee break around five-thirty.

I must confess that I've been reading my Dick Francis book at intervals between looking at the scenery and writing. I can't say I'm very enthused about his book. I've followed Dick Francis from the time he was a great Steeplechase champion jockey and later became a very good author. He wrote some great stories around the world of Thoroughbred horses, trainers, owners, and jockeys. But Dick, when you started to stray and began writing about espionage, Russian spies, and delving into politics, you lost me as I know you did so many other of your readers. In this latest book, Decider, you again introduce so many different characters I just can't keep up. Maybe you will revert back to your earlier format which was more interesting and easier for your readers. Not withstanding Dick Francis is a great athlete and writer. He is one of my favorite people.

After dropping off some people at Eugene, Albany, Salem, and Woodburn, we were finally on the way to Wilsonville where our son is waiting to pick us up. Our bus pulled into the Holiday Inn, Wilsonville at a quarter after eight, just a few minutes later than usual. Our son drove us home and we were in the house comfortably by eight-thirty.

That's just about how our trip to Reno went. I hope you found it a little interesting just following me around on the trip. Who knows, one day you may go on one of these bus tours to Reno and perhaps you'll enjoy it just as much as I do.

It takes a couple of days to get back on track once you've been out of town for a few days. Meanwhile, keeping up with current news. The Winter Olympics are now over and I'm sure most of you kept up with all that transpired. Affecting us on a local level, of course, is the outcome of the Nancy Kerrigan-Tonya Harding issue. I certainly don't wish to belabor the point anymore except to say, now that the skating is over, Kerrigan will go on to bigger and better things with the experience of being a millionaire to comfort her. As for Tonya Harding, her future both in skating and private life seems at this time to be a little uncertain to say the least. In the game of life, however, there will always be winners and losers. As always, in the final analysis, life does go on.

Once again it's back to our normal everyday routine. My wife will take care of things around the house and other things, in addition to getting together with her family. As for me, I'll start up with my regular workouts—swimming, jogging, and walking. Of course I will begin attending my synagogues again. No matter how good of a time I have when I go to Reno or the beach, it's always a comfortable feeling to be back home again. Perhaps you feel that way too.

It's now the day after getting back from Reno, and we'll just sort of ease back into things. Seems like we left all the warm sunshine back in Reno since it's raining here in Portland. However they are predicting better weather ahead.

It's another day and I had my first regular workout after getting back. It sure feels good just to be back in the gym once more. It's especially good when you know all your body parts are feeling good and you get through a good workout just as I did today. Sometimes most of us will take for granted a normal workout, but I learned my lesson not to do that many years ago.

Back when I was working out with George Pavlich, I was late getting away from work. When I finally made it to the gym I went running down to the basement and saw a bar with 380 pounds laying on the deck where someone was doing a dead lift. Without even bothering to change into sweats or warm up since I was feeling strong, I lifted the bar. I did get it up, but I could almost hear my back give out. It was normally an easy lift for me but certainly not this way.

I was through for the night and had to ease up on my workouts for over a month before I was back to normal. It was a lesson I've never forgotten, and with that in mind I'd like to offer you readers who are thinking of starting into body building or weight lifting some suggestions you may find helpful, especially those of you who are fairly new beginners.

1) First things first. Get an okay to start from your physician.
2) Select a reputable gym, one that gives beginners instructions.
3) Don't look for instant results. Be patient. Stay with the program.
4) Exercise should be combined with eating sensibly.
5) Avoid smoking. Drinking alcohol is not recommended, but if you must then moderation is the key word.
6) Make working out an everyday part of your life.
7) Finally, remember that not having time to exercise is a poor excuse. One can always find time for being sick.

Now if you are really serious, go for it and good luck.

Today is a beautiful mid-March morning, and they are predicting a warm and sunny seventy degrees. Since it is a weekend it's just the kind of day that back in Manchester my wife and I would pack a bag with some food and drink (lemonade) and set off to spend a full day at the Lancashire County Ground situated out in the country of the Old Trafford area. The crowd at a good cricket match will average between fifteen and twenty thousand, and there may be many more for a Test Match between England and another country. The biggest attraction by far is always England versus Australia, and just like baseball over here, once you learn some of the rules of cricket you'll love the game. As for me, I just can't wait to see a good cricket match once again.

One of the sports I dearly love is boxing. Naturally with my brother, Joey, being a pro and of championship calibre, and also being active in the ring myself up to the age of sixteen, I have sort of been brought up with a boxing background.

Whenever I think of boxing it always makes me think of a conversation I had many years ago with a very good friend of mine who was just one of the nicest chaps one could ever wish to meet. His name was Benny Harris. I say was because he passed away a number of years ago.

I can recall with clarity, even though it's been many years ago, an interesting conversation I had with Benny. I would like first of all to give my readers a little background on this wonderful person who was indeed a true philanthropist in every sense of the word. He, along with his brother, Ockie, and business partner, Dick Powell, the one-time television and movie actor/singer, owned the Tick-Tock Restaurant on Sandy Boulevard, the Three Star Restaurant on Barbur Boulevard, and other business ventures in California.

Benny Harris was always into sports, and especially boxing. He was instantly recognized by most people, and it was such a pleasure just talking with him. Which brings me back to our conversation.

It was a very hot September afternoon many years back, I believe it was in the 1950s or early 60s, and it was the very first day of the Jewish New Year. Benny and I, being members of the same synagogue, Kesser Israel, were sitting outside the front of the building where there used to be a wooden bench. Benny at that time was the vice president of the congregation.

He told me that he had been appointed by the American Amateur Athletic Boxing Commission to manage the American boxing team going to England to compete in an international boxing tournament. Since he had never been to England before he was concerned about the type of clothing to take along for that time of the year.

I proceeded to fill him in on what I thought would be best and we covered a few other minor things. I then asked him what kind of a boxing team he was taking and if they were a good team. He told me they would do very well over there, but he was extremely excited about a young heavyweight who I think he said was about seventeen years old at that time.

He told me this youth had the fastest hands he had ever seen on any boxer. He was very cocky and yet very respectable, and he was always addressing Benny as "Sir." Then Benny went on to tell me, "I predict that one day this kid may be the heavyweight champion of the word." How right he was. The name of the young boxer at that time was Cassius Clay, whom we all now love and respect as Mohammed Ali. Knowing the kind of person Mohammed Ali is, I'm almost sure he would still remember Benny Harris. I know I always will.

If you think that this book leans a little towards sports, then I'd say your observations are correct. As I've previously stated, I enjoy sports in any shape or form. Next to sports is my love for music. It doesn't need to be a certain type of music just as long as it's wholesome and clean. As you may have gathered from my memories of some years ago, I'm not exactly a young person. Nevertheless I like music of any kind, even the songs that the kids come up with today. I must admit, however, that some of the present-day music and words often leave a lot to be desired. Very often many songs that are a hit today are sometimes forgotten in a matter of weeks, never to be heard again. One of the exceptions to this was the music of the Beatles, whose songs, most of them anyway, remain as popular today as when they were first played or recorded. They were a talented group.

As much as I like present-day music, my overwhelming choice of good music belongs to the days of the big band era. I enjoy the music played in this country by the bands of Glen Miller, Guy Lombardo, Kay Kyser, Sammy Kaye, and Les Brown just to name a few. In England the well known big bands were Billy Cotton, Bert Ambrose, Stanley Black, Roy Fox, Jack Hylton, and many others. Singers in those days were much more crisp and clear in their delivery. Listening to Frank Sinatra, for example, one has no trouble picking up on the lyrics. Not so with some of today's present crop. There are the exceptions, I suppose, but they are very few. Although some of today's music is not all bad. The music of the big bands era, however, will continue to live on as it does today.

Getting back to the Dick Francis book I took with me on my trip to Reno. I finally gave up on it just over the halfway mark. I just couldn't get into it. Sorry, Dick, it just didn't do it for me.

Just a few days from now we will be observing the Jewish holiday of Passover. It lasts for eight days and celebrates the Exodus of the Jewish people from Egypt and their escape from the tyranny of King Pharaoh. I'm sure most of you have read about or have knowledge of Passover, but just to refresh your memory, some of the basics are as follows:

The holiday lasts a full eight days, during which we do not eat any grained food, especially bread. We do eat unleavened bread (Matzoh). The first two nights are very special, with special prayer telling the story of the Exodus (Haggadah) and special foods. Also singing and games take place. It is a very happy holiday.

What makes this Passover even better is that Easter comes right in the middle of Passover. This means I can enjoy both holidays along with my many non-Jewish friends and that makes me very happy. I always try to share some Passover treats with my friend, Father Pio Ridi. It is a time of great joy, and along with my family, I always look forward to it with great anticipation.

Returning once again to the subject of health care, I would like to share with you a conversation I had just a week ago with a young lady who works out at the Loprinzi Gym. She sometimes runs on the treadmill side by side with me. She began telling me of a problem she was having with stiffness in her hands and arms. She immigrated to this country from Colombia along with her husband and children. She visited her doctor and was told she possibly had a type of arthritis. He referred her to another doctor who scheduled a complete physical two and a half months away. Meanwhile she continues experiencing much discomfort. My question is, why does she have to wait so long just for a physical? Whenever I discuss national health care with people I am always told, "Yes that's all very well, but in England or Canada, doctor's offices are always backed up with patients and sometimes they have to wait weeks for an examination." Who's kidding who here? I can tell you for a fact that it's not like that at all.

When it first started in England before WWII, the program did get off to a very shaky beginning and it took better than a year or so before it finally settled down. I can tell you this for sure, in England if a person has a medical emergency, they are given complete priority and that is a fact. I also doubt that any patient would be kept waiting two and a half months for a routine physical examination. Incidentally, the case I'm talking about is not an isolated one either. Surely the medical authorities over here should be able to take steps to improve this type of situation. There simply has to be a better way. Hopefully it will come sooner rather than later.

I have some final information on certain points that I need to clear up so that I can be accurate in passing on my information to you. I have been in direct communication with the people of Eurotunnel regarding matters concerning the Channel Tunnel and they are as follows:

1) *Absolutely no driving through the tunnel.*

2) *The center tunnel is for service vehicles that help maintain the tunnel.*

3) *Any person may go through on the shuttle without a car. Fare is not yet finalized.*

4) *The outer tunnels being single track means that one shuttle will go to France from England while the other one will be returning from France.*

5) *There will be four trains every hour both ways.*

6) *The cost per car with driver will be $185.00 to $450.00 depending on when you go, peak period, the length of time you stay, etc. Car drivers can stay in their own car if they wish or get out and stretch their legs inside the train (shuttle).*

7) *There is a separate crate compartment for large trucks, RV's, etc., attached to the shuttle, but truck drivers must get out of their vehicles and wait in the lounge area of the train.*

I hope these final notes help clear up any questions you may have had on the Channel Tunnel.

I have to tell you about an unusual thing that happened to me today. I received a summons for jury duty in my mail. I say that it is unusual since I am not an American citizen, therefore, I am not a registered voter and I am not eligible for jury duty. How they picked my name is as much a mystery to the Judicial District of Hillsboro as it is to me. I did call in about it and I must return the jury summons along with a copy of my alien registration card as proof of my not being eligible to serve on a jury. To be quite truthful, however, I really would be a good juror since I know I can be fair and impartial in most all things. Still, it was nice just knowing that they selected me.

It's another day and I've spent the best part of the morning calling the different airlines trying to line up the most reasonable price with the best possible conditions and the least restrictions. Not an easy job by any means, but it's a happy one just the same.

I enjoy helping people whenever possible and if any of you are contemplating an overseas international flight in the future, then I would like to offer some advice. Have everything jotted down on paper such as flight dates and any questions you may have. Also, be prepared with your credit card if you are planning to use it, plus your name, address, and a phone number where you can be contacted in the place overseas where you will be staying. Above all make sure whether or not there are any restrictions on your tickets and if so make sure you fully understand them. I do hope this little bit of information will help when booking a major flight in the future.

Anyway, after calling the four major airlines that have flights to England, I was able to get tickets for my wife and myself at a very fair price. I also found that each of the airlines had different prices and restrictions with the highest fare being $135.00 more than we paid for our tickets with American Airlines flying direct from Portland to Manchester, England via Chicago, and returning by the same route.

We will leave Portland on June 27, 1994 and will return to Portland from Manchester on July 21, 1994. I'm very hopeful that I'll be able to finish this biography by the time we return. I hope you won't mind if I once again take you on a trip via my pen and pad.

It will be just great seeing my family and my wife's remaining sisters again. It should also be very interesting to see what changes, if any, have taken place.

I called Jonathan Nicholas today for some advice since he is a Welshman from the United Kingdom. After exchanging some pleasantries I asked for information on how I could get from Manchester to Treardurr Bay where I spent two years of my service in the army and made so many friends among the public civilians. The Welsh people are some of the most friendly people in all of Europe. Anyway, I needed to know how I could get into Treardurr Bay from my hometown of Manchester. Even a lot of Welsh natives are not familiar with the name of the town or its location, including Jonathan. He agreed to get the information for me, and in less than ten minutes he was back on the phone with all the correct information. I of course thanked him for his speedy response. That's typical of Jonathan Nicholas. He incidentally was born and raised in the tiny Welsh town of Merthyr Tydfill. I always read his column, which for the most part are always very local and very interesting. Jonathan is a real class act.

I'm here at home on a Saturday evening, sitting in front of the television in our living room, going around the channels, trying to find something to keep me interested for an hour or two. On any given Saturday evening an interesting show is not always easy to come up with, but I got lucky when I turned to the Oregon Public Broadcasting Service (OPBS). They were just about to begin a show called "Judy Garland (The Concert Years)" a full ninety-minute program. What a great show it turned out to be. She was the greatest female entertainer it has been my fortune to ever see or hear. Some singers perform like they are doing the audience a favor. Not Judy. she was exactly the opposite. It was as if she were saying, "You've paid big money to hear and see me perform, and I fully intend to give you your money's worth and more," and did she ever!

It was no surprise to me when Judy Garland played the London Palladium in the 1960s and the British public just went completely crackers over her. She became the darling of the British tabloids and press. She seldom failed to put out on any performance. She really died much too soon, but she left us with some wonderful memories on both film and on tape for which we will always be grateful. She was just a tremendous person and an amazingly talented performer. Her three children, Lisa, Lorna, and Joey, carry on the Judy Garland tradition of wholesome entertainment.

I can remember just one other American entertainer whom the British audiences acclaimed, and that was Danny Kaye. I was just a youth in my teens when he performed in my hometown of Manchester at the Palace Theater on Oxford Road. (Entertainment Row). Danny Kaye was one of the most energetic performers I've ever seen. I was lucky enough to get a couple of tickets for his show, and I took my longtime boyhood friend, Jack Gore, along with me. Naturally Danny was on stage almost all of the time and what a scintillating performance he put on. The audience just wouldn't let up, and what is normally a one and a half or two hour show went on for a little under three hours.

What I remember best about this show was something he did which was unique. I'd never seen it happen before. Midway through the show he came to the edge of the stage and sat down. That in itself was unusual but even more so was what took place after he did that. One of the young girl usherettes brought him a cup of tea from the snack bar and he began chatting it up with his audience while drinking his tea. For the British people it was a first, and they loved every minute of it.

It seemed to me that what Danny Kaye did that night set a precedent for other performers to follow, and today you'll find most of the television talk show hosts drinking and talking. Just two exceptional performers, Judy Garland and Danny Kaye.

I guess that by now you can tell I just love seeing good entertainers. As I mentioned earlier in the biography, I was practically raised in show business surroundings coupled with a football (soccer) and cricket background. If you were to add these activities to my religious practices, along with body building and weight training over the past forty to fifty years, then you have a pretty good idea of what my life is all about. There is one other very important ingredient of course, and that for me is my number one priority. I'm referring to my dear wife, Rose, and my good son, David.

While I'm on the subject of seeing something unique in show business, a la Danny Kaye and his tea-time break, I saw another one last night in a boxing show being televised from the Milwall F.C. Football Ground, London, England. There was a young promising middleweight from Durban, South Africa, named Gary Ballard. He fought barefoot (no shoes), and he won by a K.O. in four rounds very convincingly. Could this probably be a trend of boxing fashions in the future?

Speaking about the sport of boxing, it seems to me that the sport has regressed somewhat these past few years. It used to be many years ago that the winning of a world title really commanded a good deal of respect from the boxing public. Nowadays, however, almost every main event fight, and sometimes a co-feature fight, is for some odd world title. If this continues then the great sport of boxing could end up in the same category as pro-wrestling. Witness for instance some of the weird hairstyles and the boxing shoes, shorts, and robes contestants are stepping into the ring with nowadays.

I feel sure that what boxing fans all over the world would like is just one boxing organization instead of a W.B.C., A.B.F., I.B.F., W.B.A., and W.B.O. Let's also get back to the original format of just one world title holder in each weight division. Then we would indeed have a true world champion in every weight class. At the present time, we have so many world champions that it becomes very confusing. Every fight on television nowadays is for some title or another.

What boxing really needs is a singular world boxing commission headed by a reputable individual with a great knowledge of the sport and who is a good disciplinarian. I can only hope it will happen before too long since it's so obviously needed.

As I sit here and write I begin to wonder what methods the very professional authors use when writing a book. I truthfully have no idea. I often wonder if people who enjoy reading books ever give much thought to what goes into the process of writing a book, getting it published, printed, and ready for sale to the general public. It is not a very easy task I'm sure.

I can only assume that most writers use today's modern high-tech equipment of computers, word processors, copiers, etc. Since I don't profess to be a writer in the true sense of the word, I can only tell you how I am doing this.

In the first place I have serious doubts about this biography ever being published, but if it happens it will be something I can leave for my son to read whenever he wishes to know what made his dad tick, so to speak.

My writing methods are rather very simple but honest, and I try to get to the point as quickly as possible. I write from memory as I go along. If I think of something further along than the time frame in which I am writing, then I'll jot it down on a note pad and pick up on it at the proper time.

I'm writing this in longhand. I turn in a few completed pages at a time to my son's legal secretary, Jodi, who in her spare time (which is not plentiful) runs them through the computer and gets them back to me already typed.

I then read through them as soon as I can and proceed to make any corrections. Most errors are due mainly because of my handwriting which makes it awkward for her to decipher sometimes, but we eventually get it right. It's never easy to read someone else's writing.

Having done the corrections, I then make sure that all I have written is essentially correct as to times, dates, and facts as much as I possibly can, and then, and only then, will I put the pages together in numerical order. When I get a good batch of pages together, I take them to the gym (Loprinzi's) on my workout day and ask my young friend, Michael, to read through them. That way I can get fairly accurate feedback. Naturally, if I were to ever get a rather unfavorable reaction from Michael, I would no doubt discontinue this biography. So there you have it, dear readers, my rather primitive methods of writing this book. I hope that it will work for me.

We are well into the Jewish Passover holidays. It's also a beautiful, warm, and sunny day. There is not a cloud in the clear blue sky, and the weatherman has predicted a high of seventy-five degrees.

It's a wonderful time of celebration, commemorating the freedom from slavery of the Jewish people under the powerful Egyptian King Pharaoh. This holiday is generally well publicized each year by the media, and it is also well documented to some extent in the book and the movie Exodus.

This coming Sunday, April 3, 1994, is the eighth and last day of Passover and it is also Easter Sunday, which of course makes it an even happier time since our non-Jewish friends will be celebrating too. It's always a very happy occasion when our holidays come together this way. The children have a great time and that's just the way it should be. Just like Christmas and Hanukkah, it's a very happy time and people seem to come together more so at times like this.

I know it's a complete 360 degree turn around of subjects, going from happy holidays to violent and sometimes fatal crimes, but I picked up my morning Oregonian newspaper this morning and there must have been at least half a dozen shootings, a couple of them being fatal. One can read the morning paper on any given day and there will generally be reports of a few shootings. It seems to me that as great of a country as America is (it is able to successfully transplant human organs, send men to the moon, and have such powerful high technology), it has not done a very good job of gun control. It is a very serious problem that needs to be tackled head-on with the utmost expediency.

I can well remember as a young boy attending elementary grade school that our teachers would always tell us what a great country America was, what a great friend it had been to Great Britain, and that the American people were as good as the country in which they lived. I still believe these things to be true, but it really saddens me to see how completely out of control the weapons are in this country. We need to move faster on this issue so that thousands of lives can be saved each year. I hope that something can be done to improve the safety of our streets. It's often said that it's unsafe to walk the streets at night, but now we also hear how often people are shot at while driving or how an argument between drivers results in a shooting and in broad daylight. I'm sure some of you reading this may have wondered why I favor gun control and indeed almost a total ban on all types of guns. As I've related previously, for almost seven years of WWII guns were my constant companions. I can barely recall a single day when I didn't handle a rifle, pistol, or machine gun. However, to go much further than that, I've also had to face a sawed-off shotgun pointed directly at my mid-section. It happened one night in 1980.

This is the way it all came about. It was a February evening on a Friday, which was a night our shoe store remained open until eight o'clock. It was approximately five forty-five. The cinema less than twenty feet across the street from our store was having a first showing of a movie called The Fly, which was the attraction for about one hundred and fifty people lined up in the street waiting for the opening at six o'clock.

Anyway, at just about this time our store had emptied out of customers. My wife, our son, and I were working the store since we always made a point of not asking our employees to work the late evening hours. The three of us were just getting ready to take a break when in walks this young man who was fairly decent looking and probably in his early thirties.

He had told my wife he was looking for a pair of shoes for himself and if he liked what he saw he would bring his dad around later to buy them for him. It seemed to me, however, that he spent more time just looking around the store than he spent looking at the shoes. He just didn't look right to me, but after about fifteen minutes he left the store saying he may come back with his dad later. He certainly kept his promise but not in the normal way of doing things.

As I have said, I was not exactly comfortable with the way the young man had looked over our store. In any event, just after he left my wife decided to make some tea for all three of us. She had just started to do this when in walks this huge hulk of a man. He was well over six feet tall and built like a huge football defensive tackle weighing well over two hundred pounds. He was wearing a black and navy watch cap and wearing a top coat which almost touched the floor. He was carrying a small tartan overnight bag from which he pulled out this old and ugly looking sawed-off shotgun.

He was immediately joined by his two accomplices, one of them being the young man who had been looking the store over. They began by telling the three of us to lay face down on the floor, and then they started screaming and yelling for money. "We want your money! Where is the day's money?" Fortunately we had just previously deposited the day's take in the wall deposit of the near-by bank. We only had some loose change in our cash register which they took. I remember our son, David, telling them not to hurt his parents and they could have all the money on his person. He had almost thirty-one dollar bills which he kept for change. They took that of course.

All in all they were in the store about five or six minutes, and their total take was about thirty-six dollars. That was not much since it was considered to be an armed robbery. The final outcome of this was that all three of them were picked up and arrested the following day for armed robbery and assault on a pharmacist at his place of business just a few blocks further down from our store. They all pleaded guilty to that and other robberies and received sentences of two to five years.

Having been through the WWII years, always handling weapons, and having been faced with a gun pointed at me does, I believe, give me a good reason for my lobbying for gun control. I truly feel that with a total ban of all guns crime would take a considerable drop. We should at least give it a try.

I have tremendous respect for both the Oregon State Police and especially our own Portland Police. As a matter of fact, it is common knowledge among their peers that the Portland Police are listed pretty high in the nation for serving the public with courtesy and efficiency. We are indeed fortunate to have such good protection. However, when they come upon a situation involving a moving vehicle violation, a domestic quarrel, or a crime in progress, there's always that danger of shots being fired. I can only hope that the powers that be in this country can get beyond the talking stages and, as Nike athletic shoes suggests, "Just Do It!"

In any event, Portland must consider itself fortunate to have Charles Moose as its chief of police. He is so very well respected by his peers. The chief of school safety police is Captain Mac Lockett who is a veteran on the force, and he is still a fairly young man who is always in great physical shape. I have known Captain Lockett for over twenty years since we both work out regularly at Loprinzi's Gym.

As a matter of fact, the two of us have worked out together a few times. Two of Portland's finest are Chief of Police Charles Moose and Chief of Portland School Safety Police Captain Mac Lockett.

We are now well into April, and the signs of spring are so very obvious. It's a beautiful sunny day. It's a good feeling just walking outdoors and seeing all the flowers and trees blooming while deriving great benefits from the exercise.

I decided it was high time I called my dear friends Sam and Helen Loprinzi. We had quite a nice chat for more than an hour. They are both doing very well and enjoying retirement. They work out three times a week in a beautiful gym they built when they built their home in southeast Portland. They also swim twice a week.

I am well aware that I've mentioned Sam Loprinzi early on in this book, but I would like to give you a little extra personal and up-close information. He remains, as always, such a very humble person.

There were four Loprinzi brothers, Gus, Sam, Joe, and Phil. There were also three cousins, Gus, Tony, and Dave. The Loprinzi boys, along with George Pavlich, Harry Shleiffer (Broadway Furniture), and television exercise guru Jack La Lanne, were all serving together in the navy base at Treasure Island where, with permission from their commanding officer, they put together a gym for weight training. This took place during WWII in the years of 1943 through 1944.

I've been told by Harry Shleiffer (an ex-Mr. Pacific Coast) that it was really something for people in downtown Treasure Island to see six to eight of these well-developed body builders walking all abreast down the main street. It was some awesome sight I'm sure.

After serving his term in the navy, Sam came home to Portland and for a while and worked in an iron and welding factory along with a couple of his brother and George Pavlich. It wasn't too long, however, before Sam decided on opening a gym. With the help of his brothers he accomplished this, and in 1948 he opened up a gym on Grand Avenue. Many athletes often worked out there, including one of Portland's well-known boxers Denny Moyer. Remember him?

As the gym began to flourish and his clients began overflowing, Sam purchased some property on 41st and S.E. Division in 1963 and built Loprinzi's Gym where it still continues to operate under the people who purchased the gym from Sam. They are a very nice couple, Ed and Jane Kenworthy.

Just a few more words about Sam Loprinzi before I leave this topic. It is my opinion that Sam deserved much more recognition from the people of Portland and indeed the State of Oregon for being one of the pioneers in weight training and body building. Sam and I were workout partners for the last three years before his retirement. It was almost impossible for me to keep up with him since, just like Jack

La Lanne, he hardly every stops for a breather. His lovely wife, Helen, was always so very supportive and active in all he did, and she still is. Helen also works out regularly.

The Loprinzi Gym is noted for its famous slogan, "The Doorway to Health." Many celebrities have passed through these doors—so many wrestlers, football players, baseball players, boxers, bowlers, and often television and movie stars. My recollection brings to mind my meeting with television and movie star Richard Jaeckel. You may remember him as the gun toting, crew cut sergeant in the film The Dirty Dozen along with Lee Marvin. Richard was making a movie in Portland and police officer Johnny Howard brought him to Loprinzi's for a workout. Johnny was always the one chosen to give celebrities the Portland tour.

We got to know one another and after our workout, just before leaving, I asked Richard how old he was since he was in such excellent shape. He told me he was, at that time, forty-seven years old, but I've never forgotten his parting words when he said to me, "Remember, Barney, that age is just a number." What a nice unassuming person he is.

I still vividly remember organizing Sam's retirement party in 1981. I was greatly helped in my efforts by Police Chief of School Safety, Captain Mac Lockett; Tom Van Dorne, an all-around Portland athlete who is now caddying for Karen Noble on the ladies' pro-golf tour; Bob Mullins; and also a Portland chiropractor whose name escapes me at this time.

The event was held at the Monte Carlo restaurant in southeast Portland which is now owned by one of my workout buddies, Tony (Luigi) Salmonese, another very nice Italian whom I classify as a good friend. The party was attended by approximately two hundred fifty people; most of course were patrons of the Loprinzi Gym.

I had the honor of introducing Sam to the crowd, and I did it by reminding them that he was the runner up in Mr. America 1946 held in Detroit and winner of Most Muscular 5'6" to 5'8" at this same contest. It was indeed a great evening. It was one to be remembered and it was so well deserved.

Just one last word before leaving off. Sam's younger brother, Joe, who is so very well known throughout the weight training population in the U.S.A., is doing very well and feeling great. He still supervises weight training three days a week at the Multnomah Athletic club in Portland, Oregon. He is now into his fifty-sixth year with the MAC Club. How's that for longevity?

As for Sam's wife, Helen, I know she was teaching ladies' classes on Tuesday and Thursdays at the gym doing aerobic exercises without the music long before the word aerobics was associated with exercising.

Finally, it is my belief that the Loprinzi name will always be synonymous with exercising. In the fall of 1994, Loprinzi's in southeast Portland changed hands once again. Ed and Jane Kenworthy, owners for twelve years, sold the gym to Mr. Bob Hill.

Bob is a fairly young looking man in his early forties and he is in top physical condition being an avid bodybuilder. He has worked out at Loprinzi's for at least the past fifteen years or more, and he will be good for the ownership of the gym. I wish him well in this new venture, and I'm sure the gym will continue to flourish.

I paid a visit to my original weight training coach, George Pavlich. I'd heard he suffered a concussion due to a fall stumbling over some steps leading into his basement at home. Actually he wasn't looking too bad when I got to see him. He was in fact almost back to 100 percent of his normal self. It was good to see him since we don't see as much of each other as we used to.

George is the person I'll always remember for helping turn my life around. I'd only been in the U.S.A. for a very short time when I first met him and it was at a bad time in my life for me and my family. I had indeed given up quite a lot to come over here from England. I found myself working very hard at a very different job that I had to learn, and my earnings were barely enough to help us survive. I felt very despondent, not really knowing which way to turn.

George Pavlich not only instructed me well in weight lifting. Having learned of my situation he, along with his lovely wife, Eleanor, gave me much encouragement both with the weights and my personal life. He constantly told me that one day I would really do well in this country. We have remained very good friends ever since. I really enjoyed seeing him again, and he was looking very well.

I can recall winning my very first trophy in a weight lifting contest, and George was as happy and excited about it as I was. He's such a super person, as is his wife. From that time on things changed so much for the better. I began to feel more confident in myself, and I also developed a much different outlook on life. I also developed a much better liking for the U.S.A. which, over the years, has turned into a love for this country. My family and I feel very privileged being allowed to live in this great country.

I'd like to take just a few minutes if I may to write about an individual who has been a source of inspiration and encouragement to me and my family. It was in the year 1960 that my son, David, celebrated his Bar Mitzvah (he became thirteen years old) at the congregation Shaari Torah. It was very shortly after this that Rabbi Yonah Geller, accompanied by his wife, Lisl, moved from a synagogue in Texas to assume the leadership of the congregation Shaari Torah. He has filled this position with so much faith and enthusiasm, and he has been, and of course still is, a pillar of strength to all of the people in the community. As I've previously stated, I attend this synagogue on most weekday mornings, and Rabbi Geller often gives me the privilege of leading the prayers. He remains to the present day as active and as enthusiastic as ever. He can be found on so many occasions engaged in affairs of the community, helped by his wife, Lisl. What a great asset they have been and still continue to be to our people. May they continue to do so for many years to come.

Since I'm writing about individuals who have helped our community, one person I'd very much like to mention is Augusta (Gussie) Reinhardt. Gussie, as she is known by most everyone, is an octogenarian with the heart and spirit of a sixty year old. She is a tremendous activist, and she is always there when charity organizations call on her for assistance. She also happens to be the recording and correspondence secretary for my synagogue, Kesser Israel. She has held this position up to the present day for thirty-five years. In her younger days Gussie was a modern dancer and performed with the famous dancer Martha Graham.

Her dad, Oscar Kirshner, was one of the original founders of our eighty-two year old synagogue, and he was the president for forty of those years. Gussie is well known by so many people in the Portland area and in some other towns in our state. Hopefully she will continue to be as helpful to everyone as she has been and still is today.

I went to see my dermatologist, Dr. Albert Larner, whose office is in the Lloyd Center. I was first referred to Dr. Larner many years ago by our family doctor, David Duncan, when I developed a bad sunburn. He took good care of that with no problem since he is an excellent dermatologist. I was having a problem with irritation of the skin on both arms. It was nothing serious really, and he is once again taking care of this for me. It was good to see him again, and my wife and I actually enjoyed the appointment which turned out to be a nice friendly visit.

Dr. Larner has much in common with myself in that he goes through some hard workouts at the Multnomah Athletic Club, and he is also an avid marathon runner. He is from English parents who were raised in the small town of Blackheath in the county of Kent (England) whose ancestors were Welsh people. We consider him a good friend, and even though we have never met Mrs. Larner I'm sure she is every bit as nice of a person as Dr. Larner. Compared to most people we may not have too many friends, but the friends we do have are all, without exception, quality people. We are indeed fortunate to have Dr. Larner as a friend and doctor, and he is always there for us if and when we need him.

I don't know exactly why but my thoughts today have turned to back home and my dad whom I loved and respected so very dearly. He was a very quiet and shy sort of man who possessed a terrific inner strength.

We often used to walk together before I was conscripted to the army in WWII. During these long walks he would talk tome about life in general, things that he did when he was in his teens, and also some religious teaching. I've never forgotten the advice he constantly drummed into me, put into his own words, "Be the best possible person you can be in this life." I've really tried to live up to that, and I can only hope my efforts would meet with my dad's approval. Perhaps this sounds a little contrite, but even to this very day I miss both my mom and dad so much. Whenever I'm watching either boxing, football, baseball, or whatever and one of the athletes says, "Hi, mom" on camera, I think it's just the right thing to do. I'm sure that our struggles after getting over here from England were almost nothing compared to what my parents often told all the family they had to go through making it from Warsaw, Poland, to Manchester, England.

My mom never was able to master the English language, but my dad did get to speak English just a wee bit. In any case they were two very special people in my life, and they prepared me very well for the life ahead of me, for which I've always been grateful.

Did you ever get up in the morning feeling sort of drowsy, lacking your usual zip when you awake? You just feel like going back to sleep and letting everything else take second place. Do you know that feeling? Well it's rather unusual for me to get up in the morning feeling that way. Its was quite some time ago, I can assure you. Anyway I awoke this morning feeling exactly as I've described. There really is no reason for it, but experience has taught me that you just don't lie down and give in to this feeling. On the contrary, you just sort of dig in and fight it off. Since this mid-April Wednesday morning is my workout day at Loprinzi's, that is just what I did.

After a shave, a quick shower, and a change into sweats, I was headed on I-5 going north and keeping an eye on traffic at five o'clock in the morning. I got to the gym and parked the car at five-thirty. Then I went for a jog and a walk for the next half hour until the gym opens at six o'clock. I had a good brisk workout, showered, changed, and was back in my car headed south on I-5 by eight o'clock. I got home by eight-thirty and never felt better.

The point that I'm trying to get across to you is that if you ever wake up feeling just as I did this morning, try doing exactly as I did. More often than not it could eventually turn out to be one of your better days. Sometimes if you ever feel a slight cold coming on, try fighting it off. All I'm saying is try to work through it instead of taking medication and going to bed. You'd be surprised at what you can do for yourself if you really sort of fight it off. Sure, it may not always work out, but at least it's always worth giving yourself a chance. There is plenty of time to lay on your back or in bed when you are really sick. Throughout all my years of working out, some of my best and strongest workouts have happened when I was feeling a little down on myself.

Try to remember, if you are ever feeling a little on the down side, try working it out. You may be glad you did.

I received a couple of sporting newspapers sent to me by my nephew, Graeme, from England. Though they are almost 100 percent sports news, they do have some side-bars of regular news. One of these side-bars caught my eye. It was in effect something about the British Army upgrading physical fitness and skills in the use of weapons.

When I read this item it brought back memories of my thoughts of the British soldiers in the times of peace well before WWII. I can still recall as a young boy seeing soldiers either marching in parades or just walking through town individually or in pairs. They looked very clean and very neat. They walked very smartly, and in those times they were issued swagger canes which they tucked under their arms while marching or walking. I couldn't have been much more than ten year old at the time, and it made me feel very safe just knowing we had men like them to take care of us.

I have to be honest though and tell you that when I got called up when war was declared and I was sent from the recruiting depot in Preston to Scotland (Strandaer) to ship out to Ireland, my group, which was already a checked-out platoon (thirty-six men), was met by a Sergeant Giddens who informed us he was to be our escort and training sergeant throughout our recruit training.

He was a regular peace time soldier with ribbons on his chest for service in India and Palestine. He must have been at least forty or forty-five years old and he was terribly overweight, but he was a really nice person. His pants had a sharp crease, his boots shined like mirrors, and his sergeant's stripes were pure white.

However, his instruction left a lot to be desired, and his assistant corporal, who was younger and slimmer, was not much better.

You have to remember that these were soldiers who had served at least ten years or more and were supposedly very well trained in every phase of infantry. I got the same reaction from guys I'd gotten to know in other platoons in our company, and they said the same things about their instructors.

It seemed to me at that time that our peace-time army was top grade in the spit and polish department but sadly lacking in weapon skills, field tactics, and especially physical fitness.

I very much feared that at this time, in the first couple of months of 1940, Hitler was really going to invade England just as he did Poland, France, and those other countries. I just didn't believe that our peace time army was all we had been led to believe it was. I can only assume that Hitler was badly advised and that they looked at the English Channel as a deterrent. For whatever reasons he decided against invasion, and I'm so happy he did. Being Jewish I was terribly concerned for my mom and dad and my three sisters. As for my four brothers, I knew they would be able to handle whatever happened. We were raised in a fairly tough neighborhood.

Anyway, as raw recruits and with limited instruction from our peace-time instructors, we all somehow managed to gain proficiency by practicing, or you might say training, with any spare time that we had.

Eventually, after about six to eight months, some of us were selected to attend Cadre School to become instructors. After just a year we were now on our way to becoming full-fledged instructors.

I started off as a lance corporal assisting my sergeant, and by this method I became a full sergeant instructor after two years.

It was now 1942 and the British Army had completed an almost full 360 degree turn around. Most of the peace time NCO's and instructors had been given their discharge, and replacing them were young men such as myself from all different walks of life. We were now full-time army personnel for the duration, and we had no way of knowing how long that would be.

Gone was the emphasis on spit and polish; now it was fatigues, camouflage, and fitness. Every man we trained was fit; skilled in the use of all weapons; and adept at field tactics, aircraft recognition, and gas warfare. Using a soccer term, they were "Match Fit."

Our aircraft factories were now in full swing. We now had well-stocked ammunition depots. Our supply of weapons was being increased daily. We were now a solidified army, and above all we were ready.

Since Hitler was not prepared to invade our island via the English Channel, he carried out his large, or I should say massive, air attack later termed The Battle of Britain. Though he did tremendous damage to our towns, our casualties among the civilians were fairly low.

Our Spitfire and Hurricane planes dealt the German Luftwaffe severe losses from which they never really recovered.

So the point of all this is that I hope the British Army brass really will make sure that the peace time army can deal not only with peace but with war too. Let's just hope it never comes to that again. I'm always amazed, however, when I think about it how little time it took for us kids to come into the army from civil life and turn ourselves into such a great fighting army. We were well inspired by a hands-on sir Winston Churchill.

I happened to be listening to the radio sports station KFXX Portland, Oregon today, and ex-Trailblazer Michael Thompson was interviewing the number one tennis star, Pete Sampras. Pete was talking about his expectations of playing well at the French Open this summer. He talked about going from the French Open to London, England, two weeks later to play, as he pronounced it, at Winbleton. For all you tennis fans, announcers, and for you, Pete Sampras, it is pronounced and spoken Winbledon with a hard d. No more Wimleton please.

Since Soccer's World Cup will be upon us in next to no time, there is no other sports term I would like to clarify for you. Many Oregonians naturally and with good reason are a little put out at some versions of pronouncing this lovely state of Oregon that in which we live. They are gradually getting it right.

We now hear American announcers doing play by play on soccer, and by and large they do a reasonably fair calling of the game. It's when I hear them call a play whistled down by the referee as a call for off sides that I feel I must correct. The correct call is off side. Side is singular not plural. I can assure all you soccer fans out there that by the time the 1994 World Cup is all through, American announcers calling the game will be very good at it. You sports fans out there will learn to love the game and become familiar with the rules and terms of soccer. I sincerely hope you will enjoy the World Cup and get a chance to see the very young American team in action. I know I'll enjoy watching the game, and I'm very hopeful that the appropriate authorities will be able to keep control of the large and very vocal crowds. You'll also enjoy seeing some of the very colorful dress of the supporters of the various teams and the singing chants for their teams. As they say in entertainment circles, "The house will be rockin'."

We are now well into the month of April 1994, and today being a Wednesday, I returned from my early workout not too long ago.

As I was driving along the freeway at about five o'clock, I noticed traffic was very light and I was able to relax a little. I couldn't help thinking just how many of us take so many things for granted, even the cars we drive, the homes in which we live, and indeed even the wonders of freeways. Even more freeways are now undergoing construction throughout the U.S.A. I guess what I'm really trying to say is that we should never take anything for granted, and we should give thanks for all things in this world of ours. Personally speaking I've learned to do all that since my return from WWII. It would be nice if some of my readers could do the same thing.

I'm sitting in our living room at home with nothing real pressing on my agenda for the day since my son, David, does not require my services today. I know I've mentioned earlier how I met my wife, Rose, but I refrained from going too deep into our relationship since I've always been very low key on that; just as my wife is too. However, on thinking about it some more, I feel I would be remiss in not sharing what she is all about with you.

As I may have mentioned earlier, my wife had two brothers, four sisters, and her mom and dated; there was a total of nine. I had four brothers, three sisters, and my mom and dad; a family of ten in all.

While still a fairly young child, my wife, Rose, developed a serious illness which required constant attention and a lot of love. This was given to her by her mother and her older sister, May, who eventually moved to the U.S.A. and married an American boy from Portland, Oregon.

Rose had almost no schooling of any kind since she was about eighteen years old before she was fully restored to health. She truly is a remarkable person in that she had to learn most everything, even reading and writing, simply by watching and listening to people.

Anyway, I'm getting a little ahead of myself here. Since we are talking about taking things for granted, it gives me a reason to talk about my dear wife. Come on now, let's be honest. How often do you go to work, or play some ball game or another with your buddies and sort of get lost in your thoughts about the outcome of the game or the job you are working on and you don't give much thought to your wife? I know it's happened to me too. We all love our wives, it's true. They are always there for us no matter the situation—good or bad. That's why I learned a long time ago never to take things for granted, especially my wife.

Anyway, once Rose was back to normal health she resolved to give back some of the constant loving care given to her, especially by her mother who herself was now in failing health. My wife decided to stay home, take good care of her mother, take care of the upkeep of the house, and prepare meals for the large family which was working during the day. I've written earlier what eventually happened to her family. My wife has one brother left and he resides in Seattle. Three of her sisters are living here in Portland, Oregon. One sister remains in England.

I would just like to say that my wife has been, still is, and hopefully will be for years to come, the love of my life. It's just a great joy to share my life with her. I wouldn't change it for the world.

As for our son, David, he is a very good young man who respects and loves his parents, although he is not very demonstrative about it. I can understand that since I was just like that, and yet I loved my parents very much. They both understood me just as I do David.

It's the 15th day of April, 1994, and I'm here at home on a Friday morning relaxing a little after coming back from my early morning workout at the gym. There is not too much going on for me today other than my usual routine on the treadmill. As for my wife, she always seems to be doing something especially on Fridays which is a busy day for her. First she cleans the house and I help a little with that. Then she has to prepare the evening meal for the Sabbath which begins each Friday evening ending on Saturday evening. She also has to prepare a Sabbath Table with candles, wine, and bread (Challah) for the blessing of the Sabbath. This is always done by the woman in the house, although it's often done by the man of the house too. Preparing for the Sabbath is indeed a lot of work, but then again it's a labor of love.

This day is also a very important day for most American residents. It is the final day for paying one's taxes. Now I'm surely no efficiency expert on the subject, but my observations with regard to taxes are rather simple. If you as an employee or employer are making good money at what you do, then you should be prepared to pay your taxes. When all is said and done it is your taxes that help keep this great country in such good shape.

I can well remember back in England sitting at the desk in the office of our upholstering factory with all the annual tax papers in front of me stating the amounts due on them. Perhaps you may not understand my thoughts when I tell you in all honesty that I always felt a great sense of loyalty to my country whenever I'd write out these checks. Not only did we make a fair profit on the year, but in essence we were giving something back to our country. After all it is our taxes that help keep our country in a financially healthy position, be it in England or the U.S.A.

Whenever I read about someone being found guilty of tax evasion it sort of upsets me. Every once in a while you come across these cases in the daily newspapers. Perhaps in some instances there are exceptional circumstances, but for the most part my thoughts on the subject of taxes remains the same. If you make enough money in the year, then be ready and happy to pay your taxes for that year.

I've often heard the words "tax audit" mentioned in conversations and on television talk shows, but I never gave it too much thought until one day about two years before we retired from business when we received a notice in the mail advising us that the books of our racehorse venture were to be audited at a date to be agreed upon. I was really more surprised than I was worried since I never even thought that a small business such as ours would attract the attention of the IRS, and my only concern was that I had done a good job of bookkeeping.

Anyway, I called up our accountant, Bob McMillen, of the firm of Perrin, McMillen, and Miller and advised him about the audit. He told me just to go ahead and set up an appointment with their inspector, give them all the information they may require, and everything will be just fine.

We eventually met with the IRS inspector at our house, since our shoe store had no office in which to work and it would be very inconvenient. After the inspector had spent almost two hours of checking out books, invoices, receipts, etc., and also calling up our accountant, Bob McMillen, a couple of times, he was finally all finished.

Just before leaving he shook hands with both my wife and myself and his parting words to us, as much as I can remember them, were, "Mr. and Mrs. Wagner, I have to tell you that if all my audits were like yours, my job would be so much easier." He also asked me where I'd learned to keep books like I did. I could only tell him that I'd done books this way since being in business in England. He was a nice young man, and he was very good at what he did. He eventually left saying, "Good–bye and it's been a pleasure."

I felt so good with the way he had conducted himself during the audit. I seriously considered sending a letter to the IRS commending this young inspector for his kindness and courtesy to me and my wife while conducting his audit, but on second thought I didn't think it would be a proper thing to do.

You can perhaps imagine my surprise and my feeling of deep pride when about three weeks later we received a letter in the mail from the IRS. In essence the letter said that the IRS had completed an audit of our books, which showed everything to be in good order, and the IRS commended us on keeping such a good account of our business.

Sure it could have been a form letter, but it was our name and the name of our business that was printed on the letter. I felt so good about it that I drove to the southeast office of our accountant and gave him the letter which he read and then placed in our files. Bob McMillen was very pleased, but he said he knew we had no worries since, as he put it, we were in his words, "Good people." My wife and I have always been that way.

Incidentally, Bob McMillen has done the accounting for our shoe business and racehorse venture for many years, and at present he does the accounting for our son's law practice.

Bob is just a super guy. He is extremely efficient, very clean and neat in all his work, and above all, and this is something I always like in a person, he is very honest and very fair. You just couldn't ask for a nicer person. My wife and I often go to visit Bob at his office. My wife likes to know that Bob is taking good care of himself and taking time off to rest up.

As you may have surmised from all of this, paying taxes in this country is something I've always enjoyed doing. You just have to believe me on this because that's exactly how I feel about it. I hope many of you felt as I did when making your IRS returns today.

We are now into the last days of April 1994. Soon it will be time for my thoughts to be directed towards our trip back to England. As I begin to do this, I can't help but wonder how many people travelling overseas to a strangely different country ever give much thought to the value of the American dollar in the country to which they are going.

I do know that the last time I went back, the exchange rate at that time was 1.86 dollars to one pound sterling. In other words it was almost half the value of the English pound (100P). Today's rate of exchange on the foreign currency market is 1.47 dollar to one pound sterling, which in essence means that this time we will be able to buy much more with our dollars. I can't help thinking how nice it would be if the dollar was an even exchange for the pound by the time we left our journey. That's just not going to happen, at least not in the immediate future.

Before I leave you on the subject of foreign currency, I think it would be a good idea for anyone visiting another country to check the rate of currency exchange before leaving. Just one final piece of advice if I may, and this comes with a lot of experience. Whatever else you may do, please be good to yourself and only cash in your dollars and traveler's checks at a well established bank. You will be assured of a fair rate of exchange.

I had a couple of phone calls from England today. One was from my sister, Sonia, in London telling me she and her husband will be coming over to the U.S.A. since her husband's relatives living in New York have a wedding in mid-August. They will be arriving in Portland August fourth. They will be staying with us for about ten days and then going on to New York. We will be back from England well before they get here, so I hope it will all work out well. She also told me they were having cold weather, and it even snowed a few days ago.

The other call was from my nephew, Graeme, informing us that the weather in Manchester was awful. They had three inches of snow last week. He was concerned that we might run into bad weather again on our visit, but I reassured him that it just wasn't going to happen again. He already obtained tickets for my wife and I for the first day's play in the Cricket Test Match: England v. New Zealand, and we are looking forward to that. We had a nice exchange of conversation. All in all it turned out to be a very satisfying day.

I was reading the newspaper today and there were a few different stories supporting weight training, walking and jogging, and also swimming using alternate strokes. They have all become very popular not only with the younger folks but with the middle-aged also and indeed lots of seniors too. I just think it's great for everyone involved. Seems to me that it's not too many years ago that people would come up to me and say to me, "What are you trying to prove?" My stock answer, of course, was that I was not trying to prove anything but I was just trying to take care of my body. This would often draw some sarcastic remarks, but I would never let it bother me. Now just look at the fitness revolution today. As I once said to my friend Sam Loprinzi, "We were just a generation before our time."

Having said all this, I can tell you that I'm always more than ready to help any new beginner in the gym. It's just great to watch the steady progress they make, and some of them do make great strides in just a few months. So once again, I would urge any of you who are not into any of these forms of physical fitness to give it a try. You may enjoy it more than you know, and remember, you are really never too old to start. Just to remind you once more, be sure to get your physician's approval. If you think I am putting too much emphasis on these exercise programs then you are right. It's only because I believe it would be very beneficial to you throughout your life.

It's May 1994, and looking back on things that happened in the month just past, a couple of items stand out. The most important one of course being the sad passing of President Richard M. Nixon at the age of eighty-one. Rather than pinpointing Watergate, I would prefer to remember him for opening up communication between China and the U.S.A. He was a very tenacious individual. He was very intelligent and very diligent, and he had the will to win always foremost in his mind. May he always rest in peace.

One other item I'd like to mention is the defeat of Evander Holyfield by Michael Moorer for the Heavyweight Championship of the World. It has been well noted by the media with reference to the decision to fight. As for me, the wonder is how Holyfield survived twelve tough rounds of boxing with a heart condition. I must say, however, that in all my years of being a devout boxing fan, I consider Evander Holyfield to be one of the classiest boxers I've ever seen both inside and outside the ring. I hope that, along, with his family, he will enjoy a long and health retirement. He has certainly earned it.

This promises to be a very interesting month, but one of the most important days is of course Mother's Day on May sixth. Every mother in this life has to shoulder a great burden of responsibility, and most of them do this without a word of complaint. They more than deserve to be honored on this special day.

Also this month will be the official opening of the Channel Tunnel linking England to France on May sixth. I have already given you the details of this previously.

One more important event for many people in the sport of horse racing is the Kentucky Derby. This is a race for the top three-year-olds in the country, and it is run at Churchill Downs in the state of Kentucky. This race always reminds me of just how close we came to having our colt, D.B.'s Dream, entered to run in 1976. However, as you have already learned, it just wasn't meant to be, and I've always blamed my lack of experience, being a comparative newcomer to the thoroughbred industry at the time. Sill, I enjoy watching the race on television and trying to choose a winner.

It's hard to believe that the first round of soccer matches of the 1994 World Cup are just around the corner. It's really too bad that neither Oregon nor Washington are to host any of the games. Anyone wanting to see a game live will have to travel to Stanford, California. Excitement for the World Cup is slowly beginning to build up. Once the fans start pouring in from the visiting countries like Germany, Brazil, Italy, Colombia, Spain, etc., then the tension will increase. If American sports fans think they have seen fanatical spectators, wait until you see these soccer fans. They are really into it and they are indeed a part of all the glamour of this 1994 World Cup. It promises to be a great time for everyone. American sports fans will see soccer being played on a highly competitive level. Some of the skills of these brilliant soccer players will leave you breathless. I predict that these games will leave an indelible impression with American sports fans and that the game of soccer in this country will begin to flourish.

We are almost into the middle of May 1994. Now it is official. The House of Representatives has finally passed a ban on all types of assault weapons. I hope this legislation will result in fewer deaths by shooting in this country. However, this is just a beginning, and it's my belief that the majority of people would support a ban of all types of firearms. Since the Constitution gives people the "right to bear arms," this could be a long way off, but perhaps one day it may come about.

Now if we could just make some headway on health care reform, what a year this could turn out to be for President Clinton and his very efficient first lady, Hillary Clinton.

I firmly believe this presidency will do so much good during its current term of office. They certainly are not lacking in doing their very best to move quickly on important issues. Vice President Gore and his wife play a very big part in all of this, and both are very close to the president and his wife.

However, all of the above is just my opinion, and since I'm not much into politics, I'm sure some people's opinions will be much different from mine. That's what make life so interesting.

It's a Sunday afternoon and I'm at home watching television. My hometown team, Manchester United, is playing Oldham Athletic in an F.A. Cup Semifinal with the winner going on to meet Chelsea F.C. in the Cup Final 1994 at Wembley Stadium. The game is being played at Maine Road which is the ground of Manchester City F.C. which was eliminated early. Manchester United is leading 2-0 at the moment.

I played on this very ground when I was a schoolboy of eleven years old playing for my school, Waterloo Road, in a Manchester Schoolboy Cup Final. We lost 3-1 against a school called St. James before a crowd of over three thousand.

The Maine Road ground recalls for me another time in my life when I was about eight years old. My favorite team, Manchester City, was to play Stoke City, the team led by the great Stanley Matthews, in the sixth round of the F.A. Cup. A friend of mine, Harry Fink, and I decided to walk the eight miles from our home having no money for tram fare or to pay to get into the ground. We knew we could get in for free when they opened the gates with fifteen minutes left to play. They do this at all football (soccer) games in England.

We set off with knapsacks on our backs containing sandwiches and cold drinks. It was, as I recall, about eight o'clock on a Saturday morning. The kick-off time for the game was two forty-five, standard time for all games. We arrived outside the ground around two o'clock. It had been a warm day and we stopped many times along the way. We just sat outside once the game started and we could tell by the roars of the crowd of 84,000 people that our team was not doing too well. As a matter of fact, when they opened the gates at three quarter time we were down 1-0 to Stoke City.

I can still remember the crowd at the very top of the terrace steps rolling my friend and I from the very top until we got down to the ground level where the police allowed all of us kids to sit on the grass just outside the playing pitch. It was a great sight for us, and we were seeing the great Stanley Matthews playing at the top of his game. Stoke scored once more and Manchester City was out of the cup, losing 2-0. It was a day in our lives that Harry Fink and I would always remember.

We did in fact see while we were both serving in the army, and we did get to talk about this memorable day in our young lives. As I write I'm also watching the game on television, and Manchester United has defeated Oldham 4-1. It's on to Wembley where they will meet Chelsea F.C. in the Cup Final.

It's difficult for me to believe that I've witnessed this game being played on the same pitch on which I played many, many years ago as a schoolboy. It sure does bring back sweet memories.

I'll be looking forward to watching the F.A. Cup Final, which is to be on pay-per-view television next weekend.

I've always parked our car in a Lloyd Center parking lot for years without any problems whatsoever. The law of averages caught up with us a couple of days ago. When we got back to our new 1994 Honda after shopping, we looked around the car and it had been badly damaged in the right front fender. It would be naive to think that this was done without the person responsible being aware. They obviously just didn't care enough to leave a note of any kind. Where oh where did the age of honesty, chivalry, and integrity go? Seems to me that people nowadays do not live up to the principles of years ago. I'm sure there are still many decent people who would have done the right thing in a case such as this. There is simply no defense against this happening to your car when you are parked in any parking lot. Do you suppose that we can ever get back to the values we once cherished, taking an evening stroll, not having to lock up your home like a fortress, driving in your car without fear of being involved in an altercation possibly even where shots are fired? When did it all start, and will we ever get back our pre-WWII principles? Your guess is as good as mine, but certainly there remains much that is so very good in this country. I hope the ban on assault weapons is a step in the right direction. We must continue to go forward.

I decided to drive up to the coast along with my wife. Today being a Monday I expected heavy traffic. We left the house at nine o'clock in the morning, having returned from my workout at the gym shortly after eight o'clock. I quickly changed into casual clothes, had a cup of tea and a slice of toast, and we were on our way. Traffic was surprisingly light.

We arrived at Seaside, a very popular northwest coastal town, at about ten-thirty. It was a beautiful sunny morning. There was not a cloud in the clear blue sky with the temperature in the sixties. The very first thing we did was take a nice brisk walk along the promenade and circle the main center of town. It took us well over an hour. There were not too many people out at that time of the morning, and the air felt so very refreshing although there was still a slight chill in the air. We both enjoyed the exercise.

We sat down on one of the benches on the ocean front and just watched the calmness of the great vast body of water. Everything seemed so very peaceful. I couldn't help thinking that whoever said "The best thing's in life are free" really wasn't kidding.

As I gazed out to the horizon I began to wonder how many people knew the difference between the ocean and the sea or a channel. I'm trying to recall my geography teacher's explanation when I was in elementary school. As I recall it was along these lines.

A sea is a smaller division of the ocean, but it is partially enclosed by land, such as the Irish Sea, the North Sea, and the Red Sea.

An ocean is the whole body of saltwater that covers nearly three-fourths of the surface of the globe. For example, the Atlantic, the Pacific, and the Indian, when totaled, would make up the three-fourths.

A channel is the deeper part of a navigable river or harbor.

I hope I didn't confuse you on these definitions, but it's sometimes self-satisfying just to know these things. I just hope my recollection of my school day teaching was in order.

Needless to say it turned out to be a beautiful, sunny, warm day and we really had a great time. We got back home in the late afternoon. I got on to my one hour on the treadmill, and my wife followed with her half hour.

We then had a very nice but light evening meal, and we were able to relax afterwards. All in all it was the end of a very nice day. Some days are almost perfect. It's the days when things don't go too well that sometimes exact a toll on you. I personally try to always keep a positive attitude. It's so much better for you that way.

I read in this morning's newspaper about an attorney who was out walking his dog in a suburban area of Portland and was held up at gunpoint by three masked men. They made him return to his home and they proceeded to take his cash, jewelry, video equipment, and other goods. It's true that it was late evening, and most of you will say he shouldn't have been out walking alone at that time of night (ten o'clock). What a sad reflection on our society. I've said it before, I'll say it now, and I probably will say it again: As long as there are guns out there it just isn't going to get any better. There simply has to be some strong action taken to improve this situation. The problem is a very serious one, and something needs to be done quickly. President Clinton has made a start, and now let's hope he goes much further.

I just got back home after a good workout with my friend, Deputy Chief of City School Police Mac Lockett. We had not seen each other for a few weeks since he works out at odd times due to his always being available for anything that crops up. I had mentioned about my writing, and just on a whim I decided to check up on his rank since I've been referring to him as Captain Lockett for quite some time. He told me he is now Deputy Chief, and so from now on I will call him by his proper rank. It was good to get together again.

I had rather a bad let down this past week. Our local cable company had been advertising during the past two weeks for a pay-per-view English Cup Final between Manchester United and Chelsea United. The cup final is played at Wembley Stadium in London, generally before a crowd in excess of one hundred thousand. It's equivalent if you will to the Super Bowl of American football, except the English soccer teams are even more outrageous in dress and vocal output.

Anyway, I had ordered the event a couple of days before the game was to be shown at eleven o'clock on a Wednesday morning. I made sure that all my appointments had been cleared or put off, and I settled in at that time hoping to see a very exciting cup final.

Eleven o'clock arrived and the channel comes on with a couple of Italian teams playing a game termed as the European Cup Final. I called into the cable company and I was told that since there were not enough requests for the English Cup Final, they decided not to show it and my order was canceled. Within a couple of minutes the screen went blank.

The following day I called the cable company asking for some clearer explanation since I felt badly, missing out on an event I'd waited so long to see. This time I was told that had I left the channel on for another ten minutes or so then the English Cup Final would have come on. I told them that the very least they could have done was tell me what was going on. I was then told the marketing manager would call me back to explain, but it's been a couple of days and I have not received a call. I will still try to find out what happened even though it is now much too late for that. Anyway, with luck one of the family back home taped the game and I'll get to see it on television when I go to England at the end of June.

Incidentally, one of my nephews called to tell me that Manchester United beat Chelsea and looked great doing it. Now they have completed a great year winning both the League Championship and Cup Final. They really are a super soccer team, and as of now I'd say they are probably the very best team in the world.

A couple of days passed without any call from the cable company, but I finally was able to contact the lady in charge of programming pay-per-view. She was able to explain to me that I had been misinformed and the only game shown by them was the Italian Cup Final. She told me they have to take whatever a company called Uni-Vision sends them. Incidentally, she also told me the game didn't sell very well. She finally apologized for the inconvenience and disappointment. She really was very nice about it.

Television coverage for the World Cup in June will be very well taken care of, and I'm very hopeful that it will draw the record viewers which this sport badly needs. I'm keeping my fingers crossed.

When we had our shoe store during the 1960s, a young man, probably in his late teens, would hang around our store and talk to my wife and some of the customers. He was a wonderful person. He was very polite and ready to help anyone who needed it. He was, to be truthful, a little slower than the average person on most things, but he was able to converse on a normal level. We just knew him as Eddie, and one of the girls who worked for us, Betty Griffiths, was Eddie's mother's friend. My wife always took care of Eddie in many ways, such as giving him shoes, a little cash, or at times some food. He was just a great kid who didn't have any kind of a bad side to him.

We were deeply shocked to read the headlines of our Oregonian this morning with a picture of Eddie. He was shot and killed it seems by three individuals early yesterday morning. The three men then sped off in their car. Why anyone would want to do this to him is beyond me. His full name was Eddie Morgan, Jr., and he was forty-nine years old. What a tragedy for his mother and family. There are so many out there who are still convinced that guns don't kill people. Try telling that to Eddie's mother. He stayed around the area of our store until we sold the business in 1981. The very last time we saw Eddie and spoke to him was just about a year ago. It's so sad to see him go this way. May his dear soul rest in peace.

We are now into the month of June, 1994. Time has a way of creeping up on me, and it won't be long now before June 27th, which is the day we leave on our trip back to England and our family.

However, before that time comes around there are so many things to do. Those of you who have been overseas may be familiar with the kind of preparation it takes, but for the many of you who have not and perhaps may do so in the future, here are just a few of the many important things that need to be taken care of.

Of course the most important thing is to make sure that your passport is in order and up-to-date. In the case of a non-citizen of the United States, as in my case, you also need your alien registration card complete with a fairly recent picture of yourself. Next, be sure to check your flight tickets for times and dates. You will also be required to pick up a boarding pass at the airport within thirty days of your flight. At that time it would be a good idea to get enough luggage tags from your airline. Also be sure to check on how much luggage can be taken on the plane and stored and how much can be carry-on luggage. You will also need to know the dimensions of such luggage since there are usually restrictions.

Then there is the packing of luggage, which should be done in such a way as to make it easier for customs inspection. Then there are traveller's checks to be purchased plus a small amount of the currency of the country to which you are going. It's also a good idea to keep all your documents handy in one special holder since customs is sometimes like a zoo and it's so very easy to misplace things when there is confusion.

Having listed all the main things in preparing for an overseas flight it's not uncommon to miss out on some things, but hopefully that can be taken care of with the help of good family members you are visiting. If you've done your homework in preparation for such a flight, then you can just sit back once you are on the plane and really enjoy your journey.

Just one more thing. Should you be thinking of calling back to the U.S.A. from the country to which you are travelling, then you need to contact a good telephone company who handles international communications. They will set you up with the appropriate instructions for making your calls. In my case I've chosen AT&T. They did such a great job for me on my last visit; however, the choice is up to you.

It's June 6, 1994, and today the whole world will observe the fiftieth anniversary of the landing of the allied forces on the beaches of Normandy in France under the command of General Eisenhower, U.S.A. It's both a sad day and yet in so many ways a happy one. It's sad because of the many who lost their lives for the cause of freedom and, on the other side of the coin, it is a happy time because democracy in the world in which we live today strives to make it even better.

Today's event has been very well covered by all the media, so rather than dwell on it I would just like to make one final comment. All those whose lives were touched by the young servicemen who perished that eventful day on the beaches of Normandy and are living today should feel proud knowing that, because of their sacrifice, we are able to live in a free world. They must never be forgotten. I lost some very close friends with whom I served in the Normandy landings, but I also lost many more while they were prisoners of war in Japan and were forced on those awful death marches thirty miles a day with no food. Some of the stories of WWII are really awesome. It's not very easy to forget things like that, but as they say, life must go on, and that is what we must do.

It is only a matter of a few days now before we will be taking off on our trip to England. There is so much that needs to be done before such a trip. Those of you who have been overseas know exactly what I mean. Like so many other men I am very fortunate in having a good wife who takes care of such things, and I take care of packing our luggage and ensuring that we go through the airport and customs with some form of organization.

Today we went out to the airport to pick up our boarding passes for the flight. Yesterday I went for a physical exam which in my opinion one should do before departing for another country. I believe in this even though you may be feeling okay. Anyway, I feel so much better now that it is done, and I look forward to enjoying our visit to our country of birth.

It will be interesting to see what changes, if any, have taken place since our last visit. In any event it will be good to be back with my family once again.

While I'm over there I will do my best to bring you up-to-date with what is going on in England, and I will be finishing this biography when I've completed my visit.

Remember my telling you a little while back about my experience trying to watch my hometown soccer team, Manchester United, play Chelsea for the English Cup Final at Wembley via pay-per-view? Well it seems that our local cable company must have really listened to my complaint. They decided to show a taped replay of the game this afternoon as a regular part of programming.

It was good just to sit back and watch my team pitted against this very tough London team. Chelsea played very well in the first half to 0-0 score. The second half, however, was an entirely different story. Two quick penalties resulted in a 2-0 lead for United. It was all downhill for Chelsea from that point on, and the final result was MANCHESTER UNITED–4, CHELSEA–0.

Along with 80,000 spectators who were there, I enjoyed the game very much. Just a few years ago this Cup Final Game was always a sellout with 110,000 spectators but for safety purposes some of the terraces (standing room) have been utilized for seating and this cuts down on the maximum crowd allowed. In any event it turned out to be a very enjoyable afternoon for me. I just couldn't help thinking that between these two teams there were about eight players who would be playing for their respective countries in the World Cup, but naturally none of these players are English since England was eliminated from the World Cup in qualifying play.

Talking about the World Cup of Soccer 1994, there will be an avalanche of television exposure beginning this weekend, and it will continue for about four weeks. I hope that most of you will get to see a few games and watch how some of these soccer fans get behind their teams. Who knows, maybe you'll even catch soccer fever. I know I'll be watching as many games as I can before we take off on our trip to England. It will really be interesting to see how our young and inexperienced American team performs. I truly believe they will give a good account of themselves. Anyway, here is hoping they do well.

You may not perhaps see it as such but the 1994 World Cup is going to be one of the biggest major sports events in America sports.

No doubt most of you must have been rather shocked by the news concerning the death of O.J. Simpson's ex-wife and a male friend. Most of the circumstantial evidence so far makes O.J. a person of interest to the Los Angeles Police. It seems as if so many tragic things have happened in the world of sports recently. We will all have to wait and see how this one unfolds. O.J. Simpson has been arrested, taken into custody, and been indicted on two counts of murder. It would be a good idea for all of us to just sort of back off and allow the law to do its job.

Now, for a complete change of subject, yesterday morning I received a telephone call from my youngest sister, Sonia, with some smashing news. Every year on her birthday the Queen of England, Elizabeth, puts out a Birthday Honors List in which she names individuals who have served their cities and town above and beyond the call of duty. My young brother, Sonny Warner, was so named, and he was awarded a M.B.E. (Member of the British Empire.) The M.B.E. is a great honor, and only Her Majesty Queen Elizabeth can present this award. The investiture is to be held on December 6, 1994, at Buckingham Palace. On December 11, 1994, there is to be a huge banquet for all the families and some friend to celebrate this memorable occasion.

I remember telling my brother, Sonny, that someday his country would recognize him for not only his talent, but for his tireless efforts to raise money for the elderly, the infirm, and handicapped children. He puts on charity shows whenever and wherever possible. He celebrated his thirty-fifth year in show business just last year. Not only is his name Sonny, but he has one of the sunniest dispositions. No matter how bad things can sometimes get, he always manages to see a positive side to everything.

When we visited England a few years back I can still remember being in my brother's home, and his wife, Pamela, decided to run a video of Sonny's shows for us. They were performing at a huge nursing home complex for the elderly. There was this one lady who was well into her eighties seated a couple of rows from the front of the stage. The audience was having a good time singing and laughing and really enjoying the show, except for this one old lady who was practically in tears. The nursing supervisor got word to my brother while he was on stage. She said the old lady suffered from severe depression, and as much as they tried they couldn't seem to help her much.

My young brother stopped the show after one of the acts had finished. He then took one of his favorite instruments, his ukulele, and went up to this lady and started to sing one of the "oldies" backed up by a chorus from his show. The tune was "Let Me Call You Sweetheart" and do you know that after just a minute or so he had this old lady singing along and there was a nice smile on her face. His award is indeed well deserved, and knowing my brother he couldn't be happier. The twenty-plus members of the cast of "The Sonny Warner Show" are very happy to be a part of it.

When I was just a young boy and my brother, Joey, was a flyweight boxing contender, I was mostly always known as "Kid Joe's brother." When I go back this time, which is just a few days from now, I'm almost sure I'll be known as "Sonny Warner's brother" and that's fine with me. I'm so very proud of Sonny and I love him dearly. I hope he will continue to entertain for many more years.

I hope that many of you have been able to watch some of the World Cup soccer games. Some of these players' skills are simply amazing. The various countries' supporters were as colorful as I had predicted, and yet they were surprisingly well in control of themselves. I hope they will continue to maintain control throughout the tournament. The crowds at these games are wall to wall, with little if any vacant spots. The American team opened up with a tie and a win, and if they can win against Romania tomorrow to advance into the next round of play, I truly believe it will have a tremendous effect on the American people's view on the game of soccer. I've heard so many good things about the games from individuals who have seen live soccer on television for the first time. I feel convinced that there will be a professional soccer league in the U.S.A. not too far down the road. I firmly believe that after this World Cup is concluded, steps will be taken to start things moving in this direction. If you are thinking that I love the game of soccer (football), you are 100 percent right.

It is now the evening before taking off on our long journey back to our original home. We are all packed and ready to go, and yet like most of you going on a trip, we keep wondering what we may have forgotten. Although we can always get what we missed from one of our families, there is nothing like having your own, if you know what I mean.

That's it then. We are all set and I will join up with you once again when we begin our journey.

Today is the fist day of July, 1994, and I must confess it's been almost a full week since I've added to this biography. I felt sure that my next writing would have been on an American Airlines plane speeding to Chicago. I'd definitely made up my mind that I'd finish my writing in England and that would be the end of it. However, this biography is a little different than most others since there will be no real happy ending, except for the truth of the events that led up the cancellation of our trip on the very last day before leaving for England.

We were to leave, as you may recall, on Monday, June 27, 1994. We did all our packing, beginning on the previous Friday. We were all done except for some small items by Saturday. It was on the Saturday evening while sitting and watching television that my wife, Rose, mentioned to me that her right eye felt sort of funny. When I looked at her eye and saw no signs of irritation, I placed my hand over her left eye, and she could see hardly anything while using her right eye only. I put some eye drops in her eye, and by then it was after eleven o'clock. I thought for sure that a good night's sleep would take care of this problem. However, I was wrong about that. The problem still persisted on Sunday morning, and although she didn't feel sick or anything like that, the fact remained that she still had little or no vision in her right eye. This being a Sunday and the day before we were due to take off, it presented a very serious problem to say the least.

We tried contacting our family physician, Dr. Clifton, but he was out of town. His stand-by suggested a visit to the emergency room at the hospital, but he didn't hold out too much hope of an eye doctor being available.

It was at this time that I decided to try and contact our ex-doctor and dear friend, Dr. David Duncan. I was both surprised and relieved to hear him answer my call since it was early Sunday morning. After explaining Rose's situation, Dr. Duncan said to first of all forget England for now. He then told me to hang up the phone and he would get back to me as quickly as possible.

He called back within a matter of minutes and explained that he had been able to contact a friend of his who happened to be his own eye physician and surgeon. His name was Dr. Marvin Green and he would be on the phone to us very soon.

After another few minutes Dr. Green called, and after hearing our problems he said to drive to northwest Portland where he had an office clinic building. We immediately took off, and in less than half an hour we were at the clinic where Dr. Green was waiting for us.

He immediately went to work examining my wife's right eye, and he seemed to be very thorough in doing so. After about forty minutes he told us that he suspected there was a blockage of the main artery to the eye. He also told us that a friend of his, Dr. Peters, who is a retinal specialist, happened to be somewhere in the building and he would get him on his beeper to come over and take a look at the eye.

Dr. Peters showed up in a matter of minutes. After taking a good look at the eye, he confirmed Dr. Green's diagnosis and said there should be absolutely no travel for now. Dr. Green gave us a medical note for the airline to help us get a refund on our tickets, which we did. Here is a complete version of the medical note:

Marvin F. Green, M.D.

June 26, 1994   Re: Mrs. Rose Wagner

TO WHOM IT MAY CONCERN:

This morning Ms. Rose Wagner and her husband, Barney, were to fly to ENGLAND. It was necessary that I examine Mrs. Wagner yesterday when she had a rather sudden loss of vision in her right eye. Her vision was limited to a small island in the temporal periphery where she could count fingers at a distance of 2 feet. The cause of this was found to be an occlusion of the central retinal artery. I was fortunate in being able to have a retinal specialist examine her at the same time. It was our conclusion that she not go on her trip until she has a general medical examination with special reference to the status of her heart and carotid arteries in case she needs to prevent the vascular problems.

I trust you will take this into favorable consideration for them in the cancellation of their trip.

Sincerely,

MARVIN F. GREEN, M.D.

I just can't begin to tell you how wonderful those two physicians were to my wife and I. They really gave up the best part of their normal day off for us, and to say we appreciated it is putting it very mildly. We will never forget them and also our very dear friend Dr. David Duncan for what they did.

Anyway, to follow upon their recommendation, we got an early morning appointment with our family doctor on the following Monday. Dr. Clifton looked over Rose and wasted little time in referring us to my friend and cardiologist Dr. John Wilson. We saw him that same afternoon, and after a complete cardiac examination he ordered a series of tests to enable him to pinpoint the cause of the damage to the eye and where it had originated.

Consequently, my wife has been undergoing tests each day of the week, and on Friday morning she completed the last of the tests. At about six o'clock last night (Friday), the cardiologist, Dr. John Wilson, called and gave us an initial report of the sum of all those tests. Expecting the worst, we were very relieved when he explained all of the results. It really wasn't that bad except of course for Rose having a 75 percent loss of vision in her right eye. She also has a little thickening of a minor artery in her neck and a slight murmur in her heart, but her heart action is very good.

Overall, in view of what had happened, we were very happy to hear these results. After the July Fourth holiday she has to see Dr. Wilson for a final check-up and medication treatment. We Hope, things in our home can get back to normal by next week.

Lots of calls have been coming in from England, and so it really was no surprise when my brother-in-law, Alec, called on this Sunday of the July Fourth weekend at about two o'clock in the afternoon, which would be ten o'clock in the evening in London. I thought he was calling to ask how my wife was doing and about the trip to our Tualatin home on August 4th. I was completely wrong.

It seems that my sister, Sonia (Alec's wife), had blacked out while driving; she finished up by hitting a tree and she was hospitalized with severe bruises. Alec said nothing was broken, but they were keeping her in the hospital to give her an evaluation to find out what caused the black out. Talk about things happening in bunches. Hard though it may be, we have to learn to accept these things as a part of life. Alec told me that they have had to postpone their trip to the U.S.A. We had been looking forward to their visit.

I watched the World Cup soccer game between the U.S.A. and Brazil. This game was played before a crowd of almost ninety thousand people. Surely they were not all Brazilians. The U.S.A. Soccer Federation would have to be very pleased by the crowds that have been attracted to the game. Unfortunately, the game itself ended with a 1-0 victory for Brazil. The American team should not feel sorry for themselves. They played fairly well against a world-class team. Their attacking game was just not visible on this day. This American team has done so much to help promote the game in this country, and I predict that soccer, on a professional level, is not too far off.

We just got back from the doctor's office, and the doctor talked about the overall picture of all the tests my wife underwent. Her general condition, he said, was not nearly as bad as it could have been. Naturally, the heart murmur she has had for over sixty years still remains but with very little further damage. What does exist, of course, is a large percentage of lost vision in her right eye caused by, he said, a blockage in a major artery leading to her eye.

He has prescribed medication to thin the blood to try and keep the arteries clear, and he will monitor her progress weekly by blood tests until he is completely satisfied that the treatment is doing the job.

All in all my wife feels much happier now, but of course we missed out on our trip. Perhaps we will try again before this year is out. The main thing of course is my wife's health, and in that respect she seems to be doing so much better after hearing Dr. Wilson's report.

It has been almost three weeks since we canceled our trip. My wife, except for some loss of vision in her right eye, is feeling fine. To say that these past three weeks have been a rough time for us is putting it mildly. I know that relatives and friends wish my wife well and encourage her to keep a positive attitude. It is great advice, but it is certainly very difficult to follow.

Anyway, the good news is that the results of all the tests my wife took are now in, and except for some loss of vision in the right eye, her overall general health is good. She can carry on doing all the things she did before, and she can also travel whenever she feels like it.

Initially, when I began this biography, I had my mind set on finishing it during my visit to the United Kingdom. I also planned on giving you insight into how things were over there and bringing you completely up to date with everything going on in Great Britain.

Since I've obviously been unable to do this and I am still bent on giving you as much information as possible, I have been in direct contact with people who have a hands-on approach to many things that are going on in the United Kingdom.

The main news I have to tell you is that England, and the United Kingdom overall, is doing fairly well, especially England where there is not a great deal of unemployment nowadays. However, the cost of living is rather high, and the average worker, even living well within his means, finds it almost impossible to save any money. This has not changed any since I was last over there three years ago.

I must point out, however, that if a worker is ever laid off (declared redundant), then he or she has about three or four government agencies that assist them. This seems to work well for everyone. I will tell you, however, that the average American worker seems to live better and has much more than his British counterpart.

As I promised previously, I will now bring you up to date on some of the main issues that prevail in Great Britain.

THE LAW

The basics of English law:

1. A person is innocent until proven guilty.

2. An accused person is entitled to a jury of twelve peers

English judges have become more accessible to the average person.

A *Queen's Counsellor (Q.C.)* is appointed by the court to prosecute for the realm. A Q.C. is appointed by the court for the defense. A Q.C. is generally a title given to senior barristers. A *Barrister* is usually a specialist advocate with direct contact with the client. A *Solicitor* is a qualified legal advisor. A *Magistrate* is usually a lay person of impeccable background who will preside over minor criminal cases. *Plea bargaining* is when the court may sometimes allow a defendant to agree to plead guilty to a lesser crime. A *life term*, depending on the circumstances, can be twenty, twenty-five, or thirty years or more. The count for a guilty verdict by a jury can be 10–2 or 12–0 at the discretion of the judge. Trial procedure is very similar to the American closing statements, and the Q.C. for the realm (prosecutor) is allowed the last word.

Gun Control: Military and police are allowed to carry firearms when it may become necessary. However, a license to carry firearms in certain extreme situations may be given to a civilian. The bottom line is that any or all persons bearing firearms must be licensed. The law is very strict on gun control.

Health Care Reform: Both employers and employees pay a portion towards the Employees National Health Insurance. This is an excellent system and everyone is fully covered, except for drugs obtained by prescription from the doctor. Since there has been such a vast increase these last few years for the cost of drugs, all patients are now required to pay the standard fee of four pounds and seventy-five pence (approximately $7.20) per prescription item regardless of the true cost of the drugs. Any British citizen who is a permanent resident in the U.S.A. is entitled to free medical privileges in Britain, providing they hold British medical cards and national insurance numbers, and more so if they are drawing a British Retirement Pension.

Freedom of Speech: In the past decade, the law on this has somewhat mellowed. Freedom of speech is allowed in Britain, and anyone can say more or less what they like in public always providing it is not libel or slander. This also applies to Royalty.

Movies, Television, and Stage: All movies are rated similar to those in the U.S.A. Extraordinarily violent movies are normally cut. Any kind of bad language may not be shown, seen, or heard before 9:00 p.m. This applies only to the above mediums. To control all of this the Internal Censorship and Complaints Procedure exists.

Since I first began to write this biography about a year ago, there have been some changes made in the criminal justice system in England. The very major ones have been introduced these past few days. I would be remiss if I did not bring them to your attention.

The main changes are:

1. Previously, anyone being questioned by the police had the right to remain silent. Anyone refusing to answer questions can still do so, but judges and juries may take a defendant's silence into account when determining guilt or innocence.

2. The new law now allows police to stop and search vehicles and pedestrians.

3. The police now have the legal right to disburse squatters, trespassers, and illegal campers. There will be no more free assembly.

4. The new law now increases the government's censorship of all videos, especially targeting the ones with violence and sex.

I might point out that most of the above rights previously allowed but now being curtailed were adopted by the British government centuries ago and were in fact the basis for the U.S.A.'s Bill of Rights.

Anyway, it will be very interesting to see what effect these changes have. My own opinion is that they can only improve things. Time, of course, may or may not prove otherwise.

So there you have it, just a little extra information about Great Britain. In case anyone has any doubts about how England is doing, I can tell you that England is very much alive and well under the guidance of Prime Minister John Majors and his cabinet of ministers. Just as the song title says, "There'll Always Be an England."

Now it is time for me to bring my lifelong odyssey to a close. In order for me to do this properly I would like to stray a little from the conventional way of finishing a biography. As I told you when I first began what I thought might be a wasted effort, I am not a good writer and I certainly do not claim to be an author, I am just someone who has a life story to tell.

Anyway, I'm sure you are aware by now that throughout my experience I have never mentioned any of the businesses at which I worked by name. This was deliberate on my part so that I could quickly go over all these time periods in my life in chronological order.

Maturity started at age fourteen when I finished my crammed education at elementary school to work at the printing shop. The Bremner Printing Company was owned by a Mr. Richard Simmons. He was a fairly middle-aged man and he was very good to me. He was the person who thought I had enough talent to work for a daily newspaper. Remember?

Then I took the job learning upholstering at a small shop with just one other worker. The owner was Mr. Morris Epstein, who was a very close friend of my oldest brother, Louis. This small shop later developed into a huge factory in the space of just five years, and it became the Anchor Upholstery Company with a crew of four upholsteresses and twenty-five upholsterers. In addition it made its own upholstery wood frames using ten male frame makes. They also had three lady office workers. In all of this I was considered the lead upholsterer. I held this position until the very beginning of 1940. I was then conscripted by H.M. Government in which I served until the early part of 1947.

After my release from the army I went into partnership with my brother, Louis, trading as Wagner Bros. Upholstery. Then came my departure for the U.S.A. at the end of May 1953.

My sponsor for emigrating was a Mr. Abe Gilbert. He was the sole president of the business for which I was led to believe I would be working. The name of the business was Gilbert Bros. Furniture Co. As previously related, I never got the job, and just a couple of years later this huge, well-established Oregon business folded. To this day I can't begin to guess what caused their downfall, but it was almost a tragedy.

I then latched on to the job with the surplus store, at that time trading as Saltman Surplus. David Saltman, the ex-air force waist gunner, owned and operated the business assisted by his elderly mother, Molly Saltman, who was such a very nice, sweet lady. She is now deceased. Then David took a partner, Morris Miller, and became a wholesale and retail surplus store trading as S & M Sales.

I would just like to say before going any further that although I could never get too far ahead financially at this job, I was always treated fairly and with great respect by both partners. Morris (Morrie) Miller was an avid outdoorsman and he loved fishing and hunting. He was very well known through the Northwest. I am sad to say he died at a rather early age. As for the other partner, David (Dave) Saltman, I've always felt obligated to him for giving me my very first job in the U.S.A., which was something my wife's relatives failed to do. I must also say that one does not need a written contract from Dave Saltman. His word and a handshake is every bit as good.

From there it was on to join my wife at the shoe store in 1964. Our registered business name was B&R Family Shoe Store. We remained in business until our retirement in 1981. Our store was located in Northeast Portland, and we remained in the same location all those years. Because of our association with Nike athletic shoes we became well-known on the pacific coast.

As for me personally, my given birth name is Barney Wagner, my wife is Rosie, and my son is David Barry Wagner. David, incidentally, is a fairly well known criminal attorney.

Now it's time for me to wrap up this story of my many journeys through life. I sincerely hope it has been an interesting journey for you also. Some of you may perhaps have learned from a few of my experiences. In any event I'd like to thank you all for taking the time to read my autobiography.

Speaking for myself, what I have learned about this great country, the U.S.A., is that it offers wonderful opportunities for everyone. You can be whatever you want if you just want to be. Sure there are many other good countries, but they just don't offer the same opportunities.

Finally, I must confess, it seems as if it has been a long journey with lots of peaks and valleys along the way. It's almost as if I've led six different phases of life. It is my sincere hope that you've enjoyed reading about it just as much as I've enjoyed sharing it with you.

May all of your lives be as full as our lives ("We Three") have been. I'd very much like to end my autobiography if I may, by wishing you all a very happy and healthy year.

So until our paths may cross once again...
Peace and shalom.

Monday, May 8, 1995

This is the day that marks the Fiftieth anniversary of the end of WWII, and I'm here in the living room of my home in the U.S.A. watching the television ceremonies taking place outside of Buckingham Palace in London, England. There are thousands of people gathered for this spectacular outdoor ceremony, and I'm sure many of them are surviving veterans of WWII.

Queen Elizabeth I (The Queen Mum) appeared on the outdoor balcony of the Palace flanked on either side by her two daughters, the reigning Queen Elizabeth II and her younger sister the lovely Princess Margaret. Dame Vera Lynn who serenaded the troops during WWII is now doing the same for this vast throng of people with one of the songs from that time, "The White Cliffs of Dover." Dame Lynn has lost very little of her beautiful voice. Even the Royal Family joined in the singing. There is also a fly-over of planes from the WWII era. Some Spitfires and Hurricane fighter planes are among them.

It is a time for joy but also a time for sorrow when we think of the many young service men and women killed during WWII. If there was anything missing from this glorious occasion, I can only bring to mind two famous people—one of course being the reigning monarch of that time, King George VI, and the other that wonderful leader of our nation during those many dark years, Sir Winston Churchill.

Upon reflection I honestly believe that it was a war worth fighting, especially since the German plan, fronted by its Nazi leader Adolph Hitler, was to exterminate all the Jews of the world. Being Jewish, serving my country was much more than just my duty. It was something I wanted to do to help protect our very existence and in some small way help repay the great loss to all our relatives burned in those ovens in the Nazi death camps.

May 7, 1945 was the day that the leaders of Nazi Germany signed the declaration of unconditional surrender. However what I fail to understand today is how countries we defeated such as Germany and Japan both enjoy a much better economy than the victorious British people? I just don't know the answer to this. What I do know for sure is that funds from the original Marshall Plan estimated at approximately three billion dollars are being used to re-build Eastern Germany.

Many Jews left Germany after the war. Those that survived were indeed fortunate. The largest Jewish population in western Europe at this present time is in France where there are about seven hundred thousand Jews, mainly Moroccans, Algerians, and North Africans in addition, of course, to the French and Germans who relocated. Consequently France enjoys many kosher butcher shops, bakeries, delicatessens, and of course numerous synagogues.

Saturday, July, 2, 1995

Upon reviewing my book I had the distinct feeling that it still was not complete and that I had not delivered to you, my readers, what I had initially promised. That of course being the trip I had planned in July 1994 to visit my family in England. As you were well aware, we had to cancel due to the problem with my wife's vision in her right eye.

It has been almost a year now since that happened and now my wife has been fully cleared medically to travel. Once again we are booked for an American Airlines flight from Portland to Manchester, England leaving on July 11, 1995. We plan on staying one month. I hope to take you along with me via my pen and note pad. I will try to keep you right up to date on the different things I observe during my trip. We actually leave Portland just a few days from now.

Tuesday, July 11, 1995

We arrived at the Portland International Airport just after eight o'clock in the morning and was pleasantly surprised that it was not as busy as it usually is. Our son David had driven us to the airport which is about twenty-five miles from our home.

It didn't take very long for us to have our passports and other documents checked and after that it seemed that in no time at all that they had commenced loading passengers onto the plane. The plane was filled to capacity, but we had good seats.

There were no problems on take-off and its now almost twelve noon. It doesn't seem as though we have been airborne about two hours. Lunch is now being served and they are serving a choice of shrimp salad or chicken. I'm afraid my wife and I have to pass on this food, which is no doubt very good, but it is not in accordance with our Jewish dietary laws. We are, however, served a plain breakfast bun and a cup of coffee, and that's good enough to sustain us until we get to Chicago.

It is a beautiful day for traveling. We are high above the clouds over Billings, Montana. There is very little to see and nothing much happening around us so I will try to get some sleep (hopefully) and rejoin you in Chicago.

We are here in Chicago after a nice smooth flight. Our plane to Manchester does not take off for another two and a half hours, leaving at 6:10 P.M. eastern time, and we are scheduled to arrive in the U.K. at 7:45 $_{A.M.}$ Wednesday, Greenwich time.

Passing the time away in Chicago's airport is a mixture of people watching, coffee drinking, and reading. We will be on our way to England before too long. I will catch up with you later.

Its now seven o'clock and our plane is just about to take off. Its almost an hour late, but that's not bad at all for O'Hare Airport. In any event, we should be getting into Ringway Airport (Manchester) somewhere round eight-thirty tomorrow morning (Wednesday, July 12). Its approximately an eight hour flight.

They plan on showing the CNN news and a movie after serving dinner and they will serve a light morning breakfast, so the flight should not be boring. This large, wide bodied Boeing 367 is a very nice and comfortable plane.

Its rather difficult to whip up something of interest to tell you when one is sort of bogged down in one place for such a long flight. However its exciting just thinking of meeting my brother and sisters and all the very many nieces and nephews.

The pilot has just announced the present weather conditions in Manchester. Wouldn't you know it, it is raining! And the temperature is in the sixties! I guess its about what I expected, but I will not let that stop me from enjoying a very pleasant visit.

Its getting just a little choppy now so perhaps this is as good a time as any to leave you for a while. I will get back perhaps when we have settled down in Manchester.

Wednesday, July 12, 1995

It's early in the morning, six o'clock, and I'm up and ready for another day. As for yesterday, "what a day this has been" from a song I recall, seems to be an appropriate summation. We got into Ringway Airport at eight-thirty in the morning, but by the time we had recovered our luggage and gone through customs it was after ten o'clock. My brother, Sonny, and our nephew, Graeme, were waiting for us at the customs exit.

We drove back to my brother's, that's where we were to be staying, and Sonny's wife, Pam, was waiting to greet us along with Graeme's lovely wife, Janat, and her three children. The girls, Zoey and Jenna, and the boy, Lee, are ages eleven, eight, and three respectively. It was just great to see them all again even though it had only been about three years since we had been back.

The weather was sunny and warm and that was a pleasant surprise. After a brief rest and a very light snack we then went to see my sister Sadie and her husband, Leslie. After about an hour or more we were on our way once again, this time to visit my long time friend and best man at my wedding, Louis Gore, and his dear wife, Olga. We had a great time reminiscing about our younger days and the time passed quickly. We then went to visit Louis' sister-in-law, Freda Gore, who had two weeks ago lost her husband, Freddie Gore the brother of Louis.

We talked for some time, and by the time we left Freda was feeling much better than when we first came to see her. The day had been hectic and it was now after seven-thirty. After going back to the flat for tea we spent the rest of the evening at my nephew's home along with Janat and the children.

We were back at the flat by ten-thirty where we sat and talked until eleven-thirty. By that time we were both almost too tired to sleep. "What a day this has been" really says it all.

Thursday, July 13, 1995

We went to downtown Manchester along with my niece Janat in her white Range Rover. She proceeded on her way to the office after dropping us off in the City Center. Even though it was early morning there was a lot of hustle with people milling around all over the place. The stores had just begun to open for business and guests were already forming queues to be served—a truly British custom.

One big difference that became very apparent to me was that there was no sales personnel to help people find the things they were looking to purchase. The only employees around were the cashiers who sat constantly on their seats by the cash register ready to check you out. How they all manage to find what they want is beyond me but somehow or another they do manage. However they all have return or exchange of goods centers and the lines forming in these departments are very long. That's what happens, I suppose, when there is no sales person to help the customers.

We stopped at a McDonald's for a cup of coffee. If you believe that McDonald's is the same in England as in the U.S.A., forget it. There is just no comparison whatever. The one we went to on the main street of the town Market Street had their service counter on the ground level but seating was in the basement two flights of stairs down so one had to carry his or her food on a tray down the stairs. It was sort of a weird arrangement but somehow or another they all manage to cope with the situation.

It started to rain in the early afternoon so we took a bus back to the flat. The rain stopped quickly.

We went to a musical comedy show in the evening which included four of our nieces and one nephew. They really are a bunch of talented kids and the show was great. We had a good time, and after getting back to the flat we had a nice cup of tea. After about an hour of chatting with Sonny and Pam it was off to bed—the end of a nearly perfect day.

Friday, July 14, 1995

Today we had arranged to go to Treardur Bay on the Isle of Anglesey via Holyhead in Wales. After making arrangements to go by train, since there is no bus service to Treardur Bay, we had the radio on and found out that a railroad strike began at midnight and would last for at least twenty-four hours during which period all trains were canceled. It seems like they do a lot of this over here. Anyway we were told that we could book a return ticket via rail and they would try to get us there by special charter bus and hopefully return in a couple of days by train.

Right now we are waiting for our nephew Graeme to pick us up for a ride to Picadilly railway station. It's quite a large railway station with plenty of amenities such as restaurants, coffee houses, news stands, and rest rooms.

The bus was loading passengers and we were rolling along to Holyhead in good time. In no time at all we were in Wales.

All signs, towns, and any other information along the way are both in English and Welsh. When I was in the service I picked up quite a bit of the Welsh language. Now I was beginning to remember some of it.

The bus took almost three hours to arrive, but it was a very pleasant and informative trip. Treardur Bay, which I now know is spelled with only one "r" and is in North Wales not South, is a fifteen minute bus ride from Holyhead. It was almost two o'clock in the afternoon, and it seemed as if the bus had dropped us off in the middle of nowhere. Remembering my days in the service here, I was not surprised.

As soon as I got my bearings we were able to relax a little. It was an overcast day with some periods of sunshine. We sat on the beach for a while and then I began the tedious job of searching for any Treardur Bay native whom I could remember or who would remember me.

I finally got lucky and was able to locate an eighty-four year old man by the name of John Jones. I had not known him as well as I knew most of the people in Treardur, but he seemed to know all about me. However, at times, his mind wandered. He really was a warm and kindly man. During a lengthy conversation Mr. Jones told me that a person I had been very friendly with, Nat Chamber, had just passed away but his wife was still living in Holyhead. We finally said good-bye.

We decided to get back to Holyhead. Once there we looked for a bed and breakfast place. Because of the railway strike nearly all of the rooms were booked, but just when we had almost given up, we got lucky and found a nice clean home within five minutes from the British Railway line and the town center. The streets in the middle of Holyhead are so narrow that its difficult for people to pass one another. Its from this town of Holyhead that ferries cross regularly to Ireland via the Irish Sea. This is a journey which takes about three hours.

After a light snack we walked around the town and, since we had been on the go most of the time, we decided to go back to our bed and breakfast residence and call it a day. We were in bed and fast asleep by nine o'clock. We were more tired that we knew.

Saturday, July 15, 1995

I didn't awake until seven forty-five in the morning. It was a beautiful sunny morning with a nice breeze. The breakfast being served was cereal, eggs, sausages, and bacon with tea, coffee, and toast. We did very nicely with the tea and toast. It was delicious.

After searching around the center of Holyhead, I finally located the widow of Nat Chamber. She was living with her thirty-six year old daughter and her family. They showed me pictures of him. He was easily recognizable, but since he had re-married after the death of his first wife, I didn't know his widow. However, the daughter, who looked the image of her dad, was by his first wife whom I had known very well.

I left them each a few American dollars as souvenirs of our visit and after about a one hour chat we were on our way again. The price of everything in the British Isles is so high that I really don't see how the average working person makes it. After talking to many of them, they all seemed to convey the same message. Its very difficult but they do manage.

We checked out of our room and made our way to the railway station. The trains use the twenty-four hour time system, and at exactly 1500 hours (3 P.M.) we were on our way back to Manchester where we would arrive at 1758 (5:58 P.M.) after changing trains at Chester.

We arrived at exactly six o'clock at Picadilly railway station. Unfortunately we exited at a different place than where my brother Sonny was waiting to pick us up. We were finally able to locate the bus station where we took a bus back to the flat. My brother and his wife Pam were already back from Picadilly where they had been waiting a half hour for us. However, it all turned out well and it had been a great couple of days for me. After a shower, a change, and a meal the four of us sat and talked until nearly midnight. Then it was off to bed feeling very tired.

Sunday, July 16, 1995

I got up a little later then I generally do on a Sunday in Oregon but this is a different place and time. We will be going for a workout at ten o'clock this morning with my nephew Graeme and his friend Steve. I think the two of them have been waiting to set me up for this workout. I'll try my very best to keep up with them. They will be along soon to pick me up to go to the YMCA.

I had a great workout which lasted almost two hours. I gave my nephew and his friend a good workout. In addition to that, the three of us took part in a forty-five minute group workout led by an instructor consisting of jogging four minutes with sit ups, push ups, and various aerobic exercise intermittently. I can tell you I could feel it by the end of the workout, but it was also very satisfying.

We got back to the flat around two-o'clock this afternoon and spent the rest of the day visiting family. All in all it was another great day. Tomorrow we will be going to Liverpool to visit my wife's sister. One of the girls from the Sonny Warner Show will be driving us down. Her name is Suzanne Kay and she is a vocalist and musical arranger. She will be picking us up at seven o'clock in the morning.

Monday, July 17 1995

Suzanne came by right on time and we were on our way and arrived in Liverpool at about seven forty-five. We had a nice visit for a couple of hours and then I went to the passport office in the city center to try to renew my passport. There were about four hundred people waiting to be served and they told me I would have to wait about two and a half hours. I got the information I needed to obtain a renewal and decided to do it when I got back to the U.S.A.

It was a beautiful sunny day with a slight breeze blowing. We stayed in town for a few hours and returned by bus to my sister-in-law's home around three o'clock. We had some more conversation with my sister-in-law, Sadie, and her daughter, Janice, who lives with her mom and takes care of her. My sister-in-law suffers from a severe case of arthritis and has much difficulty walking.

Suzanne arrived to take us back to Manchester. We said our good-byes, but we may of course be back again during our stay in England.

We spent a rather quiet evening reminiscing with my brother, Sonny, and his wife, Pam. It was almost midnight, and feeling very tired we decided that it was time to turn in for the night. It was a wise decision.

Tuesday, July 18, 1995

My brother-in-law, Alec, along with his wife, who is my sister Sonia, drove by the flat at about nine o'clock in the morning to pick us up for the long drive back to their home in Middlesex. Middlesex is a county just a few miles from London Town. Traffic was heavy because the British Railways were having another one of their one day strikes. By doing this they hope to create chaos more than a prolonged strike. In any event, it caused a massive traffic jam and it took quite some time before we could get onto the MI motor way to London. Its fortunate that we were able to do that without any mishaps.

We finally arrived at my sister's home at about one o'clock. The service centers they have there, which are located about every thirty miles, are comprised of a restaurant, a large gift shop, nice rest rooms, and of course a full service station. These centers are absolutely crowded with people and the parking lots are really full.

After freshening up at the house, we had a light snack and went for a walk. The weather was not too bad. It was slightly overcast with some breaks of sunshine and a little on the muggy side. The temperature was seventy-three degrees, and the humidity was rather high.

The rest of the day was spent getting together with my sister's children and their families. We had lots to talk about and many things to see. The day went by rather quickly and we didn't stay up late.

Wednesday, July 19, 1995

I was awake by six o'clock. The weather was slightly cloudy with a promise of afternoon sunshine. After a light breakfast my brother-in-law, Alec, and his wife, Sonia, drove us to a huge complex about sixty miles away. It was called Lakeside. In some ways, it was similar to American malls. There were plenty of stores, gift shops, and restaurants with the addition of a huge mile long lake with lots of ducks and swans swimming around and plenty of seating all around. Its situated in the beautiful countryside of Essex.

We had brought a light lunch along with us which we all ate as we sat by the lake. After lunch we did some shopping, but the price of goods make it almost impossible for tourists to make any substantial purchases. We finally left around two-thirty and we were back by four o'clock.

The afternoon was very warm and the humidity was very high. The temperature was a rather soggy seventy-five degrees. We were able to visit with my sister's children and of course all of their children, numbering seven in all. Their ages ranged from two to eleven. My sister's son-in-law, Paul Zneimer, is the Rabbi of the large Kenton Synagogue. Along with his wife, Elizabeth, they have three girls and two boys. Another daughter, Suzanne, and her husband, Arthur, have a boy and a girl. All of these children are very bright and talented and they are crazy about English football (soccer), which they all play. Yes, even the two year old boy who actually will be three very soon plays football.

We had a great time with the children and after they had all gone it was time for supper (dinner), a late chat, and then off to bed. Sleep didn't come easy this night since it was very muggy and they did not have air conditioning, which is somewhat of a luxury in these parts.

Thursday, July 20, 1995

I awoke early this morning. The sun was shining and it was rather warm. We had our bags packed ready for our return to Manchester by bus. Getting to the bus station was an adventure. It consisted of taking a walk to the entrance of the underground then taking the train to Charing Cross, changing trains to Victoria, and finally walking twenty-minutes to the main bus station.

The bus station was packed wall to wall with people of all kinds waiting to board a bus for their different destinations. We finally boarded our bus which was a double decker. The trip to Manchester took four and one-half hours and we were able to purchase refreshments on the bus. By the time we got to Manchester we were very tired and sort of dirty from all the travel. It was a nice and very welcome surprise to see my nephew Graeme at the station waiting to drive us back to my brother's flat.

Once we got home, I took a nice hot shower and made a full change of clothes. After that we went over to Graeme's home to spend an evening with his wife Janat, and their three children. The two girls were awake but the two-year-old, Lee, was already fast asleep. We played around until about ten-thirty in the evening and Graeme drove us back to the flat.

Friday, July, 21, 1995

I awoke this morning with a slightly sore throat. I can't make up my mind if I caught a virus or perhaps its from too much talking. It was raining when I got up, but now the sky is clearing and they are predicting fair weather again.

Its Friday and we will be leaving here around two o'clock this afternoon to drive up to Blackpool for a weekend at my brother Sonny's caravan. It's only a stone's throw from the beach by the North Sea. We will be staying until Sunday, so it should be a very nice weekend.

It took about an hour to drive to the caravan. The sky was clearing and the sun started to break through. I had a shower and changed into clothes more suitable for the warm sunshine. After some lunch we went down to the Lytham village. Lytham is where the British Golf Open Championship is often played and it is just a mile or better from the well-known seaside town of Blackpool.

We did some sight-seeing and a little shopping. We went back to the caravan which is situated on a huge recreational vehicle park with over a hundred others of various sizes and descriptions. I met some people I knew many years ago and we swapped some nostalgic stories. I watched some television, read the English newspapers, and by ten o'clock I was in bed and asleep almost as soon as my head hit the pillow.

Saturday, July 22, 1995

I was awake by five-thirty. Its a beautiful sunny morning. It is still a little on the breezy side, but it promises to warm up by mid day. After a very light breakfast of tea and a morning bun, my wife and I took a walk around the very picturesque countryside. It really is beautiful around these parts.

My brother drove us down to St. Annes which is a small town just a mile from the caravan site and by the beach. Perhaps I should have told you previously that a caravan is the English equivalent of a mobile home. There are numerous caravan sites all over Great Britain.

I had a very pleasant couple of hours in the town and returned to the site where my brother and his wife had invited some friends for lunch. These included some people I knew who had a permanent home both here and in Florida.

We had a great afternoon and continued partying and talking until about eight o'clock in the evening when most of the visitors had to drive back to Manchester. After they had all left we all took a hand in cleaning up and made ourselves some tea and scones. We sat and watched some television until after ten o'clock. Feeling rather tired we turned in for the night.

Sunday, July 23, 1995

Its a beautiful sunny Sunday morning and its still early, almost seven o'clock. We will be leaving here this morning about eleven o'clock to head back to the flat where we are staying in Manchester. It seems that my nephew's wife Janat is giving a surprise party for her aunt's seventieth birthday and she wants us to be there at two-thirty. We should be back just after noon and have enough time to change and freshen up.

Meanwhile, my wife and I will enjoy an early morning cup of tea and a toasted tea cake and then it's off for a nice leisurely walk. I ought to explain that these English tea cakes and scones are absolutely delicious. As a matter of fact, the patiserries, as they are called over there, are bakeries which do their own baking and retailing. The selection in most of them is absolutely fabulous.

We went out to the nearby deli and bought some bagels and buns. We walked around a little and then drove back to the caravan for some tea and a bagel before leaving for the drive back to Manchester. I will read the Sunday morning News of the World which is very popular over here.

It took us less then an hour to get back to Manchester. Traffic was fairly light on the motor way and the weather, though not very sunny, was dry and fairly warm. Now its time to take off for the surprise party I referred to earlier. I guess they need to have everyone there so the surprise will be a good one.

We were still thinking about the wonderful weekend at the caravan. Some of the people we met and sat around with included Barry Ancill, an agent for entertainers, and Eric Deleney, a well known drummer who leads his own big band now performing for the summer season here in Blackpool. We will be taking in a couple of shows later in our stay.

The surprise party was really just that. She is the Aunt Nita of my niece Janat and lives in a retirement haven for widowed women. There were probably around forty people assembled in my niece's home and as the time for her surprise arrived the guests gathered into the outer garden. Meanwhile my nephew Graeme had told them that when they heard the music on the loud stereo he was operating they were to troop single file into their very large dining room to offer congratulations to Aunt Nita.

Promptly at three o'clock, to the sound of "For She's a Jolly Good Fellow," the guests came in and did the honors. It was very effective and to be truthful, it was done in very good taste. After much talk and a huge array of refreshments, a huge birthday cake full of colored lit candles was marched in to the tune of "Happy Birthday." They really put on quite a show.

It was only after I'd spoken to my nephew Brian, the leader of the Lemon Tree Band, that I realized a good many of the guests were entertainers from television on the Blackpool pier shows. No wonder it all looked so professionally orchestrated. Anyway, we had a great time and after a couple of hours Sonny, Pam, and Rose, and I all went over to Brian's flat. He had just moved in a few months ago.

We had never been there before and it turned out to be one of the most unusual little houses we had ever seen. I say small, but in reality it was more of a luxury home big enough for a single person such as Brian. However, it did have two large bedrooms. One of the telephones was shaped in the form of a black and white piano, correct in every detail, which played tunes depending on the number you were dialing.

There were all kinds of unusual things in the house which easily identified the occupant as a person in the world of entertainment. We really had a great visit, and Brian's business partner and lead female singer, Maxine, joined us later. She is a very striking young blonde. She is a very nice, soft spoken woman and a very good singer and dancer. Maxine had done the layout of the house.

It was getting late and time to go so we said our good byes and drove back to the flat for a cup of tea, some television, some more talk, and finally off to bed. It had really been a very busy but most enjoyable day for us.

Monday, July 24, 1995

We were up early and by seven o'clock had showered, changed, and had a light breakfast by the counter in the kitchen. This flat of my brother's is so very cozy and has everything in it you could wish for.

My nephew Graeme will be coming by to pick us up on his way to his downtown office. He will drop us off at the bus station where we will get a bus to take us to the seaside town of Southport where we will be going to visit my cousin Sadie. She is in fairly good health and is in her early sixties. She resides in a home for retired people. She has never married. We will visit with her and probably take her out for lunch. The trip to Southport takes approximately an hour. Its a fairly nice morning so hopefully we may get some sun later in the day.

My nephew Graeme picked us up at eight-thirty and dropped us off at Picadilly where we were able to get the nine-twenty train to Southport. We arrived there just after ten-thirty and went straight to the retirement home to visit my cousin. She was in the lounge relaxing. She was, of course, very pleased to see us. We sat and talked for a couple of hours. I gave her some spending money which I generally mail to her from the U.S.A. and then we took our leave. She did not feel well enough to eat lunch out.

It was a very nice sunny day, and after a light lunch of lettuce and tomato salad, some hovis bread, and a pot of tea, we were ready to spend the rest of the day enjoying the sights and sounds of the Holiday Makers at Southport's seaside.

During the afternoon we sat in the large floral gardens right on the promenade to listen and enjoy a very nice Wurlitzer organ concert. The crowd we quick to join in the singing of all the popular tunes being played. The show finally concluded at about five o'clock in the evening.

We stopped at a small tea shop for some tea and scones. By the time we were done and had a short walk it was time to head towards the railway station for our journey home by train. We left at seven o'clock.

We got into Picadilly station in Manchester at exactly 8:20 P.M. where my nephew Graeme and his daughter Jenna were waiting to drive us back to the flat. Back at the flat I quickly showered and changed completely. I had a nice hot cup of tea and a bagel. We all stayed up until eleven o'clock just watching television and talking. Then it was off to bed again after another busy but splendid day.

Tuesday, July 25, 1995

Its six-thirty Tuesday morning and it promises to be a very nice warm summer day with the weather forecast to possibly reach eighty degrees. They use the metric system in England and all the temperatures are given in Celsius, all the measurements are in meters, and their weights are in kilograms.

This morning our friend Suzanne Kay, she is the girl who sings on the Sonny Warner Show, will be taking us to Liverpool and dropping us off at my wife's sisters home for a short visit.

I must stop and reflect on some of the things I've noticed during my stay in the United Kingdom. Contrary to what you may have heard, things over here are not bad at all. As far as I can tell, the economy seems to be holding up. More about that later.

Wednesday, July 26, 1995

Its a really great morning. It is sunny and warm with the weatherman predicting temperatures into the eighties. We are really having a heat wave over here. What a stark contrast to our last visit three years ago!

My sister Sadie and her husband Leslie will be coming by to pick us up around ten o'clock this morning, and we will be spending the rest of the day with them. I should mention at this point that my sister-in-law, Pamela, who we are staying with, has been keeping a diary for us with all our appointments. She tells me we are almost booked up for the remainder of our stay. I never thought that I was so much in demand!

Anyway, it should turn out to be another very interesting day which I will recall for you later. As for now, its just after nine o'clock so I will relax and read the Daily Mail and find out what's going on in sports and in the world in general.

My sister and her husband came by at eleven o'clock. They drove us back to their bungalow. This is a small two bedroom building all on one level with the same type of building directly attached on one side, very similar to our duplex type of building. We had tea and scones and sat and talked for a while. After that we went up to Bury Market which is both indoors and outdoors. It was very busy and the crowds are much larger than in the average American mall. The shoppers also seem to be in more of a hurry too. In any event, we browsed around for a couple of hours buying one or two small items we never see in the States. Then we left the market and went to a very unique outdoor coffee place. It was unusual in that it was located at the rear of an extremely large nursery. Here in England nurseries are called gardens and they sell a vast array of trees, plants, bird baths, statues, and all kinds of seeds. All of this is spread over a very large area.

The tea was very good and so were the tea cakes. The sun was nice and warm and people around us seemed to be having a good time. We left the gardens around five o'clock, then drove back to my sister's bungalow. She gave us some gifts to take back with us to the States for her daughter Annette who lives in San Francisco. She will be visiting us in Tualatin for a weekend in September along with her two children. We will give her the packages when she arrives.

They drove us back to my brother's flat. We then showered and changed and spent the evening at my nephew Graeme's home. We enjoy being with his wife Jan and the children—Zoey, Jenna, and Lee. We stayed until after eleven o'clock and Graeme drove us back to the flat. We stayed up until almost midnight just talking about family and things in general. Then it was time for sleeping. I must have fallen asleep as soon as my head touched the pillow.

Thursday, July 27, 1995

Today is Thursday and the day that my wife and I will be going to the Cricket Test Match. Its a five day event or it may be less depending on how long each team takes when up to bat. Its also a best of five game series, and as of now the West Indies team is 2-1 up on England. Today, being the opening day of this fourth game, could be very significant. As a general rule, the team that wins the toss tends to bat first, assuming that the condition of the pitch will deteriorate as time goes by.

Graeme will be taking us to the game around nine-thirty this morning. The match begins at eleven o'clock and the end of the day's play is at six-thirty. We are taking a cold insulated bag with water and orange juice with us. We are also taking a large thermos of tea, some bagels and scones, and some fruit. It will be a sold out crowd of about thirty-thousand people and getting refreshments would mean more queuing.

Incidentally, talking about queuing. I met a lady in Liverpool while I was in a queue waiting to be served in a Marks and Spencers store. I explained to her that we rarely had to form long queues to be served in the States. She then told me how queuing got its name. It seems that many Chinese men wear their hair long and braided in a sort of pony tail in the back called a "que." The British people picked up on this and the long lines they form are like the long pony tails. They expanded on the word and called it "queuing." This lady happened to be the Head Mistress of a junior high school so I'm assuming that her explanation was well researched.

Its just after nine o'clock so I'll leave off for now and get ready to go to the Test Match. They are predicting some sun with a shower or two. Hopefully the showers will hold off since any rain at all suspends play. We will get back together after the game. I forgot to mention that we will also be taking a pair of binoculars, sun glasses, lotion, and sun hats to the game. We will also take a brolly (umbrella). That's the lot. We are ready to go!

Getting to the game was not that easy. Traffic was extremely heavy, especially as we approached the Cricket Ground. It has been more than fifty years since I last went to Old Trafford to watch a game. Finally I'm back here again where as a young boy I enjoyed many full days of cricket.

We had our nephew Graeme take us to our seats once we got to the ground. He was with a business group and was sitting in a different section than us. He came by periodically during the day's play just to see if we were alright or if we needed anything. We had great seats and the huge crowd was already in a happy mood.

Play began promptly at eleven o'clock and by four-thirty the West Indies team had completed their innings with a total of 216 runs. By the close of play at six-thirty England had scored 65 runs for the loss of 2 crickets (2 batsmen). Play will resume tomorrow morning at eleven o'clock. It had been a great summer's day and the cricket was excellent with an appreciative sell-out crowd in a very merry mood.

Years ago the crowd at a cricket match would applaud gently at any appropriate time. Today, however, the crowd acts very similar to the way a crowd at a soccer game acts. There is a lot of singing and shouting and all types of bells, whistles, and horns.

We really had a great time today and it was something I had hoped to do during all the years I've been living in the States.

Graeme drove us back to the flat where he gave me a large plastic bag full of souvenirs he had obtained for me. There was a couple of England's Cricket

Color ties, some badges, pens, and a lovely colored program of the game. He really took good care of me.

I had a shower and changed and by that time it was eight o'clock and my brother and his wife Pam were taking us to their son Brian's house where his girlfriend and lead singer Maxine had prepared a nice dinner for us.

The six of us were right in the middle of eating when the front door chimes went into its thing. They had arranged a surprise for me. The visitor was a school chum of mine whom I had not seen for about sixty years. He is a very well known sports celebrity as a television announcer, interviewer, and boxing promoter and officiado. His name is Nat Basso and he is a very young looking, fit sort of guy at seventy-nine years old.

Nat had brought along a bunch of photos of all kinds of sports celebrities. You name them and he had them along with himself in the picture too. He's a great story teller and he has many American friends, especially in the world of sports. His official title is Secretary and Commissioner of the British Boxing Board of Control Council. It was great seeing him again.

All in all, it had been a great day topped by a splendid evening with our wonderful hosts, Brian and Maxine. They had taken a night off from the entertainment circuit just to spend an evening with us. Tomorrow they are playing somewhere in Yorkshire. The Lemon Tree is a stage band in great demand in the U.K. and they are to play at a reception given for John Majors, the British Prime Minister, sometime in September.

So there you have it. Another almost perfect day gone by and our days in the country of my birth are gradually dwindling down.

Friday, July 28, 1995

I had a very good night's sleep. I must mention something I forgot about yesterday. Just about an hour before Graeme was to come by to take us to the game my voice was still very scratchy and I felt very uncomfortable. My brother Sonny's wife works as an accounting secretary for a couple of doctors just around the corner from the flat. She made me go into her place of work and within just a few minutes she had one of the doctors take a look at my throat. He said it was inflamed and he prescribed medication which I had filled at the pharmacy next door to the doctor's office. All of this took place within about ten or fifteen minutes and the cost of course was absolutely free. I'm still covered by the NHS (National Health Service) and of course, being as they say in this country, a pensioner, I am not required to pay for any prescribed medications. Incidentally, I was prescribed penicillin tablets and they were improving my voice.

Today my wife and I are going to the popular seaside town of Blackpool where we will be staying until Monday afternoon. Graeme (my nephew) will be picking us up at eight-thirty this morning to take us to the bus station downtown. The bus leaves at nine-thirty and arrives in Blackpool at eleven-twenty. The weather is still good and hopeful it will stay that way for the next few days. We really have had a great time so far, along with some very good weather.

We arrived in Blackpool and found the same hotel where we stayed three years ago except it was now under new ownership. The previous owners retired. The cost was about the same as our last visit, thirty pounds per night which is approximately fifty American dollars per night.

Having once settled in to where we would be staying, we then went out onto the promenade, for which Blackpool is famous. Talk about crowds, it was almost back to back with a wall of people. The weather was almost a perfect ten!

Anyway, we went about booking our seats for shows on Saturday night and Sunday night. Friends of our families were headlining each Show. We thought maybe we could get together afterwards depending on what they have committed themselves to. In any event, we understand that it may not be easy to do that.

We purchased tickets, had a quick snack, and spent the rest of the day either walking along the prom or just browsing the numerous small stores along the way.

It has been a long and busy day for us, so by ten o'clock I was back in our hotel. It wasn't too long after that and i was in bed and fast asleep in no time.

Saturday, July 29, 1995

I slept a little later than usual since I have no gym to go to. I'm really missing my workouts and I will have to work in gradually when I get back to the U.S.A.

I was out walking along the prom at eight o'clock this morning. Its the best part of the day for me when the air is still fresh and there are not too many people around. The sun is already out and it promises to be another warm and sunny day.

They served breakfast at nine o'clock, and what a large meal it was. However, we just had our usual—hot tea, toast, and jam (my wife likes jam). The actual breakfast consisted of orange juice, cereal, eggs, toast, sausages, and bacon along with tea or coffee. Not a bad meal, don't you think?

Having finished breakfast, my wife and I walked along the front and decided to take the electric tram to Fleetwood, which is a fishing town about six or seven miles from here. The fare on the tram was two pounds for each of us one way. This is equal to about three dollars and thirty cents just for a six to seven mile ride. Are we spoiled in the U.S.A. or what?

I must admit, however, that the trip was worthwhile. The pier was very interesting and colorful. Boats in the harbor were leaving for Ireland and the Isle of man. We spent the rest of the morning and early afternoon just browsing around the town. We headed back to our digs (the hotel) around five o'clock with just enough time to shower and change and cover the half hour walk to the north pier where my friend Frank Carson was the star of a music hall type of show.

When we got to the show it was almost show time. I was able to get one of the ushers to tell Frank's manager we were there. He then arranged for us to see Frank at the intermission when he had a break before his featured act in the show. Frank Carson is one of the most popular comedians in Great Britain. He is very busy with radio, television, and stage shows. He is an extremely funny man on stage. He is a full-blooded Irishman.

During the intermission we were led backstage to Frank's dressing room where he was relaxing on a couch. I could hear his first words as we were climbing some steps up to his room: "Who the bloody hell is there in the U.S.A. that I owe money too!" As I said, he is a very funny man and he had my wife and I in stitches laughing for most of the twenty minutes we were with him.

He sent us on our way with a couple of his latest photos. One was for our nephew Brian who has appeared with Frank many times. He signed "Miss you Brian" "From Big F. News at 10 Sober." It has to be an inside joke which I'll find out about from Brian. Our picture was signed "to Rose and Barney. Love Ya! Frank."

We went back to our seats and watched the rest of the show. We were out by nine-fifteen when it is still daylight here, and we took a pleasant walk along the prom. We stopped at a small cafe for scones and tea at a fairly reasonable price then went back to our hotel and turned in for the night.

All in all it was a very nice day and an extremely pleasant summer evening. The weather predicted for tomorrow is much more of the same—dry, warm, and lots of sunshine. Suits me just fine.

Sunday, July 30, 1995

Once again I awoke early to another fine warm and sunny morning. Even the people who live in Blackpool Town can't believe this beautiful weather they are experiencing.

I had a breakfast of orange juice, dry toast, and tea. We decided to take the electric tram to the town of Cleveleys which is another resort area just a few miles from here with a promenade about two miles long. Arriving there we found that the tide had gone way out and the North Sea appeared rather calm.

Walking in the heat can make you very thirsty and there are no fountains at all that I could see. When I ordered a pot of tea I asked for a glass of cold water and I was told it would be 50 P which is about 81 cents! I learned from this that they all charge for cold water thought at different prices according to where you may be. I often wonder if the average American realizes how fortunate he or she is to live in the U.S.A. I know my wife and I are and we are not Americans!

We spent the day at Cleveleys mostly walking, sometimes sitting, and again browsing around all the many little shops they have around these parts.

We arrived back at the hotel five-thirty where we showered, changed, and left for the long walk to the opera house where we had booked seats to see our friend Barnaby, the very young comic, who is destined for stardom. He was appearing for a one night stand only. I decided that since the show didn't start until seven-thirty and we arrived at the opera house at six-thirty, that I would try to see Barnaby before the show started. I got lucky because he was just coming to the stage door as I got there.

He was so glad to see us, and after exchanging greetings we talked for about fifteen minutes. Then it was time for him to get ready for the show.

Barnaby is just a very young comedian who is very athletic with a quick fire delivery, and he is still on his way up. It was a great show which we thoroughly enjoyed and it was good to see my friend again.

We had a nice long walk home along the Blackpool prom, which was crowded with people even though it was ten o'clock. We were home about ten forty-five and it was just about bed time. What another great day it has been. They say the weather will be the same for tomorrow, which will be our last day here since we will be leaving on the five-thirty bus for Manchester.

Monday, July 31, 1995

I was awake at almost six o'clock. I took a nice cool shower and changed, and by seven o'clock I was out on the prom enjoying a nice walk in the fresh sea air. My wife was right along with me of course. We went back to our hotel for a nine o'clock breakfast of orange juice, dry toast, and some nice hot tea. The tea here has a much better taste than ours back home.

After an enjoyable breakfast we walked back up to the prom and sat for a while, just relaxing and watching the early morning sun bathers and the many children and some adults frolicking around in the sea. Its surprising how the time goes by.

We also did some more browsing around the stores, making a couple of purchases to take back as gifts for some friends. It was another extremely hot day for England with temperatures in the mid-eighties, and for this country that is considered to be a heat wave.

We had some afternoon tea and shared a scone between us. Soon it was time to get back to the hotel where the lady of the hotel had allowed us to leave our luggage until we were ready to leave at five o'clock by bus back to Manchester.

We got into the Manchester bus station at ten minutes past seven where my nephew Graeme met us to take us back to my brother's flat. My brother Sonny and his wife Pam were waiting to welcome us back from our four day trip along with our nephew Brian who was taking a week off from performing because his lead singer and dancer Maxine's daughter was being married in France this week which meant that she would be out of the country for a week.

Anyway, shortly after we got in, Pam made a nice table of tea and a selection of all kinds of buns and tea cakes.

After that we sat and talked until shortly after ten o'clock. My brother then told me he was going to play a video tape which Graeme had taken especially to let us see the final day of the West Indies—England cricket match. It ended on the fourth day (Sunday) with a huge victory for England. During this final day a record was equalled by an English bowler which had been established well over seventy years ago. The bowler, whose name is Dominick Cork, dismissed three West Indies batsmen with three successive balls, thus completing a natural hat trick. It was a great performance any way you look at it, and believe me, it was well worth looking at. I know most of you readers may not understand the rules of cricket but it really is a great spectator sport, especially in weather like we are having over here.

In any event, the time was flying by and it was after eleven-thirty when we all decided to call it a night. It was a rather muggy evening so I took a warm shower. Once in bed, I just slept like a log.

Tuesday, August 1, 1995

This morning we are off to Liverpool again for one final visit to my wife's sister Sadie and her daughter Janice. Suzanne will be picking us up a quarter past seven for the half hour drive on her way to her office in Liverpool. Its now almost seven o'clock so i had better leave off and get ready. I'll be back later.

Suzanne got us into Liverpool around a quarter past eight. We visited with my wife's sister and her daughter for a couple of hours. We then took the bus into the town center where we went shopping for all kinds of food to take back for them since they are not blessed with a lot of wealth and its not easy for them to get any shopping done. We also stayed downtown to eat lunch. We arrived back at the house at about three o'clock and sat and talked until Suzanne came by for us at four-thirty.

We said our final good byes to the both of them since we would not be returning to Liverpool. However we will phone them, of course, before leaving to return to the States.

After arriving home we took showers and changed. The day had been hot and very humid and it felt good to get under the shower. I decided to stay in the flat for the rest of the evening. Brian came by, however, and told us that we were going to dinner with some friends not too far away from the flat. This turned out to be a very nice lady by the name of Margaret Addy who has been like a part of the Warner (Wagner) family just as our Liverpool chaufferesse Suzan Kay is.

Margaret has had a really tough time of it lately. She lost both her husband and her son in the space of a couple of years. She is still a fairly middle aged woman working as a social worker. She suffers from a type of chronic arthritis. In spite of all these serious setbacks, she is a very upbeat person and she turned out to be an excellent hostess.

There were eight of us at Margaret's flat for dinner, and after the mash Brian's twelve year old daughter Nichole entertained us with some comedy routines mixed with singing and dancing. Incidentally, Brian's son David, who is seventeen years old and is away on Holidays in Spain, is a terrific young drummer. If he decides to follow in his Dad's footsteps, David could make a fine career for himself. Brian's entire family is very talented. Nicole is also very good on the flute.

After we left Margaret's lovely house and got back to the flat, Brian was waiting to play us his latest Lemon Tree Show which he had video recorded especially for us. We were unable to travel with the band on this trip so this was the next best thing. We enjoyed the video very much. My brother Sonny had also taped a couple of his last shows for us, and we spent the rest of the evening being entertained by video tape. It had been another great day for me. The weather remained warm but very humid, and since very few people in England have the luxury of air conditioning they simply suffer the heat as best they can.

Wednesday, August 2, 1995

Its another great morning with the sun beaming down and its still early, just after eight o'clock. This morning we are on our own, so we will take the bus to the city center.

We got downtown (Manchester) just after nine o'clock and most of the people around were going to work. We just browsed around all the different stores and different places. The weather was still hot and humid. I should point out again that most of the buildings here do not have air conditioning.

During my time spent over here I have been able to talk with many people in a friendly sort of way. Most of them were people who were strangers to me. Among the many topics I discussed with them and one of the main things they talked to me about was this unusual weather they have been and still are having this summer. They nearly all agree that they can never recall a time in their lives when the weather has been this hot, eighty to ninety degrees, for such a long period of time.

I also was able to talk with many women who were the mothers of children of various ages. We discussed how the government assists them financially to care for the children. First of all, when a woman becomes pregnant she does not have to pay for any medications. When the first child is born the government gives the parent or parents nine pounds (approximately fifteen dollars weekly until that child finishes his or her education or marries. For each and every child after the first one the parents are allotted seven pounds (approximately twelve dollars). They all seem to convey to me the fact that in general the NHS (National Health Service) works very well for them. There are flaws in every country's health program, but in Great Britain the NHS seems to be doing fairly well for everyone.

We returned to the flat from downtown by one-thirty to get ready for a two-thirty visit to a person I had not seen since I was about sixteen years old. His name is Jack Kay and his wife is not feeling too well I'm told. Jack is four years older than I am, but he has a full head of white hair and looks fairly young and fit for his age. He is well known in Manchester, and as a young teenager he was a great soccer goalkeeper. Jack would easily have become a professional if not for his lack of an inch or two in height.

I used to watch Jack play whenever I could. We had a great reunion and he was as pleased to see me as I was to see him. A couple of hours passed by very quickly. Then my brother Sonny had us in the car again, this time we were headed for a home for retired and disabled people. It turned out to be a massive, new looking complex called Heathlands.

"The Sonny Warner Show" performed for the residents free of charge once every year. As we toured the huge building, escorted by the young lady director, some of the residents would call out to my brother saying, "When is the next show Sonny," or "Congratulations on your MBE, Sonny." It makes me feel so very proud of all the things my wonderful brother has achieved.

This establishment is a state of the arts building. It really has everything. It is well equipped with full medical facilities, dining halls, all types of recreation areas, and living quarters which are really excellent.

It turned out to be great seeing many of the residents who remembered me. We had cold drinks served to us and had to turn down an invitation to lunch since it was time to be heading back to the flat.

Brian dropped by to see us along with my friend Nat Basso's daughter, Irene. I had met Irene on my previous trip to England. She is a fitness instructor and works one on one with most of the actors and performers in England. She is fifty-three years-old but looks to be in her thirties! We were only able to visit with Irene for about thirty minutes since she had to get away and so did we.

I had promised Graeme that I would watch him play a match of tennis against his forty-eight-year-old partner Johnny Manson. Johnny is very well known in Manchester as an ex-football player. We drove to his home where he has a full, regulation size tennis court.

The match was played at a fast pace. Johnny is surprisingly fast and powerful for his age, but my young nephew Graeme is a very good player and he was able to win rather handily 6-0, 6-1. The quality of play was just slightly below the play of the pros.

After the game Graeme drove us back to his home where we were having dinner along with my brother Sonny, his wife Pam, and nephew Brian. We enjoyed a nice meal and some after dinner talk. Sonny took us back to the flat around ten-thirty.

We stayed up late watching a taped video of Sonny and Pam's Ruby Wedding which was hosted by Brian and a surprise show put on by The Lemon Tree. In addition to this, Suzanne and Brian had arranged a "This is You Life" for Sonny and Pam which was full of surprises and appearances by performers live and on tape. It turned out to be a two hour video show of excellent quality. It was really a great show and a fine tribute to two wonderful people.

We went to bed well after midnight and I was asleep very quickly. It had been a very busy day for me.

Thursday, August 3, 1995

Its just another beautiful morning and it promises to be another hot day. There is no telling how long this weather will last, but we will take full advantage of it while it does.

We had an early breakfast and then decided to take a bus ride to the nearest town. Its a place called Bury and its about eight miles from here. The people who live in this small town speak with a little different accent, than the folks from Manchester (Mancunians).

After wondering around the town, we stopped at a small cafe for tea. The price was 76P (approximately $1.20) for a pot of tea for two. This is not a bad price, really. Anyway, the tea here is excellent. We also purchased a large eccles cake which is a thin pastry about the shape and size of a tea saucer that is filled to the brim with black currants. We shared this between us and it was really delicious. I just want to explain that the Eccles Cake got its name from a very small town just outside of Manchester where they were first made and introduced to the country. Now they can be found in most all of the bakeries in Great Britain.

We returned to the flat by bus. Since it was just twelve noon it seemed like a good time to catch up on my writing and also to rest up a little. I'll be going out again at two-thirty this afternoon to visit with my sister Sadie and her husband. I will catch up on things later.

I enjoyed seeing my sister and her husband again. I stayed inside their flat and we talked for a couple of hours. Then we left. It was another hot day and we all felt a little tired, so we drove back to the flat where we were staying with my brother Sonny. Once we were back we immediately showered and changed. Then we relaxed for a few hours since we would be going out early in the evening to meet up with the remainder of my family that i had not yet seen.

I will be going to another small town outside of Manchester called Altringham. Its about twenty-five miles from where we are staying, and Sonny and Pam will be taking us in their car. Actually they have been taking us everywhere we wished to go.

When we arrived in Altringham it was at the house of the remaining nephew and niece I had still not seen while I had been here. They are the son and daughter of my sister-in-law Gertie who is the widowed wife of my late brother and business partner, Louis. He was my partner in the upholstery manufacturing factory we had in England.

There was quite a crowd of people I had yet to meet. First of all there was my sister-in-law Gertie; her son Anthony, who is a lawyer; her daughter Rosalind, who dabbles in real estate; and her husband Victor, who is an oral surgeon and a very nice, down to earth sort of guy.

Anthony and his wife have three children and Rosalind has four. The Warner (Wagner) families are a large group when they are together for a party or celebration. Most of the children are very talented and play several instruments. They can all sing and dance. Its just great to see and hear them entertaining.

I had a very nice evening and by ten forty-five Sonny was ready for the drive back to Manchester. I said good bye to all of the family in Altringham since i would not be seeing any of them again before leaving. It was a pleasant drive back. Once we arrived at the flat we relaxed, had a nice drink of tea, a quiet chat, and went off to bed.

Friday, August 4, 1995

I woke up this morning bright and early feeling very refreshed after a sound night's sleep. The sun is already out and its going to be another warm day.

Graeme will be swinging by to pick my wife and I up at eight-thirty this morning for a prearranged tour of the Manchester City Football Club at Maine Road. This is, if you recall, the very same ground where I played in a Cup Final as a schoolboy, which we lost. But the joy of playing on the same football pitch as my idols was compensation enough for me.

I must explain to you how the invitation to tour the facility came about. My nephew Graeme and his friend and business partner Johnny Manson are involved in the health care business. They provide supplementary coverage to large groups such as factory employees, computer industries, and some premier football (soccer) clubs such as Bolton F.C. Just last week they were awarded the contract for Manchester City F.C. So that's how our visit came about. (F.C. is the abbreviation for Football Club).

We arrived at the City ground just after nine o'clock. Waiting to greet us at the main entrance was the head gateman and security chief, Charles Phillips. After a brief introduction and an exchange of handshakes all around, Charles turned us over to a very wonderful, vibrant young lady named Tracy Digby. Tracy escorted us all through this huge facility.

We sat in the luxurious sky suites. We also toured the brand new Kippax Stand which has seating for 12,000 and took well over a year and a half to erect. After Tracy had shown us about 90 percent of the club she led us onto the playing pitch where Graeme took pictures of us. What an unbelievable thrill to be back on this pitch once again!

The only things remaining to be seen were the dressing rooms and physiotherapy room. We had to have a special person to take us through this part of the tour and he turned out to be an ex-player for City from the 1960-70 era. His name is John Clay and he has been involved in the City organization now for almost twelve years. Incidentally, the security chief, Charles Phillips, has been with Manchester City F.C. over forty years!

Anyway, John Clay took us through the various dressing rooms including the separate dressing rooms for the referees. In this room the Chief Referee has a buzzer which he presses five minutes before actual game time to let the players know that he is on his way through the tunnel leading to the playing pitch.

John was with us over an hour telling us about the various rooms of this great facility. It was indeed very impressive. We were introduced to Alan Ball, the ex-player who captained England's team not too long ago. This will be his first season as manager of the club. He spent some time chatting it up with us and he mentioned that he once played in Portland, Oregon against the Portland Timbers when he played a season for Vancouver, B.C. He also took time to have some pictures taken with us. He was just like the rest of the Manchester City organization—a really nice person—and I wish him all the very best of luck in the 1995-96 campaign which begins August 17, 1995.

Among some of the other people we met was Alex Williams, a fine strapping young man who appeared to be about six feet three inches tall. He is an ex-City goalkeeper who is now helping coach in the youth program. We also met Keith Barnes, another old time City player who is doing some Public Relations work for the club. We were also introduced to Mike Summerbee, a very popular ex-player whose son Nick is now playing for the Club.

We finally returned to our hostess and escort for the tour, Tracy Digby. She arranged for us to have tea in one of the club's lounges. After some more photo taking we finally had to say good bye to her and we extended a great "Thank You."

What a great thrill it had been for me to be able to tour those facilities, meet those people, and be back on the very same pitch where as a young boy I had been lucky enough to play. Manchester City F.C. is indeed a wonderful organization. There very well may be bigger and better clubs, but for me Manchester city represents all that is good in this great European sport of soccer.

We spent over three and a half hours touring the facility and it was now almost one o'clock. Graeme's wife Janat drove us to Bury and left us by ourselves. We spent a very nice afternoon just looking around the town. The evening was divided by time spent with my brother Sonny and his wife Pam and time spent with Graeme and his wife Janat. It was just another wonderful day.

Before leaving the world of soccer, I would like to tell you just how big the sport is in Europe. It has been well documented that it is the biggest spectator sport in the world. There are no doubts at all on that score. In addition to this fact, soccer has also grown into the largest business in the world of sports.

European football (soccer) has come a long way over this past decade. Today almost all of the teams have a sponsor whose name is very visible on each player's jersey (shirt). Take for example the club I visited, Manchester City F.C. They are sponsored by the huge computer firm, Brother. The firm's logo is always on the front of the shirt. The relationship between a club and its sponsor is very close. They are both in the sport to make money even though the players themselves love to play just for the game's sake. It is no secret, however, that the players, coaches, and managers make really big money.

In addition to all of the above, a huge change has taken place over the years in the equipment. Many years ago, until just around the time of WWII, players wore heavy boots with large cumbersome studs. Soccer shoes today are much lighter, not unlike an athletic shoe, with smaller built-in studs. Today's modern soccer shoes weigh about one-third as much as the old fashioned type. The players' shorts are made of a much lighter material and the guards which protect a player's shins are made of a much lighter material than the old ones. Even the jerseys are much lighter. As for the football itself—it used to be that the ball was inflated by pump and then closed with leather lacing. During a game the ball got to be very heavy if it got damp or if it was raining when the ball was not, even a simple corner kick was often difficult to do properly. Today the ball is much smaller and lighter. The ball is self-inflated, it does not have any laces. Heading the older ball, especially when it was wet, could give you a real headache if the laces came in contact with your head. I can't help but think what a player like the great Stanley Mathews would have been able to do with today's football.

I mentioned the big money being made in the sport today. Much of it is generated by the advertising for both the games and the products of the sponsors. You'll find this to be very evident if you attend one of the Premier League games. It wasn't too long ago that the players' uniforms were generally referred to as a jersey (shirt), shorts, and socks. Today, however, the uniforms are called script. This is where some of the really big money is being made now.

Although it is not a hard and fast Football Association rule, most sponsors these days insert a clause in their contract with the clubs suggesting that they change their script every two years. Each team also has a different color script for an away game as opposed to a home game. This generates a tremendous amount of income for both the sponsor and the club.

Almost everywhere one goes in England you can see young boys and girls in the streets wearing the script of their favorite team with a player's number and name on the shirt. They are the exact same shirts as those worn by the players. Many adults wear script even to the workplace. It is my understanding that both the club and the sponsor receive a percentage of anything pertaining to the club that is sold. Most clubs now have tremendously huge souvenir shops. It really has become a thriving business. So much for the game of soccer.

Saturday, August 5, 1995

Its truly remarkable how this weather is holding up. It promises to be another great weekend. Unfortunately for me it will be the last weekend before I leave for my home back in the U.S.A. on Monday. I'll miss my family over here.

I will be going to Graeme's house this morning where my wife and I will baby-sit the three children while he and his wife go to town for some last minute purchases prior to the two week vacation they will be taking to Spain. They leave on Wednesday and the children will be going, too. It should be a great time for them. They are such great people.

Just a few days back I erred in saying that we were meeting the remainder of the Warner (Wagner) clan. In actual fact, that will take place later today when we will be going to meet my nephew Clive and his wife Louise along with their three very young girls. I've never taken the trouble to count the members of the Warner family over here, but there must be close to seventy or more in all. What a great musical show they could put on if they all performed at one time. Talk about the Von Trapp family. They don't nearly add up in number to this group.

Clive and Louise live out in the country in a place called Hale about thirty miles from the flat and just a stone's throw from Ringway Airport where we will be departing from on Monday. We will be having lunch at their house and it should be a very nice visit for us.

Lunch turned out to be a wonderful meal. Clive and Louise were exceptionally gracious hosts. The three girls, Melanie, Rebecca, and Sara, were such sweet children and they are very talented. All of them played ukeleles, guitar, and piano. Each of them, including their mother Louise, were fine tap dancers.

They had a huge home with large grounds for a play jungle and for adult games. We all had a great time and the weather was perfect. We gave the children some English Pounds and a few American Dollars and spent a good part of the afternoon trying to figure out the exact amount they had been given. It was really funny.

Soon it was time to be taking our leave. It had been a great afternoon and we thanked Clive and Louise after saying good bye to the children. Sonny and Pam drove us back to the flat and it was after five thirty by the time we got back.

We will be staying home tonight to relax for a change. We seem to have been on the go constantly since the day we arrived. We have really had a great time over here, and tomorrow will be our final day here.

Sunday, August, 6, 1995

It was an early night last night. I was in bed by ten o'clock. That's easily the earliest I have gone to bed during my time here in England. This is to be our last day here and the weather is just fantastic. That's a word they use a lot over here. It used to be that marvelous was often heard.

Its almost nine o'clock and I'm getting ready for a light breakfast which my wife prepared for me. This morning breakfast is going to be half of a grapefruit, a morning bun, and tea. That does me just fine.

My nephew Graeme will be coming by about twelve noon to pick us up. We will be going to the district of old Trafford where the Lancashire County Cricket Team play all their games. This, incidentally, is the same ground where we were watching England versus the West Indies.

Graem's best friend, Steven Burton, was to meet us at the cricket ground. He won a lottery at a game there last week and was to be presented with a large trophy in the form of a statuette facially resembling Neil Fairbrother, one of Lancashire's best players.

We arrived at the ground in brilliant sunshine and Steven was waiting for us. Before going to our seats we took a tour of the many shops and places of interest inside the ground, including the cricket museum and the souvenir shop. There were crowds of people carrying huge picnic bags and bottles of water preparing for a full day of cricket. There was lots of food and drink with plenty of sunshine. It turned out to be a great day, and without going into any deep details, I will just tell you that it was a one day match and Lancashire won after a very close game.

As soon as the game was over we went to the front of the player's entrance to the field where Steven was to be presented with his trophy by Neil Fairbrother. Pretty soon Neil came running down the steps to the playing field and presented Steve with his trophy while they were photographed by the news media. One of the directors of the club asked Neil if he would join my wife and I for a picture which he was nice enough to do. He really was good about it. We had a great time and it was a wonderful experience being on the ground and meeting this fine player. Steve said good bye to us since we would not see him again before leaving and Graeme drove us back to his house to say farewell to Janat and the children. We were then driven back to my brother Sonny's flat where he and his wife Pam were waiting to join us for a dinner they had prepared. It was much later then their usual time, but Graeme had a car phone and he called Sonny and Pam to tell them that we wouldn't be back until a quarter past eight.

We enjoyed a very nice meal, after which we just sat and talked with Sonny and Pam until after eleven o'clock. We were very tired and got to sleep soon after going to bed. What can I say except that it was the end of another great day. It was our last one here, sad to say.

Monday, August 7, 1995

This morning I was up at five thirty. I looked out the window and, in accordance with the television forecast, it appears as if its going to be another great day. After breakfast we said so long to my brother's wife Pam who had gone out of her way to make sure we were very comfortable and didn't lack for anything. Having done that, Sonny and Graeme drove us to Ringway Airport where, after much waiting and producing passports, documents, etc., we finally had our luggage checked in and went to the departure gates. Now it was time to say a final good bye to my brother Sonny and my nephew Graeme. They both had seen to it that we had a great time. My brother shed a few tears, but I know he will be alright once we are gone. It has been a wonderful time for me and my wife.

Now I'm on this huge Boeing plane and there must be about three hundred passengers on board. It appears to be perfect flying weather, and amazingly enough the flight captain has come on the inter-com and said just that.

Since our eight hour flight to Chicago is in its fifth hour, this would be as good a time as any to bring you up to date with my assessment of how things are in Great Britain. I'll begin by telling you that Britain is a much better country to live in today than it was years ago. It is making a return to prosperity as it has never before experienced. Most people over there own their homes and are able to take one or two holidays a year. Most other European citizens have much less than the people of Great Britain. Take for example the people in Germany where only a small percentage of them own their own homes. However, the economy of Germany is alive and well. As for Great Britain, I can truthfully tell you that there are a great number of non-Europeans queuing up to enter the country. The standard of living here is fairly good along with the many benefits and freedoms that go along with it.

The Health Care System

I questioned scores of Brits regarding their views on the NHS (National Health Service). As I may have told you previously, this is an agency run by the government for the complete medical care of all of its subjects. Its founded by a weekly contribution deducted from one's pay check which is equally matched by the employer. Both sides are in complete agreement on this arrangement.

All of the people I've talked to seem to be of the same opinion. They all seem to believe that the NHS is a wonderful thing and that it is operating very well. As with all government agencies there may be some snags once in a while, but everything is decided by the seriousness of the patient's ailment. Consequently, patients who are in no danger but require elective surgery may sometimes have a waiting period of a few months.

Having visited a doctor while in England, I can tell you that I received the very best attention just as I do in the U.S.A. I received a prescription for pills for my throat. Being over the age of fifty-five (a pensioner), the cost was absolutely free since I'm covered by NHS. However, everyone under the age of fifty-five and gainfully employed pays five pounds and twenty-five pence per prescription. There is no charge for the doctor visit.

Before leaving this very important topic I would like to mention something that has just come to light over the last couple of days. It appears that the secretary of health for Great Britain, Mr. Stephen Dorrell, will soon release revised guidelines for doctors and other NHS hospital staff which will obligate them to report colleagues who administer poor patient care. This is in all probability a move to assure the public of the administration's attempt to maintain the complete confidence of the people of Great Britain against any lowering of standards of the NHS.

Crime and the Law

When I left my country of birth in 1953 to immigrate to the U.S.A., criminal activity in Great Britain was very low. Sad to say, however, such is not the case today. As a matter of fact, during the short time we were here, in Manchester alone there were more than half dozen murders and almost one a day occurred elsewhere! Many of the victims were small children who were sexually molested before being murdered. People in Great Britain are beginning to rise up against what is happening and it will be interesting to learn how the law will cope with it.

As for the law of the land, perhaps it would be of interest to my readers if I were to transcribe for you a question or two I posed to a prominent solicitor (attorney) in Manchester. I hope I can put it into layman's language.

Before proceeding, however, I must tell you that I failed to explain that those who are covered by NHS and are not required to pay for prescriptions from their doctors include the following:

Women and Men age 55 and over

All school children

All students

Pregnant women

People redundant (unemployed)

People who suffer with serious ailments

It is also well documented that in actual fact just under a half of the population pays NHS dues.

You must forgive me for digressing, but I will now attempt to get back on track with the Q and A session with this attorney. Here then is a list of my questions and his answers.

1. Is it fair to say the British judicial system is based on the following?
   Q. Innocent until proven guilty?
   A. Yes.
   Q. Trial by a jury of twelve of your peers or a judge?
   A. Yes, but major trials such as murder are only by jury. Minor offenses are by a magistrate.
2. Q. Is a jury challenged as is done in the U.S.A."
   A. Yes.
3. Q. What majority constitutes a guilty verdict in a major trial?
   A. Ten to two or unanimous.
4. Q. Has capital punishment been barred? If so, in what year?
   A. Yes. Around the year 1960.
5. Q. Are perpetrators who are indigent given free legal representation?
   A. Only in matters of a criminal nature.
6. Q. What is the term served for life imprisonment?
   A. Fifteen years.
7. Q. Can you estimate the average length of time required for a major murder trial?

A. Weeks rather than months.
8. Q. Are your courts still referred to as Assize Courts?
A. No.
9. Q. Do any judges still reside at these courts as they did years ago?
A. No.
10. Q. Do you, sir, believe on the basis of what you know about the American system of justice that is both fair and impartial?
A. Definitely yes.
Q. Is plea bargaining in any shape or form a part of the British judicial system?
A. Yes. As to the sentence itself, there can be no plea bargaining on the sentence.
Q. Finally, sir, do you have any specific comments you would care to make on the ongoing trial of Mr. O.J. Simpson?
A. I am very much against the use of television in the court.

It was a great privilege and my pleasure to have this interview with this attorney and I wish to thank him very much. The above questions and answers were asked by me and answered by Mr. Andrew Kormornick of Manchester. His full title is Solicitor of Supreme Court of England and Wales.

Our flight has just landed in Chicago so here we go once again. It took us almost ninety minutes to get through the various ticket, passport, and customs gates since we had to collect our luggage for inspection and get to where it would be checked in again. Then it was almost a mile walk to the shuttle train which took us to our terminal for departure. Finally we had another long walk to the gate where our plane was loading its passengers. We eventually made it just twenty minutes prior to flight time. All in all it took us almost two hours from the time our plane touched down in Chicago. Knowing O'Hare Airport, that's not bad at all!

Now I'm up and away on a slightly smaller Boeing plane on my way to Tualatin, Oregon via Portland. We should be there in about four hours and our son David will be waiting to help collect our luggage and drive us back to Tualatin. It should be a nice flight.

We are now actually three and a half hours into our flight and we should be touching down in Portland in just about one hour. It has been a fairly easy journey most of the way, and hopefully I can overcome any jet lag once we get back home.

We landed at Portland's airport almost on time at five-twenty. Our son David was waiting for us, and after collecting all of our luggage from the carousel we loaded up and headed home.

There's just nothing like being back home, especially after being in another country. We are indeed very fortunate to be living in the good old U.S.A.

It has taken a while to adjust to the time difference, but after almost two days I'm beginning to feel better by the hour.

I'd like to make some final comments regarding my trip to the United Kingdom. It was my intention to take the Eurostar train through the Channel Tunnel to France, but because of the time factor I just never got around to doing it. I can, however, do the next best thing by giving you a sort of graphic description of the service.

I'll begin by telling you that the most popular route used is from Waterloo Station (London) to Lille (France). Waterloo International has an all glass surrounding which makes it extremely hot in the summer. Employees are dressed like airport staff. The very long airport style departure lounge has all the usual shops that you see at most Airports.

The train is actually in the tunnel for approximately twenty-five minutes. The speed at which the trains travel sometimes approaches 175-180 miles per hour. The entire journey takes less than two hours. Eurostar is not only a journey by train, but it is a distinct advance in the world of technology. The average return fare, if booked fourteen days in advance, is about seventy-five pounds or one hundred and twenty dollars.

Once you get to Lille, connections are very available north to Belgium or Brussels. The Eurostar service has all of its signs printed in both English and French. Train connections are also easily made to Paris. Passengers are reminded that the time zone in France requires them to put their watches one hour ahead.

It seems, after talking with a few people who have been through the tunnel, that it has the flaws that any new project may have. But by and large it appears to be operating fairly efficiently. So much then for my comments on the Channel Tunnel.

I also had been meaning to tell you that while I was in London I phoned my friend and England's popular idol, Frankie Vaughan. His mother-in-law answered my call and we talked for only a few minutes since we do know each other. She told me that Frankie was at the Palace. I said that I had just gone by the Palace Theatre and his name was not on any of the billboards, whereupon she informed me that she meant Buckingham Palace. It seems he was there at a party being given by the Queen. Frankie Vaughan and Queen Elizabeth have met many times and they know each other quite well.

I called Frankie again around eleven o'clock the following day. The only reason he was home was because he had an afternoon appointment at the hospital for an MRI scan on an old knee injury from his soccer days that was giving him some trouble. We had a lengthy talk and he told me he was appearing at Steatham that week which made it awkward for us to get together. I called him again the next day to find out about his MRI and it proved to be negative. I also asked him about the party at the Palace. He said the party was great and he did get to have a word with Queen Elizabeth.

I've tried as best I can to cover most of the important parts of my trip to the United Kingdom. Hopefully I've been able to give you some insight into the people who live in Great Britain. Now its time for me to put the finishing touches on this lengthy biography which I began almost two years ago.

I have always enjoyed reading quite a lot, be it sports, fiction, newspapers, or magazines. You name it and perhaps I've read it. Some of the books I've read just recently have not been very interesting and they were written by reputable, well-known authors. Its almost as if they were in some kind of a hurry to get the book completed. I tend to discard such books after reading the first few pages.

This brings me to the point I'm trying to make. If you are still with me at this stage of my book, then I feel very grateful that I have managed to retain your interest. I sincerely thank you for that.

Since I said my good byes to you before taking my trip to England, I'll just close my biography by wishing all my dear readers a very happy, healthy, and long life.

God Bless.